The
AMERICAN SOUTH
in the 1960's

Edited by
AVERY LEISERSON

With an Introduction by
ALEXANDER HEARD

FREDERICK A. PRAEGER, *Publisher*
New York · London

FREDERICK A. PRAEGER, PUBLISHER
111 FOURTH AVE., NEW YORK 3, N.Y., U.S.A.
77–79 CHARLOTTE STREET, LONDON W. 1, ENGLAND

Published in the United States of America in 1964 by
Frederick A. Praeger, Inc., Publisher

The essays in this volume originally appeared in a special
issue of *The Journal of Politics* entitled "The American South:
1950–1970," Vol. XXVI, No. 1 (February, 1964).

Library of Congress Catalog Card Number: 64-19962

Printed in the United States of America

CONTENTS

INTRODUCTION: THE SOUTH AHEAD

ALEXANDER HEARD
Vanderbilt University

It is the risky habit of the Southern Political Science Association to foster periodic evaluations of the Southern situation. The Association's latest venture is the twenty-fifth anniversary issue of *The Journal of Politics* (reprinted in this volume), which probes important aspects of Southern public affairs. The nation's stake in the South—in a heretofore conspicuous, distinctive South—has always been high. It is even greater now as the many partial Souths and non-Souths of the United States become increasingly alike in their concerns. The South ahead is also the nation ahead.

Historians and other students of the South have long pointed out that many of the region's distinctive characteristics stem from the presence of the Negro. The ante-bellum plantation system was possible only with slave labor. The system of agriculture that developed after the Civil War was an accommodation to the new labor conditions created by the freeing of the slaves. The South's Democratic one-party system developed as a protective device against the threats posed by the Republican party, which had come into existence as the champion of Negro rights. The presence of large numbers of Negroes in the Southern population, outnumbering whites in many areas, has all along conditioned the social milieu. Obviously, many diverse influences have interacted with each over many years to create the modern South, but shaping their impact since before the American Revolution has been the presence of large numbers of persons of color.

It follows that when Southern Negroes change in some significant way, the South as a whole is affected. When attitudes of other Southerners toward Negroes change, for similar reasons the South is again affected. Both kinds of change have been under way.

A change in attitude among Negroes themselves toward their own state in American society has become obvious. This new attitude, which is widely though perhaps not universally held among Negroes, warrants consideration by other persons. A new spirit of independence characterizes many modern Negroes, in the South as well as in the North. Perhaps some Southern white persons will feel like the parents of an adolescent youth who one day with seeming abruptness declares his independence. The deference previously shown by one and the power previously held by the other are altered. Southern Negroes lived so long in dependence on Southern whites that both groups often appeared to accept the situation as natural. In the 1950's, basic changes in attitude became apparent—most portentously among young Negroes. Chiefly, there was less fear of the consequences of certain actions.

Many Negroes began to show an unaccustomed initiative. In sporadic actions throughout the region, they displayed a vigorous independence. For the first time, the Negro affected positively the flow of events. He had previously been largely an object of them or a reactor to them. Now he himself exerted a significant initiative in the effort to mold his own fate. Many developments of importance have occurred in the South since 1950, but none has greater import for the Southern future than this one.

The essays in this volume assess many aspects of the Southern scene. The publisher has asked, however, that a brief survey be added here of the channels through which the new Negro initiative works. Various groups mobilize and direct Negro energies in public affairs. These groups are innovators as well as reflectors of the new independence. What they do ultimately affects most aspects of Southern life.

Marked changes occurred in the organization and leadership of Negro action in the decade following the Supreme Court's 1954 public-school decision. Center stage had long been occupied by the National Association for the Advancement of Colored People. Now, other organizations competed for leadership and allegiance. The importance of white leadership in the Negro's struggle declined. Leadership positions were steadily taken over by Negroes themselves. The forms of protest increased in variety. Emphasis on "direct action" mounted, in contrast to the earlier appeals through the courts. The activist movement became more and more a mass movement. Impatience grew among both leaders and followers.

Six organizations for Negro action reflect this new (and changing) situation: the National Association for the Advancement of Colored People (NAACP), the Urban League, the Black Muslims, the Congress of Racial Equality (CORE), Martin Luther King, Jr.'s, Southern Christian Leadership Conference (SCLC), and the Student Nonviolent Coordinating Committee (SNCC, or "Snick").

Over the years, the NAACP, founded in 1909, has been far and away the Negro's most effective advocate. Negroes themselves assert this. In July, 1963, 45 per cent of a nationwide sample of Negroes over the age of eighteen named the NAACP as the person or organization that had been most outstanding in the fight for Negro rights. Martin Luther King, Jr., was cited by 26 per cent. None of the other four organizations was mentioned by more than 1 per cent.*

Led by whites and Negroes, with the latter ever more important, the NAACP carried on its campaign chiefly through the courts, appealing for what it deemed to be the Negro's constitutional rights. It sought equal treatment for Negroes in many spheres—including teachers' salaries, seating in public transportation, voting, admission to colleges and universities, public recreational facilities, housing, and the public schools. The doctrinal shift in Supreme Court decisions was favorable to Negro objectives, and culminated in 1954 in the unanimous decision that separation of the races in the public schools *ipso facto* constituted inequality. The NAACP's tenacious campaigns through the courts laid the grounds for the current efforts of other groups working through different means. In 1963, NAACP membership totaled about 400,000, scattered in 1,500 local units. Expenditures, including those through its Legal Defense Fund, have recently run to more than $2 million annually.

NAACP leaders, especially following the outlawing of the white primary in a 1944 NAACP case, led in voter registration and get-out-the-vote drives, and in the formation of Negro voters' leagues. Such political punch as Southern Negroes had and directed toward goals of racial equality was largely the result of these efforts. The organization was the symbol of aggressive

*William Brink and Louis Harris, *The Negro Revolution in America* (New York: Simon and Schuster, 1964), p. 116.

action on behalf of Negro equality and was the object of various sanctions against it by Southern legislatures and others.

At the same time, the National Urban League—now comprising over 60 local leagues across the nation—worked on a different level. It sought better jobs for Negroes and the improvement of their social and economic status. Viewed as conservative by some persons, and usually absent from the headlines, the League currently works through "action research" on such problems as unemployment, poor housing, crime, and hostile community attitudes generated by these conditions. It is the best-financed of the Negro organizations—the 1962 budget was about $3.5 million. In contrast to the other groups, it draws large support from united funds, community chests, and foundations, in addition to private donations. It has been at work for over half a century.

The pre-eminence of the NAACP in the Negro protest movement gave the movement a substantial degree of unity until the mid-1950's. In the years since, agreement on goals and means and coordination of efforts have often been lacking. Competition for leadership has been intense among organizations and individuals. Rivalries seem certain to continue.

Each of the four other groups mentioned has distinctive characteristics. Each in its own way is likely to be a stimulant and vehicle of future activity. The Black Muslims, variously estimated to number between 50,000 and 250,000 in the nation, claim that the only road to dignity and fulfillment for the Negro lies via a separate Negro society. How this pure Negro nation is to come about is not stated. Nonviolence is preached; however, Black Muslim leaders play freely upon Negro frustrations.

The number-two leader of the Black Muslims, known as Malcolm X, broke away early in 1964 to organize a Black Nationalist movement. He subsequently advocated that Negroes exercise their constitutional right to keep and bear arms—in order to shoot when necessary to protect themselves. He urged the formation of "rifle clubs" and argued that when whites commit offenses against Negroes the latter "should not wait for white investigators. They should find the guilty ones themselves and execute them on the spot." How important Malcolm will become, and how important the original Black Muslims will remain, cannot easily be predicted. But Malcolm does not hesitate to say that in the United States "you have to expect the Negroes to rise up [in revolution] sooner or later."*

CORE, Martin Luther King's SCLC, and Snick are all new on the Southern scene. They advocate nonviolent direct action and have become symbols of Negro impatience.

CORE was not very active from its formation in 1942 until 1961. Then, under new leadership, it launched the early "freedom rides." In the South, it has concentrated largely on trying to open up public accommodations to Negroes. In 1963, it set a budget of $775,000 and received contributions from more than 61,000 members. Negroes have gradually replaced whites in leadership roles.

The SCLC had a comparable 1963 budget, something over $700,000, but claimed 350,000 members through some 115 affiliates, 85 of them in the South. The organization grew out of the Montgomery bus strike of 1955, which catapulted Dr. King to prominence. It was intended as a means by which Negro clergymen in other cities might assume the leadership that King had displayed in Montgomery, but it has not always worked that way. The organization serves chiefly as a vehicle for Dr. King, without a doubt the foremost symbol of the new Negro aspirations.

The Student Nonviolent Coordinating Committee resulted from a conference called in Raleigh by Dr. King following the first sit-in actions, in Greensboro, N.C., in 1960. It was supposed to link affiliated youth groups around the South in coordinated action. It seems, instead, to provide a base of operations for an energetic leadership in Atlanta that intervenes in selected local situations when it appears propitious to do so. The 1963 budget was $160,-000. Snick has had widespread influence. More than any other organization, it is a channel for Negro youth activity, and it has more than once ignored the restraining counsel of its elders. One close observer concludes that "it has probably supplied the major drive for the civil rights movement in the South."** Another states that he "would not be surprised if Snick became *the* organization to be reckoned with in the Deep South."†

*Gertrude Samuels, "Feud Within the Black Muslims," *The New York Times Magazine,* March 22, 1964, pp. 104–5.
**August Meier, "Negro Protest Movements and Organizations," *The Journal of Negro Education,* No. 32 (1963), p. 442.
†Louis E. Lomax, *The Negro Revolt* (New York: Harper & Row, Publishers, 1962), p. 129.

The diversity of styles in contemporary Negro leadership doubtless increases opportunities for social friction. Certainly, the difficulties of negotiation and mediation between the white and Negro "communities" are heightened, and the ability to find and stick to agreements is complicated. Rivalries and disagreements among Negroes themselves (along with those among whites) add to the turbulence. Restraining mechanisms of unified leadership may be less effective in the future than in the past. A growing pluralism among Negroes inevitably follows their social, economic, and political gains. Moreover, who can doubt that with each advance will come further demands. Every barrier down exposes others ahead.

If all forms of separation based on race were eliminated, differences in social and economic status associated with color would remain. Racial equality is said to exist in Jamaica. Yet the bulk of power and prestige is concentrated in the white 1 per cent of the population. The economic middle class corresponds generally to the "colored" 18 per cent of the population. The proletariat are the 78 per cent who are black. The demands for revision of the social system, the explicit call for social revolution, are given impetus by this correspondence of color to economic and social status.*

The situation in the United States is somewhat different. The Negro population is approximately 11 per cent, compared with Jamaica's 96 per cent. Class and color are not so closely matched. Yet those who would look ahead must recognize that social and economic deprivation are associated with color in many places in the United States and the South. If all formal and *de facto* racial barriers were wiped out overnight, other differentials that cannot be wiped out overnight would remain: lack of skills, shortage of education, poor housing, deficiencies in qualifying types of social experience, unemployment, crime, family disorganization, and more. Regardless of the race of those affected, these defects deserve remedy by the society they blight. It seems probable, however, that social remedies will increasingly be framed as demands for racial justice, or even as demands for racial reparations based

*Katrin Norris, *Jamaica—The Search for an Identity* (London: Oxford University Press, 1962), pp. 61–70, 93–101, and *passim*.

on past injustices. No realist will assume that Negro aspirations for *general* advancement will easily be satisfied, or that Negro social and political action, rooted in the aspirations of Negroes as such, will soon subside.

Directly related to all this is the decline of the Democratic party's traditional domination of Southern politics. The Republican party grew up in the 1850's around a single attitude, an attitude toward the place of the Negro in American life. The Democratic party provided the South with a refuge in which unity against this common foe overrode the factors that divided the region.

The conditions that led to the one-party South are rapidly disappearing. The question is no longer whether there will be a two-party South. The question is what new Southern two-party systems will develop—where, of what kind, and how fast. Negro migrations, the growing Negro vote in the South and in strategic electoral states outside it, changing white attitudes, and a national political context that less and less permits differences on racial policy between the major national parties and their presidential candidates, have all operated to erode the original basis of Democratic dominance in the solid South. Other factors are also at work, not least among them the further diversification of the Southern economy and the growth of commercial and industrial activities. A notable result has been the patches of Republican strength in presidential elections now found in the suburbs of many Southern cities. The payoff is registered not only in a greater Republican presidential vote. It is also reflected in the mounting number of Republican candidacies in local and statewide races, the votes such candidates attract, the increased activity of Republican party organizations, their improved financing, and the disappearance in many quarters of the old prejudice against "black Republicanism." These and other changes are spotty, proceeding at uneven rates, varied by local circumstances; but in sum they constitute a major alteration in the American party system.

The rate and character of economic development in the South bear on both the changing role of the Negro and the processes of political change. Only a generation ago, the South was declared by a President of the United States to be the nation's number-one economic problem. Despite all that has happened since, and the clear absolute gains made, the region is still relatively under-developed. While its rate of development, from a narrower base, has been faster in various ways than in some of the older industrial sections, it has been slower than that of the newer Western areas.

What can the South do to move itself ahead? Many varied factors affect the rate and scope of economic development, and many of these are not subject to man's control. Exploitation of minerals may be, but not the geography of raw resources. Power development may be, but not the volume of rainfall and the drop of rivers. Energetic search for new industry may be, but not the existing concentrations of economic activity that directly affect the location of new businesses. Important characteristics of the situation and requisites for its improvement are discussed in this volume. The levers for regional progress are many, but one particularly requires emphasis in the contemporary South. It impinges on everything else, including racial matters, political processes, and economic prosperity.

This is education. The Southern lag has always reflected, and been reflected in, the low educational achievement of the Southern people. Howard Odum and Rupert Vance, in studies a generation ago, delineated the handicaps imposed by Southern educational deficiencies despite heroic efforts to overcome them. Since World War II, formal education has become increasingly crucial. More especially, the dependence of our modern scientific and technological society on highly trained, talented brainpower attaches a new importance to higher education. Universities have become, in fact, the most significant secular institutions of our society.

Here the South still lags. The lag is greater in the colleges than in high schools, and greatest of all in graduate education. In 1962, the eleven states of the Old South contained approximately 25 per cent of the nation's population. The region graduated 22.4 per cent of the nation's high-school graduates that year, and awarded 20.8 per cent of its college bachelor's degrees and 11.6 per cent of its Ph.D. and related doctoral degrees. In many Southern states, the departure from national levels of performance was vastly greater. Investments in education have a multiplier effect in their ultimate impact in many reaches of society. It is here that the South, with its limited financial resources, can over the long haul expect the greatest yield from public and private investment.

The following essays treat many aspects of the changing South. Profound institutional innovations (most notably, the court decisions affecting legislative apportionment), the formal machinery of government, election processes, public attitudes, political leadership, and much more are examined in articles that may not always agree with each other (or with this introduction), but do report on matters of consequence for the South and the nation of which it is a part.

The
AMERICAN SOUTH
in the 1960's

THE CHANGING MIND OF THE SOUTH:
THE EXPOSED NERVE

LESLIE W. DUNBAR
Southern Regional Council

I

I PREMISE THAT THERE has been such a thing as a southern folk, clearly if not definably more a single people than any other Americans, composed of two grades of persons, both of whom have been truly part of the same folk, and yet one of whom, the Negro Southerners, because they were ruled by the other did not sense and hallow as did the whites their folk integrity and their distinctness from the rest of the nation. And because white Southerners have consciously known that they were set apart, they have struggled to define themselves, have striven for self-identity, and with every Cash or Percy—or Faulkner—asking "Who am I?" have moved nearer the point which comes in every self-examination, where discovery means either release or reunion.

Who is there who is not tired of this search, who would not rather give it up before he has to choose between release, and rejection, or recoil into the mind of the South, who would rather not stop short in self-discovery and become what history makes of him? And indeed, there has been a re-directing of the South's self-study. The intellectual and artistic concern is changing, has changed, from a deep, self-combative hoeing and chopping of souls and history and eternity, and toward commitment to the active issues of the day. The dark, Faulknerian, problems recede.

The classic interpreters of the South began with the conviction that there was a "South" and a "Southerner," and they hunted for definitions. Because the interpreters were themselves Southerners, dredging their prey up through their memories and revealing it as a Protean substance, their definitions were never abstract, and they never tired of examining countless aspects. Nor did they, however, ever yield the belief that something constant and essential lay under the aspects. The Southerner was to be known as a being, and not an active one at that. Only the public figures of the South defined themselves in activity, and the interpreters tended to be less interested in them than in regarding the South's election of them as another aspect of the essential being which needed to be pondered. The essential Southerner acted occasionally, savagely and without premeditation, and this proclivity of his was another aspect to be explained. But except for this, the Southerner "was"; he did not, since the Civil War, "do."

Our preoccupation today is with how Southerners do and will act. For this is a time of testing. We are re-learning an old truth, which historians have nearly always known and social scientists have frequently forgotten, that men reveal themselves more accurately through their action than through their established feelings, opinions, and beliefs.

Another change has occurred as well. Cash, writing as late as 1941, was not really much attentive to Negro Southerners, and Percy, writing also in 1941, could say that he was "usually in a condition of amazed exultation over the excellent state of race relations in the South." James Agee, almost the quintessential New Dealer, took only an occasional and not seriously interested glance at the Negro neighbors of his white Alabama sharecroppers. Of the classic writers, only Lillian Smith had the greatness to wrestle with what the others saw, but passed by, and that was the centrality of race to the southern self-consciousness[1]

In fact, not until the sit-in movement began in Greensboro in 1960 did the "mind" of Negroes become of conscious interest to white Southerners, in the sense that an active awareness began that the southern consensus had to include Negro values and desires. Even in the titanic controversies after 1954, the actors—those who were conspicuously making history—were almost always white: Senator Byrd, Governor Faubus, and the other captains of massive resistance. Negroes appeared only as a shadowy mass, from whom now and then emerged an impersonal lawyer or a poker-faced schoolchild walking through white faces lit with expression. The state of North Carolina might well put one of its historical markers at that

---

[1] W. J. Cash, *The Mind of the South*. N. Y., 1941. W. A. Percy, *Lanterns on the Levee*. N. Y., 1941; the quotation is from p. 286 of the 1959 reprinting. James Agee, *Let Us Now Praise Famous Men*. N. Y., 1960; the book was written in the late 1930's. Lillian Smith, *Killers of the Dream*. N. Y., 1949 (revised edition 1961).

dime store in Greensboro: here is where, after more than three centuries, the white and the Negro South were finally met.

In result, they have learned to know each other better. One Negro civil rights leader remarked to me that southern racial relations in the past had been like an unfaithful marriage, which could be preserved only by the two parties not speaking the truth to each other. Negro Southerners are today speaking the truth to their white neighbors. If white Southerners can learn to live with this truth, the marriage can be continued, and may even become a fruitful one. Still today, no Southerners are more bred to the essence of the region's distinctive history, manners, and outlook than are the Negroes. If Dixie is not yet ready for its epitaph, it will be only because Negroes, freed of illegitimacy, may give it new life.

For earlier white Southerners, even for those as late as Cash, a decision about racial policies was not socially crucial. Men had different opinions and beliefs, but these were like other personal preferences, or even convictions, that were tolerable by the folk. Southern racial relations were like Hinduism, able to absorb and contain many changes and interests and ideas. The advent of industrialization, the steady immigration of non-Southerners, the growth of learning, the magnification of cities—all had come and had modified the old patterns and would surely in time overthrow them. But the endurance—what a Southerner might call the "cussedness"—of the old ways was remarkable.

But now this changes, and I know no better way to illustrate the change at its profoundest — though infrequently perceived — level than by contrasting Faulkner with that present-day southern writer who, in surface aspects, is most like him. The genius of Faulkner was such that he was able to suffuse his characters in life and individuality even though, in fact, they were little more than marionette's. They were held in the hand of God, but that hand which controlled them kept them in ceaseless confrontation with their home, i.e., with southern history, and in it they defined themselves. Miss Flannery O'Connor's characters are also marionettes and also in the grasp of God. They are Southerners too, but this is only an artist's detail. They could be anyone, they are caught directly, as simple individuals, in the human predicament, and they act directly to meet it, not, as Faulkner's characters always did, as Southerners, but as mere people.

Fundamentally, this is where Southerners find themselves today, forced to act directly without validating their acts against their history, much of which is sinking fast underneath them. Another southern writer, Allen Tate, in his novel *The Fathers,* depicts the deep psychological hurt felt by conservative Virginians in 1860-1861 when pressures from the cotton states and from the North were mysteriously pushing Virginia into severance from the government in Washington, of which over the years since 1787 they had come to feel as proprietors. Something similar is happening today over the South, as men see institutions which they had thought were theirs (e.g., the churches, the town school), relationships which they had thought secure (e.g., mistress and maid), begin to take on new shape and purpose.

All this has meant that, for today's white Southerner, an explicit rationalizing of his views about race has become the most urgent of his intellectual and spiritual tasks, and that he has had to achieve it on his own, or with new referents. He has had to attune himself, harmoniously or discordantly, to the authoritative words and practices of institutions from outside his region, such as the federal government, national church bodies, national media, and even-in fact-Wall Street. Perhaps still a man living in a remote Black Belt county untouched as yet by racial controversy may be as unengaged as nearly all of us were but a few years past. But I suspect that no white man living now in a Danville or an Albany or a Birmingham can support himself either by mores or by Faulknerian brooding. For the strong segregationist, the mores will appear too mild when the protest comes; for nearly all men, the brooding will seem irrelevant.

It is astonishing how often a southern white liberal can date his acceptance of racial equality at some specific episode in his life, much as did the ex-Communists in *The God That Failed*[2] tend to date their break with Communism with a decisive, illuminating event. It is even more notable that almost every liberal can (and often does) recount the history of his changing attitudes. This sort of keen self-awareness occurs only with those life problems deeply and genuinely felt. Nevertheless, in accepting racial equality, the southern liberal does not typically reject the South. In Turgenev's

[2]Edited by R. H. S. Crossman, N. Y., 1949.

Fathers and Sons, when Bazarov's tolerance of an older conservative is asked—"you must take into account his upbringing as well as the times in which he lived the best part of his life"—, Barzarov exclaims: "His upbringing: Every man should educate himself. . . . As to the times, why should I depend upon them: Much better they should depend on me. No, brother, all that is just loose thinking, there's nothing solid behind it!" To a Southerner, if to no one else, this is questionable doctrine, because inadequate tolerance; and rightly or wrongly, the key word of southern liberalism has been "tolerance."

Southern liberalism deserves more serious study than it has had. What, in this context, is worth remarking is the long sustained refusal of southern liberals to repudiate the South, and this is one side of the tolerance which they have elevated above all other social virtues. Few liberals have acted out their beliefs. They do not try to enter their children in Negro schools, do not usually refuse to eat in segregated restaurants or worship in segregated churches, do not spontaneously and widely mingle socially with their Negro peers. This is not well described as either hypocrisy or timidity. It is something a good bit more basic. The general conformity of the liberal to social practices which he opposes is a mark of his dogged refusal to alienate himself from southern society. He has counted himself a Southerner, with an obligation to respect the community and, so far as possible, to keep it whole. He often will, in fact, contend (and not only from polemical motives) that he—and not the defenders of segregation—represents the core of southern traditions, and he will sometimes appeal to other values acknowledged to be "southern," such as "courage" or "manners" or "individuality," against the less venerable practice of segregation. The tenacity with which liberals hold to southern culture, while endeavoring to reform it, is a quality which cannot be measured, but it would seem at least as intense as the somewhat comparable spirit of the Benthamites and later Labourites in England; they too insisted on behaving as Englishmen as they went about changing the country.

On the whole, this attitude of respect toward the community is not alien to a great many of the Negro leaders. And on the whole, this shared attitude presents the only real possibility, for those of us who want one, of preserving the South as a cultural organism, and not merely as a cultivated, but mummified, memory, analogous to

New England. It is not a very strong possibility, though the relative poverty of the region may help along its chances: poverty is a strong folk-tie. I may be wrong and shortly proved so, but I see the white South today, outside the Black Belt but even there in some measure, as disposed, though often reluctantly, to accept more and more racial integration, but wanting also to keep the community much as it has been. I see Negro Southerners wanting equality desperately and angrily, but disposed to keep the community much as it has been, if they are admitted to it.

The South that Cash sought to track down was the white South, and, assuming that Cash found what he sought, it was unprepared for 1954. That South is still here. But because, being what it was and is, it stayed distant from the black South, called itself and itself only "the South," it has become an inert thing, a mere environment. Within this environment and against it, the southern leaders of today —the Negroes—act. It is the antithesis of motion against matter, and unless it can be cured there is not even a meager chance that the South will persevere. The white South is become an object, and only subjects can, even in a Faulknerian sense, endure.

II

Myrdal remarked that, "The intellectual energy spent on the Negro problem in America should, if concentrated in a single direction, have moved mountains."[3] In truth, almost the profoundest thing one can say about southern race relations is that it *is* an old problem, toughened and complicated and made wondrously intricate by age, which has confused its diagnosis, rendered uncertain its treatment, and obscured its prognosis. Ancient as it is, it has had changing definitions, and these have, in the past, been determined by the interests and policies of white people. As Myrdal put it,

> It is thus the white majority group that naturally determines the Negro's 'place.' All our attempts to reach scientific explanations of why the Negroes are what they are and why they live as they do have regularly led to determinants on the white side of the race line. In the practical and political struggles of effecting changes, the views and attitudes of the white Americans are likewise strategic. The Negro's entire life, and, consequently, also his opinions on the Negro problem,

[3]Gunnar Myrdal, et al., *An American Dilemma*, N. Y., 1944, p. 27.

are, in the main, to be considered as secondary reactions to more
primary pressures from the side of the dominant white majority.[4]

This analysis was undeniably correct as an interpretation of the
pre-1945 period; it is no longer so. Beginning about the close of
World War II, the power to determine the Negro's "place" began to
shade off from white control. Today, the Negro grip on the levers
of social change is secure, and much more firm than the remnants of
white direction.

The race relations policy of the southern white leadership from
1619 until Reconstruction, and from about 1890 until the 1940's,
was governed by the objective, *How to get the maximum satisfaction
from the Negro population.* The policy was pursued in economic,
political, and social relationships, frequently with unsuccess. This
fairly unanimously held single policy has, in the years since the
40's, been both losing adherents and singleness of application; the
growth of Negro votes combined with pressures from Washington
are forcing on our public life policies markedly more progressive than
those which still dominate our churches and other more or less privately determined activities. Perhaps only in Mississippi today is
there near unanimity about racial policy. But it is not the old policy
of maximum satisfaction. Instead, it is, *How to maintain white control of the institutions of society.* At least, Negroes are not regarded
as instruments and tools, but as antagonists. That, in itself, is a
higher status.

If initiative has passed from the white majority to the Negro
minority, the principal cause has been the success of Negroes in
achieving a new and more stable self-knowledge. The dilemma—
intellectual, emotional, political—of the Negro, especially the Negro
male, has always been the problem of identity.[5] A man's valuation

---

[4]Myrdal, *op. cit.,* p. li.

[5]There has been a lot of recent writing on this subject, mostly by non-
southern interpreters. See the three books of essays by James Baldwin: *Notes
of a Native Son.* Boston, 1955; *Nobody Knows My Name.* N. Y., 1961; *The
Fire Next Time.* N. Y., 1963. Essays in the first book are of uneven quality and
interest, but some of them and all of the two later books are superb and required reading for insight into the Negro revolt. For the latter reason only,
so too is Louis Lomax, *The Negro Revolt.* N. Y., 1962. See also the excellent
book by Harold I. Isaacs, *The New World of Negro Americans.* N. Y., 1963.
Isaacs has an especially interesting essay in *Encounter,* August, 1963: "Blackness
and Whiteness." One scientific inquiry is B. P. Karon, *The Negro Personality.*

of himself is derived and sustained by his reading of other people's assessment of him, and at all times in a person's life there are some "other people" whom he regards as the most authoritative assessors. Because of history and color., Negroes for centuries got maddeningly confusing reports whenever they inquired of their society, "Who am I?"

With some notable variations, they adopted the social values and standards of the dominant white society. For generations, Negro Southerners had no sustained insight into white society beyond their own neighborhood, and they consequently shaped their self-portrait through the terms of local opinion. The past three or four decades have been a time, even for rural Negroes, of awareness of a larger universe of values and authoritative opinions, and increasingly they have tended to disregard local definitions in preference for more favorable nation-wide and world-wide judgments of their worth. But even in the old days, the answer to their question, "Who am I?", was far from clear. The Christianity they had been taught affirmed some things so surely that not even the utmost ingenuity of white pastoral apologists could altogether obscure them. The grand generalities of American democracy seeped into their consciousness. Their white neighbors behaved toward them with contradictory manners, producing what was (and, to a large extent, still is) surely one of the most weirdly implausible patterns of human relations ever observed. And always, Negroes were accompanied by a few stereotypes which sprang easily into the minds of white persons, even those a Negro might regard as friends, and displaced the actual Negro person they knew—or thought they knew.

The stereotypes were and are the damning judgments of white society on Negro identity. What is happening today is that Negroes are disowning the stereotypes, the white man's creations, are refusing any longer to acknowledge themselves to *be* what the white man said

N. Y., 1958; its findings and methods aroused some dispute. As a stranger to psychology I hesitate to cite writings in this field but from a dilletantish reading I might mention three pieces which were suggestive to me: Robert Coles, "Serpents and Doves: Non-Violent Youth in the South" (in Erik H. Erikson, ed., *Youth: Change and Challenge*. N. Y., 1963). Lewis W. Jones, "Negro Youth in the South" (in Eli Ginzberg, ed., *The Nation's Children*, Vol. 3, N. Y., 1960); D. C. Wilson and E. M. Lantz, "The Effect of Culture Change on the Negro in Virginia, as Indicated by a Study of State Hospital Admissions," *American Journal of Psychiatry*, July, 1957.

they were. White Southerners are confronted with a blunt demand from the Negro that he be accepted on his terms: *and this is the crucial problem of race relations today.* For years, whites have decreed that Negroes must think of themselves as the whites thought of them. Negroes now are insisting that the white majority revise its opinion of them in accord with their own, newly fashioned self-conception.

Negroes found that in the same European-American culture which had relegated them to inferiority, white supremacy had become a strand of that culture which "tends to wear away protective strata, to break down its own defenses, to disperse the garrisons of its entrenchment." The words are Schumpeter's,[6] and taken from a context which, though not analogous, is suggestive. Some other words of his are exactly applicable to contemporary Negro agitation: "Secular improvement that is taken for granted and coupled with individual insecurity that is acutely resented is of course the best recipe for breeding social unrest."[7] A concatenation of economic and educational factors, supported haphazardly and minimally by politics, produced the secular improvement; another array of political, emotional, and social circumstances caused and kept strong the individual insecurity. The social unrest is a direct outcome of the combination, and is given its specific form and intensity through the re-infusion of ideas and values into American culture by a constantly growing number of educated Negroes who have derived these ideas and values from the cultural property of western white peoples, the terms of whose inheritance require them to admit non-whites with whom they come into regular communication to equal shares in the property.

III

Lincoln began his Gettysburg Address by recalling that "fourscore and seven years ago" there had been brought forth "a new na-

---

[6]A. Schumpeter, *Capitalism, Socialism, and Democracy,* 3rd edition. N. Y., 1950, p. 143. Schumpeter's brilliant analysis (pp. 121-164) around the theme of capitalism's "crumbling walls" illuminates racial unrest throughout the world. As capitalism sponsored its own intellectual and emotional opposition, so European-American culture has sown the denials of its own privileges.

[7]*Ibid.*, p. 145.

tion conceived in liberty and dedicated to the proposition that all men are created equal." If, in this centennial year of the Emancipation Proclamation, of Gettysburg and Vicksburg, we look back four score and seven years, we confront a less happy and auspicious event: 1876, the year when Hayes defeated Tilden, or Tilden defeated Hayes, whichever it was. Hayes became President through the Compromise of 1877, and for the next 70 years or so the white South was left alone by the nation in its policies and in its relationships toward Negro citizens.

The Civil War had freed the slaves and preserved the union. It had, besides, put on two Amendments to the Constitution—the 14th and 15th—which in the years after 1876 would be, as to Negroes, well nigh meaningless: four generations of Negro and white Southerners would come and go and live without acknowledging that Negroes could and should vote, or that laws should give them equal protection. The Civil War, moreover, left all these people in a ravished region, where men would get used to desperate poverty. The War and its aftermath made the South feel its spiritual and cultural separation from the rest of the nation more keenly even than before.

Then, earlier, and now, we have defined "the South" by its differences from the rest.

Southerners and non-Southerners have been, in fact, much alike. White men everywhere ruled, and Negroes were subservient, and treated as inferiors. Society belonged—and still largely does—to the white man. Protestants ruled, dominating the economic and cultural and political life of the nation. Society placed a high sentimental value on farm or small-town culture and people, and long after the bulk of our population moved into cities the rural districts kept political power. And North and South, East and West, we all believed that *any* man who worked hard could get ahead.

These common qualities of American life, native both to the South and the non-South, are dissolving. And the present crisis in the South, which became acute in 1954, does not result from traditional differences from the nation; it results instead from the dissolution of things which have in the past united us.

Six landmark dates conveniently illustrate the changes. Although they affect the whole nation they are a special challenge to the South. Somebody—Arthur Koestler, I think—once spoke of the Jews as humanity's exposed nerve, feeling first and most sharply all the troubles and pains. Sometimes one feels that the South is America's exposed nerve, and that issues which are national in scope are most intense, or at least most apparent, here.

There was 1944, and *Smith v. Allwright,* and the ensuing erosion of the white monopoly of power to make political decisions. There was 1954, and *Brown v. Topeka,* which in its deeper import signified that the civic institutions of American society could no longer be operated as if they were the property of one race, and which, in its application since the New Rochelle case,[8] has upset the North as well as the South. There was 1960, and confirmation that non-Protestants have a share in the power to make the country's highest decisions. There was 1962, and *Baker v. Carr,* and the consequent remarkably fast crumbling of the rural fortress of political power.

There was 1940, the last year before our entry into World War II, the last year of a peace-time economy. After seven years of prodigious effort by the New Deal, unemployment in the United States was 14.6% of the working force. We went into the war and unemployment virtually ceased. We came out of the war and unemployment stayed low while the country was busily engaged in converting to peace-time needs. We had a recession in 1948, and the next year unemployment shot up to 5.9%. We went into the Korean fighting, and again unemployment declined. We had another recession in 1954, and unemployment was up again. We had yet another recession in 1958, and this time unemployment really rose—to 6.8% of the working force of this country. After each recession, recovery was slower. There has been little improvement since, and President Kennedy in March 1963, called unemployment our "number 1 economic problem," and reported that it was still about 6%; the rate for August 1963 was a seasonal 5.5%. Many economists believe that the government's way of computing unemployment seriously minimizes its extent.[9]

Neither the policies of Republican nor Democratic administra-

[8]*Taylor v. New Rochelle,* 195 F. Supp. 231, 294 F. 2d. 36 (1961).

[9]See chapter 4 of the *Manpower Report of the President and a Report on Manpower Requirements, Resources, Utilization, and Training,* U. S. Department of Labor, 1963. The statistics above are from *Statistical Abstract of the United States,* 1962, p. 215, except for the 1963 ones, which come from news reports.

tions have, as yet, been able to lick this problem. Unemployment is high despite the boosting of the economy with huge expenditures for armaments and for space exploration; without those would we be back to the 14.6% unemployed of 1940?

Here we meet a tragic irony; as has happened in the past, Negroes seem to be the victims not only of discrimination, but of impersonal history. After the first World War the country severely restricted the flow of immigrants from abroad. Up to then, American industry had grown by drawing on a boundless labor supply of European immigrants. With immigration drastically cut, industry met its need for new labor by drawing from the farms of America, including those of the South. Beyond this last large supply of white manpower, waited in economic succession the Negro. The tragic irony is that when his turn is come, the job market is declining. This is occurring in manufacturing and mining, chiefly, and these are fields which have been a gateway for new entrants into the free competition for economic advancement. No one seriously can continue to believe that America is for everyone now a land of opportunity where *any* man, unaided, can get ahead by dint of his own hard work. Some five to seven per cent or more of those people who want to work, find that there are no jobs, even though there is general prosperity in the country, and for the Negro the unemployment rate is about double that for whites.[10]

And, finally, there was 1947, when Mr. Truman appointed the President's Committee on Civil Rights, and later espoused its recommendations, even at the cost of a party split at the Democratic convention of 1948. No political act since the Compromise of 1877 has so profoundly influenced race relations; in a sense, it was the repeal of 1877. Among the consequences were (a) a shift of emphasis from Negro "uplift"—essentially a paternalistic approach—to civil rights, i.e., the achievement of more than nominal citizenship; (b) a renewal of the fateful rupture between South and non-South; and (c) the ensuing complications for economic and social reform by statute, so that, since 1948, law-making for domestic problems has fallen into desuetude.[11]

[10]See Charles E. Silberman, "The Businessman and the Negro," *Fortune*, September, 1963.
[11]The ability of southern Congressmen to act through concepts of the national interest, so long as they felt presently secure in race relations, made pos-

These six landmarks suggest, if I am not mistaken, that we shall have much more democracy in the United States. The price of that will be the ending of certain old ways and traditions. Groups who have led and controlled the country from its earliest days will have to accept a lessening of their influence. And if the South had trouble joining the old union—which, like it, was white, Protestant, and rural in its outlook and leadership—can it join this new union? The South was separated from the basically similar non-South of yesterday by a sharp enough cleavage; the new division would be a gulf.

To put it differently, the policies which Mississippi represents would not merely perpetuate North-South differences. The longer these policies are pursued, the greater becomes the alienation of Mississippi and the Black Belt generally from the American consensus. Just by standing pat, residents of these places will become strangers in their own land, because the nation as a whole is moving farther and farther from them.

IV

Over the years, Negro Southerners tried various methods of effecting change. They occasionally resorted to violence in the slave revolts of the ante-bellum period. During Reconstruction they sought the power of office. In Populist days they experimented—to their sorrow—with an electoral alliance with small farmers and mechanics. They tried the Booker T. Washington regimen of self-improvement, in the expectation that they would be accepted when their uplift was completed. They left the South, for the uncertain and often unrewarding North and West.

Finally—and with really their only success—they converted the political issue of equality into the Constitutional issue of equal rights. The "direct-action" movement has been a new force, and one of tremendous effect. It has produced results and it has unleashed and directed energies. Yet even its appeal has been to values thought to be in or implied by the Constitution, and the safety and success of the movement have been protected throughout by the procedural guarantees of the Constitution. The reform of the Negro question

sible the reforms of Wilson and Franklin D. Roosevelt. For an interesting case study, see I. A. Newby, "States' Rights and Southern Congressmen During World War I," *Phylon,* Spring 1963.

in the United States has been a striking instance of the effect of a constitution upon the life and events of a society. The constitution, created by the society, becomes a force which changes society.[12]

The Constitution becomes a revolutionary instrument, for Negroes, being political outcasts, have had to combat the government, and not merely the government of the day. Nowhere yet in the old Confederacy does a politically representative body debate and settle on policy, except in two circumstances: to shore up the legal defences of segregation; or to circumscribe as closely as possible the scope of a judicial decree when defiance is considered inexpedient. Nowhere has a deliberative body accepted the premise that social change is necessary or inevitable, and that action to guide that change is its responsibility.

None has done so, because southern political theory has been incapacitating. Although formal democracy has been in short supply in the South, the tone and practice of southern politics has been democratic almost to an extreme—among the whites. Probably no where else in the country have there been closer personal relationships between voters and representatives, at all levels of government. But a democracy which is short on formal controls and efficient methods of obtaining popular consensus, and which puts a high value on informal means of effecting accountability, is going to be a conservative society. And when not all the inhabitants are constituents, the conservatism will be, in fact, defensiveness. Thus both the democratic and the conservative spirits of the South combined to defend the folk, its monopoly of power and its cultural integrity. There is nothing to deliberate about, and to do so is betrayal. There is no relief from this paralysis except through an enlarged Negro vote, and a few municipalities of the South are already tasting this emancipation.

We may well ask again whether, when a conflict runs deep, democratic politics and its institutions can solve it. If the southern conflict is being resolved, it is because it was possible to appeal it to a constitution, whose first principle is that it itself is enforceable law. There is still some life left in the old maxim that democracy

---

[12]cf. the interesting analysis by Gerhard Loewenberg, "The British Constitution and the Structure of the Labour Party," *American Political Science Review*, September, 1958.

requires agreement on fundamentals, although it may more accurately be this: that democratic politics cannot be counted on to bridge deep chasms of opinions and values unless undergirded by a fundamental authority (e.g., a self-enforcing constitution) which is independent of parties and legislatures.

Impersonal causes—the boll weevil, farm technology and chemicals, faster-paced industrialization, communications media, and still others—re-arranged the roots of southern life after World War I. But human action did not, until the last decade.

Now Southerners are not only being moved by their environment, but are revising themselves and their manners of living with and getting along with each other. Events and change are pell-mell, and unpredictable. Whatever we say, we must say most tentatively. I note, therefore, that the case has often, even usually, been that white Southerners can and do change their racial mores when inescapably confronted by a community-wracking situation to which they must respond in one way or another. But I note further that this has not been invariably so; witness, e.g., Albany (Ga.). Those places, however, which have refused to yield to the Negro demands, modest as they often have been in the South, have been able to do so only through techniques of suppression which tear at precepts of the Constitution. They have maltreated the right of assembly, denigrated the supremacy of federal law, whored the police powers of the states.

The Negro demands have been within the Constitution. The Negro methods have been within the liberties and privileges of the Constitution; only occasionally have they violated the rules of the game. Southern communities have been tested, therefore, not only in their customs and morality, but in their understanding of and affection for the Constitution. Those many which have accommodated, and have stepped into the currents of change, have shown to us that the feelings men have do not necessarily determine their actions or reactions; that when confronted with practical choices, men discover themselves more accurately than they had before. I have to leave to others the scientific analysis,[13] but I believe we

[13]Which is, of course, being supplied. The point of view I have here expressed is consistent with that of Allport and his supporters. See, e.g., Thomas F. Pettigrew, "Personality and Sociocultural Factors in Intergroup Attitudes: a Cross-National Comparison," *Conflict Resolution*, March 1958; and "Regional

can see the mind of the white South changing through the action of the black South and the accommodating reaction of the white South, and that a new South is shaping itself through history-making, and not through history-consciousness.

Success breeds hard problems, and it seems to me that the Negro movement is courting two very serious ones. There is disquieting evidence that a great many Negroes, naturally imbued with the excitement and the power of having led America's first sustained experiment in government by the street, are oblivious to the fact that their guiding rule and their indispensable ally has been the Constitution. Secondly, the availability of the political process has been so long withheld from them that they may not learn soon to value it.

I see little or no prospect for rational answers to America's or the South's racial woes unless the channels of politics are opened up for their resolution, by Congress and by the states. This means a steady transference of issues from court to legislature. The Constitution has done its work, and the way is cleared to reach decisions through consensus. For the long run, *Baker v. Carr* may be the avenue through which Negroes, under the leadership and representation of new, political types, may bring racial issues finally into political settlement. In the nature of things, the South's practical alternative to government by the street may include the price of a half dozen or more Adam Clayton Powells, but that is democracy's age-old exaction.

In the meantime, we can note that any government has but three possible postures toward the question of racial equality: in favor, opposed, or neutral. The political theory of the South has for more than three centuries been grounded on the principle of white supremacy. It has been the cardinal doctrine. If, then, southern state governments were to follow the lead already given by some municipalities, and move from opposition to neutrality, this would be a truly historic change.

Differences in Anti-Negro Prejudice," *Journal of Abnormal and Social Psychology,* July 1959, From the former: "The success of the movement in the South does not depend—this hypothesis would contend—on changing the deeply ingrained orientations of prejudice-prone personalities; rather, it rests on the effectiveness with which racial integration now going on in the South can restructure the mores to which so many culturally intolerant southerners conform."

In fact, the border states have already moved beyond neutrality,[14] and have begun incorporating into their public policy commitments favoring equality. And of even greater historic moment, some of the old Confederacy states have begun the withdrawal of state power from the defense of segregation and inequality.

This seems to me the *sine qua non* for the preservation of the South, as a community of persons acknowledging a common heritage. There must be an end to governmental hostility toward Negro advance, and acceptance of a political theory which sees government as neutral toward the competing aspirations of all economic and social elements. Such theory has been a commonplace in American national politics since at least Theodore Roosevelt. It will have to be established in the South and will have to be founded on the conditional truth that neutrality of the governmental power has to exist if there is to be order. Hobbes may not have said the last word in political philosophy, but he did say the first: power should be independent of the competition of private interests, and, because of its recognition of the equal potential threat of every person to public order, must acknowledge the equality of rights.

V

Let us say only that as long as a large number of people sense an identity among themselves, the South as a specific, self-conscious culture will endure. As was said at the start of this essay, who is there who is not tired of struggles for more definitive answers?[15] Perhaps I could venture that a Southerner is a person who feels, as against all other people, that he is the more moral, using that word in its broadest meaning of being spiritually fit for life as it is. But this would say no more than that the Southerner shares a widespread conceit. Perhaps it would mean more if I said that the Southerner is someone who can recognize that he has lost every argument about good and evil he has ever had—and he's had a lot

[14]Delaware, Kentucky, Maryland, Missouri, and West Virginia have all legislated some minimal standards and mediation procedures for racial relations, and the governor of Kentucky has gone further with a sweeping executive order.

[15]I have been privileged to read a draft of the forthcoming book of James McBride Dabbs, whose *The Southern Heritage* (N. Y., 1958) is the likeliest candidate of recent years to stand beside the classic interpretations of Cash and Lillian Smith. Dabbs has *not* tired of the search.

—yet he *still* feels himself somehow more moral, again in the broadest meaning.

But it is safer to come back to the simple test of identification. The deepest wisdom in human relations is to accept a man as whatever he names himself. Ten years from now, or 20, will people living between the Potomac and the Rio Grande still identify themselves with each other, still feel worthwhileness in calling themselves Southerners?

I don't know. But I think we all do know some things that bear on the answer.

We know, most importantly, that politics is the way a people conducts its affairs, and that politics not only serves a group of people pragmatically but gives it unity, helps make of it a community. When the political processes cannot handle the affairs of the people, and when to settle grievances men have to act outside those processes, the polity is always hurt, sometimes to the point of death. Both Negroes and intense segregationists, including segregationist officials, have felt that they must take their causes outside the normal processes of politics.

The South is a little place. It cannot act greatly, and its survival means hardly anything to the world. Except that, as I have tried to argue, the only way it can, in fact, survive is to do something that *would* matter to the world, and that is to become a rarity, a bi-racial community at peace with itself. It can do so, I think, only by integrating Negroes into its political processes.

Southern politics is just now, as usual, full of curious things. Mississippi is experimenting with a Soviet style government, with the Citizens Council paralleling the state machine in emulation of a successful Communist Party. Southern governors have become the *de facto* executive directors of the state chambers of commerce, and spend their time competing with each other as supplicants for new plants. We have talked of state socialism and state capitalism, but what do we call governments whose chief affair it is to entice and propitiate business? And all over the South, battle lines draw close to each other, portentous of an epic contest which may never occur in any explicit, decisive engagement, but which will, one way or another, reach to the innermost desires of the South.

For southern conservatism is blending now with that of the nation at large in spirited defense against the dissolution of the old unities of American life. Southern liberalism has, and this is its good luck, no choice but to accept the Negro's cause as its own. The pains of the warfare between those who are rebelling against 30 years of history and those who want to move more rapidly into the future, will probably be most acutely felt in the South; it is the South's ancient calling to deflect pain and guilt from the rest of the nation.

Negroes have hymned the American dream, but only its battle-cries. There are other parts of it and, if we read our history honestly, the Birchites and lesser breeds within the law are responsive to them. A "nice" home; people like ourselves; Jesus, and "our" church; the righteousness of property. America is on its way, not to a confrontation with its dream, but to a study of it, a mining of its content. The cutting edge of one drill is the radical right, and the other is the Negroes. It is in the South that each will probably cut most deeply. We are likely to learn a lot about ourselves, these next few years, as the drills cut away.

THE SOUTH AS A DEVELOPING AREA*

WILLIAM H. NICHOLLS
Vanderbilt University

W HILE THIS SYMPOSIUM on the American South is largely focused on the period 1950-70, economic development (whether national or regional) is a long-run historical process which cannot appropriately be examined without reference to the more distant past. For this reason, the present paper takes 1930 as the historical turning-point between the South's long period of economic lag and the more recent period in which it has closed much of the gap in material well-being between itself and the rest of the nation. We shall therefore begin by examining the relative status of the Southern economy in 1930. We shall then discuss the historical, social, and political factors which help to account for the South's lag behind the national economy. We shall then turn to a statistical documentation of the substantial spurt in the South's rate of economic development during 1930-60. We shall conclude with a discussion of the job that remains if the South is finally to achieve full economic parity with the other regions of the United States.

I. THE SOUTH IN 1930

By 1930, the United States had already clearly established itself as the world's richest nation. Nonetheless, the Southern states—stretching from Texas and Oklahoma to Virginia and Florida—re-

---

*This article closely follows the author's oral presentation in Lesson 124 of the CBS College of the Air's series on *The American Economy,* televised on March 29, 1963, under the title "Uneven Growth Rates: Lag and Spurt in the South." Since the present manuscript was written during a year's sojourn in Brazil, the author may have failed in a few instances to use 1960 census data which would have been easily available to him had he been in the States.

[1]Where possible, I have used statistics which define "the South" as the 13-state region, embracing Virginia, North Carolina, South Carolina, Georgia, Florida, Kentucky, Tennessee, Alabama, Mississippi, Arkansas, Louisiana, Texas, and Oklahoma. From an economic point of view, West Virginia might also appropriately be included in the South while, for some purposes, Oklahoma—and more recently Florida and even Texas—might appropriately be excluded. Where Delaware, Maryland, and the District of Columbia are included here, it is only because of the vagaries of Census classification.

mained a relatively underdeveloped region.[1] The extent to which the South was disadvantaged relative to the rest of the nation (or non-South) may be illustrated by the following statistics. In 1930, nearly half (43%) of the South's gainfully employed population still remained in agriculture, almost three times the non-South's 15 percent. On the other hand, only 14 percent of the South's work force was employed in manufacturing, little more than half of the non-South's 26 percent. The South's relative urban population (34%) was also only about half of that (66%) of the rest of the nation. With crude birth rates 39 percent above the non-South and nearly identical crude death rates, the South's crude natural increase (15.1) was twice that of the non-South's (7.7).

Thus, the South in 1930 was characterized by a much heavier dependence on agriculture, a relatively rural population, and a relatively high natural increase of population. All this would not have been so bad if the South's agriculture had been efficient and prosperous. Unfortunately, 46 percent of its gross cash farm income was derived from cotton, which was produced by techniques which (like most other Southern farm products) made very ineffective use of human resources—a reflection of the relative plenty and cheapness of labor in an overpopulated agrarian economy. As a consequence, Southern agriculture contained most of the nation's low-income farm families. Typically, its farm families were poor because each had so little land and capital to work with. This perennial problem was intensified by high birth rates which exerted a constant downward pressure on farm-labor productivity and incomes.

To some extent, population pressure in the rural South was relieved by large-scale migration of its farm people to other regions where non-farm job opportunities were more plentiful. Thus, during 1910-30, the 13-state South had lost 2.0 million people by migration to the rest of the nation. Omitting Florida and Texas, which enjoyed considerable in-migration during that period, the remaining eleven Southern states had actually lost 2.7 millions by net outmigration during the two decades prior to 1930. Insofar as the South had been industrializing, some further relief had been provided for its rural overpopulation. But the South's own rate of industrial-urban development had been far from sufficient—even in combination with a high rate of outmigration—to solve the region's low-income problem. Furthermore, such manufacturing as the South attracted was largely in such low-wage, low-productivity industries as textiles, furniture, and garments which required less capital and lower labor skills than did the more desirable, higher-wage industries.

As a consequence of all of these factors, the average Southerner was in 1930 *less than half* as well off as his counterpart in the rest of the nation. In that year, per-capita income in the South was $322, only 47 per cent of the $624 enjoyed in the non-South.

II. WHY THE SOUTH LAGGED BEHIND

As I have argued at length elsewhere,[2] the South's great lag behind the rest of the United States in rate and level of economic development was largely attributable to historical and cultural factors. Prior to the Civil War, the South prospered on the basis of a dominant cotton economy, associated with a plantation system and slave labor. The consequences were several:

(1) The South embraced an agrarian philosophy which positively opposed industrial-urban development as an inferior way of life.

(2) The South took over from England the "aristocratic ideal" of a society dominated by large landholders, with a carefully stratified and rigid social structure in which first the Negro, and later the typical white, had his place.

(3) The South's political structure was based on a narrow electorate which gave disproportionate weight to the economic interests of large planters.

(4) The South's dominant socio-political leadership gradually lost its sense of social responsibility, reflected particularly in its opposition to the advancement of public-school education and industrial-urban development.

With military defeat and Reconstruction, the South reacted by re-examining its distinctive value system. It made frenzied efforts to industrialize and for the first time established a basis for the public financing of common school systems. However, these efforts were aborted by the modest results of its belated industrialization campaigns and by the use of the battle-cry of "white supremacy" to defeat the threat of agrarian radicalism, under which the interests of the rural masses of poor whites and freed Negroes were beginning

[2]William H. Nicholls, *Southern Tradition and Regional Progress*, University of North Carolina Press, Chapel Hill, 1960.

to coalesce. Thus, by 1900, the old aristocratic agrarian values were re-inforced and restored to their original dominance.

The results were highly unfavorable to the South's general economic development. The large planters were insulated from competing economic forces. The *rural* middle class, which contributed so much to the democratization and economic development of the North and West, was abnormally subordinated in the South's rigid social structure and undemocratic political structure. The South's *urban* middle class was handicapped by the slow growth of Southern cities and by a political system which discriminated strongly against industrial-urban interests. The South's rural leadership accepted a disproportionate number of low-income people as normal and inevitable. It promoted its self-interest in a cheap labor supply by diverting the attention of low-income whites, through numerous devices which at least clearly supported their claims to superiority over the Negro race.

This rural leadership also held strongly to the belief that the South's low-income people, whether white or Negro, were poor because they were innately inferior. Thus, it rationalized a policy of inaction toward the improvement of school and other public services, toward social and political reform, and toward the promotion of industrial-urban development. In such a static and stagnant environment, only by migration to other regions could most low-income people better their lot.

III. SOUTHERN ECONOMIC PROGRAM, 1930-60

Despite these severe handicaps, the effects of which were still strong in 1930, the South enjoyed a substantial acceleration in its rate of economic development thereafter. The two decades following 1940 were a particularly dynamic period. Millions of surplus Southern farm people were attracted to other regions in which they could substantially improve their economic status. Still other millions were finding it possible to obtain better non-farm job opportunities within the South itself. This new Southern industrial development received its first strong impetus during the war years when, labor becoming almost impossible to obtain at any price in other regions, the South's relatively plentiful labor supply emerged as a major asset.

Since industries now sought out Southern locations, not because Southern workers were "cheap" but because they were of higher quality than those then available elsewhere, the quality of Southern industry was substantially upgraded. In the process, old prejudices (which held that Southern workers were unsuitable for the more skilled industrial jobs) were dissipated, encouraging further movement of industry to the South even after labor supplies elsewhere became less tight. The South's relatively unexploited water, forests, and other natural resources also helped greatly to attract chemical, paper, and other higher quality industries to the region. Finally, Southern industrial-urban development was, to a rapidly growing extent, re-inforced as a prospering South became increasingly attractive as a market for industrial goods. Let us look at some of the evidence on the impressive extent of this recent regional progress.

Industrial-Urban Development

First, the growing relative importance of manufacturing employment[3] in the South may be shown by the following figures:

YEAR	SOUTH	NON-SOUTH	RELATIVE MANUFACTURING EMPLOYMENT, TOTAL SOUTH AS % OF NON-SOUTH
1930	14.5%	25.7%	56%
1940	14.8%	27.2%	54%
1950	18.4%	29.0%	63%
1960	21.3%	29.4%	72%

During 1930-60, as a percentage of the total gainfully employed, manufacturing employment grew from 14.5 to 21.3 percent in the South but only from 25.7 to 29.4 percent in the rest of the country. In the process, the South closed a major part of the gap between itself and the non-South in relative manufacturing employment—standing at 72 percent of the non-South in 1960 as compared with only 56 percent in 1930.

In this connection, it is also interesting to break down manufacturing employment into non-durable goods (which in general tend to be produced by lower-productivity, lower-wage industries) and durable goods (which on the whole are higher-productivity, higher-wage industries). For 1950 and 1960, relative manufacturing employment[3] was as follows:

[3]Based on U. S. Census of Population data, which include Delaware, Maryland, District of Columbia, and West Virginia in "the South."

RELATIVE MANUFACTURING EMPLOYMENT

	NON-DURABLE GOODS[4]			DURABLE-GOODS		
YEAR	SOUTH	NON-SOUTH	SOUTH AS % OF NON-SOUTH	SOUTH	NON-SOUTH	SOUTH AS % OF NON-SOUTH
1950	11.1%	12.5%	89%	7.3%	16.5%	44%
1960	12.5	11.6	108	8.8	17.8	49

Here, we see that during 1950-60 the South actually surpassed the non-South in the relative importance of employment in the manufacturing of non-durable goods, the relative of South to non-South increasing from 89 to 108 percent. Furthermore, while the South still lagged far behind in durable-goods manufacturing, even here it showed a gain from 44 to 49 percent relative to the non-South, indicating a continuing process of upgrading in the composition of Southern manufacturing.

Second, the South passed during 1930-60 from a predominantly rural to a predominantly urban region, as shown by the following data on relative urban population:[5]

PERCENTAGE OF TOTAL POPULATION URBAN

YEAR	SOUTH	NON-SOUTH	SOUTH AS % OF NON-SOUTH
1900	18.0%	50.0%	36%
1930	34.1%	66.4%	52%
1940	36.7%	65.7%	56%
1950	44.0%	65.8%	67%
1960	57.7%	74.4%	78%

Whereas the rest of the nation's population became more urban than rural shortly after 1900, it was only half a century later (during the 1950's) that the South's urban population exceeded its rural population. The rapid acceleration of Southern urbanization may be indicated by the fact that its relative urban population increased during the single decade 1950-60 nearly as much as during the preceding thirty years 1920-50. At the same time, the South's relative urban population moved up sharply from 52 to 78 percent of the non-South's during 1930-60.

[4]Includes industries not otherwise specified.

[5]Excludes Delaware, Maryland, District of Columbia, and West Virginia. Based on Calvin Hoover and B. U. Ratchford, *Economic Resources and Policies of the South,* Macmillan, New York, 1951, pp. 23-24; and U. S. Census of Population, 1960.

Decline of the Rural-Agricultural Sector

As the South was becoming more industrial and urban, it was of course becoming less agricultural and rural. Thus, the percentage of the Southern labor force employed in agriculture[6]—which had slightly exceeded 50 percent in 1920—declined as follows during 1930-60:

	RELATIVE AGRICULTURAL EMPLOYMENT		
YEAR	SOUTH	NON-SOUTH	SOUTH AS % OF NON-SOUTH
1930	42.8%	14.6%	293%
1940	34.9%	12.8%	269%
1950	22.9%	9.0%	254%
1960	10.4%	5.5%	189%

It will be noted that the relative importance of agriculture in the South's total employment dropped from 43 percent in 1930 to only 10 percent in 1960. While relative agricultural employment was also dropping sharply in the rest of the nation, the decline in the South was sufficiently greater so that, relative to the non-South, the South's agricultural sector employed less than twice as many in 1960 as compared with about three times as many thirty years earlier.

Meanwhile, Southern agriculture had experienced a remarkable change toward greater diversification into farm products of higher productivity. Thus, in terms of the composition of the South's total gross cash farm income, the following shifts[7] took place:

	RELATIVE SOUTHERN AGRICULTURAL INCOME FROM			
YEAR	COTTON	OTHER CROPS	LIVESTOCK AND PRODUCTS	TOTAL
1929	46.0%	26.4%	27.6%	100.0%
1939	26.7%	36.6%	36.7%	100.0%
1949	27.2%	34.6%	38.2%	100.0%
1960	18.0%	39.3%	42.7%	100.0%

Here, the most striking change was the precipitous drop in the relative importance of cotton in Southern agriculture during 1930-60.

[6]Same exclusions and sources as in previous footnote.

[7]Same exclusions as in footnote 5. Sources were Hoover and Ratchford, *op. cit.*, p. 103; and U. S. Dept. of Agri., *Farm Income Situation.*

In 1930, after reigning for well over a century in the South, King Cotton was still a tyrant, accounting for nearly half (46%) of the region's agricultural income. By 1960, when he accounted for only 18 percent, King Cotton had clearly been reduced to the status of a constitutional monarch. In substantial part, the production of cotton had become much more efficient, thanks to mechanization and other improved techniques associated with a more productive use of farm labor. Furthermore, by diversifying into other crops, Southern agriculture had become less dependent upon the vagaries of a single crop. Finally, by its notable expansion of livestock and livestock products (particularly cattle and poultry), from 28 to 43 percent, the South had also found ways to utilize its plentiful labor supply more fully throughout the calendar year, to follow better soil-conservation practices, and to raise annual farm incomes significantly.

With its rapidly increasing urban population, the South's relative rural population also declined sharply, as shown by the following figures:[8]

PERCENTAGE OF TOTAL POPULATION RURAL

YEAR	SOUTH	NON-SOUTH	SOUTH AS % OF NON-SOUTH
1900	82.0%	50.0%	164%
1930	65.9%	34.0%	194%
1940	63.3%	34.3%	185%
1950	56.0%	34.2%	135%
1960	42.3%	25.6%	165%

Since these data are simply the converse of those on relative urban population, they are presented primarily to indicate an interesting contrast with the much greater decline in relative agricultural employment, particularly in the South.

To a large extent, the much smaller drop in rural population reflects the general trend toward suburban and rural living by those employed in urban centers. Especially in the South, it also reflects the large numbers of persons who have changed from farm to non-farm occupations without giving up their original residences. While many of these latter persons have considerably increased their annual incomes, substantial numbers (again especially in the South) have probably simply shifted from employment at low wages in agriculture to employment at little higher wages in some marginal non-agricultural activity still in the rural sector. Thus, in recent years,

[8]Same exclusions and sources as in footnote 5.

part of the problem of human poverty in the South may well have shifted from its rapidly declining rural-farm sector to its rural-nonfarm sector as well as (via migration and unemployment) to the urban sector. Even so, for the most part, declining agricultural employment in the South—whether due to out-migration to other regions or to its own industrial-urban development—has undoubtedly been favorable to raising the incomes of both those who left agriculture and those who stayed behind.

That a declining agricultural labor force is absolutely necessary for the South's continuing economic development can be illustrated by turning our attention to the available data on the productivity of Southern agriculture, on rates of crude natural increase, and on out-migration both actual and potential.

Productivity in Southern Agriculture

The South's relatively low agricultural productivity in a year as recent as 1949 can be illustrated by the following comparisons between one of the best agricultural regions of the South, the Mississippi Delta, and one of the best agricultural regions of the non-South, Central Iowa:[9]

INDEX, 1949	AGRICULTURE OF		MISSISSIPPI AS % OF IOWA
	MISSISSIPPI DELTA	CENTRAL IOWA	
Average per Farm:			
Gross value of product	$3,029	$ 9,603	32%
Net value of product	$2,421	$ 6,052	41
Man-years of labor	1.62	1.42	114
Value of land and capital	$7,321	$46,197	16
Acres of cropland	36.7	136.7	27
Average per Farm Worker:			
Gross value of product	$1,870	$ 6,763	28%
Net value of product	$1,494	$ 4,262	35
Value of land and capital	$4,519	$32,533	14
Inputs per $1,000 of Net Product:			
Man-years of labor	0.67	0.23	291%
Value of land and capital	$3,024	$ 7,633	40

[9]"Gross value of product" includes all farm products produced, including an estimate of the value of product consumed on the farm. "Net value of product" is gross value less selected cash production expenses. Available labor was converted to "man-years of labor" actually used by adjusting for farm operator's work off of farm, age of operator, and seasonality, quantity, and quality of family-labor inputs, defining a man-year at 2,500 hours of actual labor input. "Value of land and capital" includes value of land, buildings, power and machinery, and productive livestock. (Data derived from Jackson V. McElveen

According to these data, the average Mississippi Delta farm had slightly more labor but only one-sixth as much cropland and one-fourth as much land and capital as did the average Central Iowa farm. Accordingly, the average Mississippi farm had a net value of product only 41 percent of that of the average Iowa farm. Perhaps in more meaningful terms, the average farm worker in Mississippi, having only one-seventh as much land and capital to work with, produced only about one-third (35%) as much net product as the average farm worker in Iowa. Finally, in order to produce a given amount ($1,000 worth) of net product, Mississippi agriculture used almost three times as much labor, but less than half (40%) as much land and capital, as did Iowa agriculture. Thus, in 1949—despite decades of large-scale shifts of Southern farm workers into non-farm employment, either in other regions or in the South—Southern agriculture still suffered from an excess labor supply and a deficit of capital, with the consequence of relatively low labor productivity and income.

Major Demographic Trends

In large part, the reason was that the rate of natural increase of the Southern population remained sufficiently high to keep its human reservoir rising in spite of a very large outflow of migrants to other regions. The following vital statistics[10] will amply illustrate the problem:

| | PER THOUSAND OF TOTAL POPULATION | | |
YEAR	SOUTH	NON-SOUTH	SOUTH AS % OF NON-SOUTH
	Crude Birth Rates		
1930	26.6	19.2	139%
1940	25.1	18.4	136
1960	24.6	23.4	105
	Crude Death Rates		
1930	11.5	11.5	100%
1940	10.4	11.1	95
1960	8.6	9.5	91
	Crude Natural Increase		
1930	15.1	7.7	204%
1940	14.7	7.3	200
1960	16.0	13.9	115

and Kenneth L. Bachman, *Low Production Farms*, Agri. Info. Bul. 108, U. S. Dept. Agri., Washington, 1953).

[10]Hoover and Rathford, *op. cit.*, pp. 23-24, and U.S. Bureau of the Census. Excluding Delaware, Maryland, District of Columbia, and West Virginia.

These figures indicate that, in both 1930 and 1940, crude birth rates in the South were more than one-third higher than in the non-South, largely the effect of the South's more rural population. At the same time, crude death rates in the South were as low or slightly lower than in the rest of the country, the effects of the fact that the South had poorer medical and public-health facilities being more than offset by the lower average age of its population. With substantially higher birth rates and approximately the same death rates, however, the South as late as 1940 had an excess of births over deaths per 1000 population (the crude rate of natural increase) fully *twice* that of the rest of the nation. By 1960, birth rates in the South and non-South had moved close together but, having gained a slightly more favorable relative death rate, the South still had a crude natural increase 15 percent higher than that of the non-South.

If, then, one looks only at the relatives of South to non-South, the results look very favorable to the South's economic development since most of the interregional difference in natural increase had disappeared during 1940-60. Such a result would not be surprising since, having become much less rural, the South might have been expected to reduce its birth rate toward the lower level of the more urban non-South, thereby relieving the historic pressures to accommodate the South's excess rural-farm population by out-migration and by internal occupational shifts. Unfortunately, in this instance, the gap in the rate of natural increase was actually closed by an opposite tendency—i.e., by birth rates in the non-South rising to the levels which had characterized the South in the pre-war period. This latter tendency may perhaps be attributed primarily to the post-war "baby boom" in the non-South and to a normal time lag between urbanization and reduced birth rates in the South. With some recent indications that birth rates in the non-South are beginning to move back toward their lower pre-war levels, plus the probability that natality patterns in the urbanizing South will increasingly resemble national norms, large interregional differences in natural increase may well have disappeared for good. Meanwhile, however, the effects of the "baby boom" in the non-South have been unfavorable to Southern economic development in the sense that the non-South, now providing a larger part of its own labor force, offers fewer job opportunities for migrants from the South than the latter have historically enjoyed. As a consequence, the South's further economic progress must depend even more on its own industral-urban development than in the past.

The extent of the surplus farm labor force in the South as late as the 1950's may be illustrated by the following data on replacement ratios of rural-farm males in the working age group 20-64 for low- and high-income farming areas of the United States:[11]

FARMING AREA BY LEVEL OF FARM-FAMILY INCOME	REPLACEMENT RATIOS RURAL-FARM MALES OF WORKING AGE, 1950-60	RATE OF NET MIGRATION 1940-50
United States	168	—30.9%
Medium and high income areas (largely non-South)	143	—28.1
Low-income areas (largely South):	(200)	(—33.7)
Moderate	169	—27.2
Substantial	206	—34.9
Serious	221	—37.1

The "replacement ratio" indicates the number of rural-farm males expected to enter the age group 20-64 during 1950-60, *assuming no net migration* into or out of the given area and no shifts to non-farm employment within the area, per 100 rural-farm males expected to leave the same age group through death or retirement during the same decade. Thus, the figure 168 for the United States means that, for every 100 rural-farm males of working age dying or retiring during 1950-60, 168 were expected (in the absence of migration or local occupational shifts) to become farmers of working age. It further means that, for the farm labor force merely to remain constant rather than increase, about 40 percent (68 out of 168) would have to find non-farm jobs either locally or (via migration) at a distance.

The above figures are very important, making it clear that, the lower the average family income of a farming area, the higher its natural increase and the greater the excess of its farm labor force, in the absence of out-migration or increased non-farm employment, over previous high levels. While they also indicate that, during 1940-50, net out-migration rates were higher, the greater the extent of rural poverty, they also emphasize the very large magnitude of the downward adjustments still needed in the farm labor force. Thus, even in the medium and high-income farming areas of the non-South, about 30 per cent of the rural-farm males had to find non-farm jobs for the farm labor force just to hold its own. In low-income Southern agriculture, the corresponding figure was around 50 percent (100 out of 200). Since Southern agriculture could im-

[11]These figures are taken from a special report of the Secretary of Agriculture, *Development of Agriculture's Human Resources—A Report on Problems of Low-Income Farmers*, U. S. Dept. Agri., Washington, 1950.

prove its low productivity substantially only by an even much larger reduction in its labor force—thereby permitting the consolidation of small farms into larger, more mechanized, and more efficient units—the need for both increased outmigration and increased local non-farm jobs was obviously enormous. While most Southern states actually succeeded in reducing their agricultural employment by 35-60 percent during 1950-60, further substantial reductions will continue to be necessary if Southern agriculture is finally to achieve levels of income comparable with its counterparts in the rest of the nation.

High Out-Migration Rates

Under these circumstances, while it would have been preferable for the South to have enjoyed a sufficient expansion of non-agricultural employment to keep all of its farm youth within the region, continued large-scale outmigration throughout 1930-60 did serve as a "safety valve" which made for more rapid regional development than would have been possible in its absence. The extent of this net migration may be indicated by the following figures:[12]

| DECADE | NET MIGRATION (000) | | |
	WHITES	NEGROES	TOTAL
	Florida and Texas		
1930-40	+153	+55	+208
1940-50	+704	—60	+644
1950-60	+1,657	+74	+1,731
Total, 1930-60	+2,514	+69	+2,583
	11 Other Southern States		
1930-40	—620	—459	—1,079
1940-50	—1,018	—1,261	—2,279
1950-60	—1,327	—1,586	—2,913
Total, 1930-60	—2,965	—3,306	—6,271
	All 13 Southern States		
1930-40	—467	—404	—871
1940-50	—314	—1,321	—1,635
1950-60	—330	—1,512	—1,842
Total, 1930-60	—1,111	—3,237	—4,348

[12]Here, "the South" includes, in addition to Florida and Texas, the states of Virginia, North Carolina, South Carolina, Georgia, Kentucky, Tennessee, Alabama, Mississippi, Arkansas, Louisiana, and Oklahoma. Data compiled from Everett S. Lee, *et al.*, *Population Redistribution and Economic Growth*, Vol. I, Philadelphia, 1957; and U. S. Bureau of the Census, *Current Population Reports*, No. 247, April, 1963.

According to these data, the 13-state South lost by net out-migration 4,348,000 people (74 percent Negro) during 1930-60. However, Florida and Texas differed distinctly from the other Southern states in that they enjoyed persistent net in-migration (gaining a total of 2,583,000 people, almost entirely white) during the same thirty years. The eleven remaining Southern states suffered persistent out-migration, losing 6,271,000 people (53 percent Negro) between 1930 and 1960 and 2,913,000 during the 1950's alone.

Since less than 25 percent of the South's population was Negro during 1930-60, the *rate* of out-migration of Negroes was obviously much higher than that of whites. This continuing phenomenon accounts for the gradual reduction in the South's relative Negro population during the last half century or more:[13]

| YEAR | PERCENTAGE OF TOTAL POPULATION NEGRO | | SOUTH AS % OF NON-SOUTH |
	SOUTH	NON-SOUTH	
1900	34.3%	2.4%	1429%
1910	31.6	2.3	1374
1920	28.6	2.7	1060
1930	26.1	3.5	746
1940	25.0	3.8	657
1950	22.5	5.2	433
1960	21.0	6.6	318

While the South in 1960 still had three times as large a relative Negro population as did the non-South, this index had been cut by more than half since 1940 and by more than four-fifths since 1900. With this radical redistribution of the Negro population, many Northern and Western cities had by 1960 relative Negro populations greater than that (21 percent) for the South as a whole and even some of its own major cities. Given its racial attitudes, the South's large loss of Negro population had probably served to ease somewhat the many race-related problems which have so long plagued its general economic development. In the process of even welcoming Negro out-migration, however, many Southerners have too easily overlooked the concomitant heavy loss of white population and have too cavalierly ignored the high cost to the region of losing people of either race when—after having received substantial private and public investments in their rearing, education, etc.—these people have chosen to move elsewhere as they entered their most productive years.

[13]Same exclusion and sources as in footnote 5 above.

Per-Capita Incomes

In reviewing the changes during 1930-60 in some of the major indexes of Southern economic development, we have found some highly favorable and others much less so. Nonetheless, if we look at the best over-all measure of economic development, per-capita incomes, the very favorable balance becomes clear. In this connection, let us look at the data on real per-capita income payments:[14]

| | REAL PER-CAPITA INCOME PAYMENTS (IN 1957-59 DOLLAR) | | |
YEAR	SOUTH	NON-SOUTH	SOUTH AS % OF NON-SOUTH
1929	$ 623	$1,335	46.7%
1939	665	1,290	51.6
1948	1,200	1,860	64.5
1959	1,652	2,391	69.1

According to the above table, per-capita real income increased during 1929-59 by 165 percent in the South, as compared with only 79 percent in the non-South. In the process, the South closed a remarkable part of the income gap between itself and the rest of the country. Thus, while the South's per-capita income was less than half (47%) of the non-South's in 1929, it had risen to 69% by 1959. However, despite these great strides, there has been some tendency in recent years for the South's relative progress to slacken. Upon what, then, does the South's further economic development depend?

IV. THE JOB THAT REMAINS

The Income Gap by Residence and Race

In order to understand more fully the problems which still remain, if the South is at last to achieve economic parity with the rest of the nation, it is desirable to break down our interregional income comparisons to allow for differences in race and place of residence. At the time of this writing, such a breakdown was possible only for 1949, the 1959 Census data not yet having become available. Even so, the following 1949 family-income data are very instructive:[15]

[14]Hoover and Ratchford, *op. cit.*, p. 48; and *Survey of Current Business*, August 1962. Data in current dollars deflated by Consumer Price Index.

[15]Here, "the South" includes Delaware, Maryland, District of Columbia, and West Virginia. Data compiled or computed from the 1950 Census of Population and from U. S. Bureau of the Census, *Farms and Farm People*, Washington, 1952.

TYPE OF FAMILY	% OF ALL FAMILIES IN REGION WITH INCOMES UNDER $1,000 IN 1949			MEDIAN FAMILY INCOME, 1949		
	SOUTH	NON-SOUTH	SOUTH AS % OF NON-SOUTH	SOUTH	NON-SOUTH	SOUTH AS % OF NON-SOUTH
Rural and urban families:						
All	24.3%	11.5%	211%	$2,248	$3,330	68%
Non-white	43.8	n.a.	n.a.	1,168	n.a.	n.a.
Urban and rural-non farm families:						
All	17.9%	10.5%	170%	$2,622	$3,419	77%
White	n.a.	n.a.	n.a.	n.a.	n.a.	88+
Non-white	34.9	n.a.	n.a.	1,389	n.a.	60++
Rural-farm families:						
All	45.0%	19.4%	232%	$1,284+++	$2,480+++	52%+++
Non-white	69.2	—	n.a.	n.a.	n.a.	n.a.

+ Mean rather than median family income, based on an estimate by D. Gale Johnson.

++ The author's estimate, based on a U. S. median income of $1,658 for non-white families.

+++ Families of farm operators only. If the families of farm laborers are also included, the median farm-family income for the United States as a whole was lowered from $1,867 to $1,729.

The foregoing family-income data indicate that in 1949, for all families rural and urban, the proportions of families having net cash incomes of under $1,000 were 24 percent in the South and 12 percent in the non-South.[16] For the Southern families, however, 45 per cent of those in rural-farm areas, but only 18 percent of those residing in the non-farm (urban and rural-nonfarm) sector, fell into this low-income category. For Southern non-white families, the corresponding figures were much higher—69 and 35 percent, respectively. While the South had about twice as many low-income families (in relative terms) as the non-South, the actual gap was much wider. Typically, the South's low-income families had small children and able-bodied male heads in their most productive years, while their counterparts in the non-South consisted more largely of the widowed, the disabled, and the aged, with fewer dependents and lighter financial responsibilities, frequently having savings or other capital resources from which to supplement their low current incomes. Thus, the South's poverty stemmed largely from poorly utilized but potentially more productive human resources, the non-South's poverty representing primarily a welfare rather than a production problem.

Let us now turn to the data on median family incomes in the preceding table. We see first that, for all urban and rural families, the South's median family income was 68 percent of the non-South's in 1949.[17] However, Southern non-farm white families (with incomes at 88 percent of their counterparts in the non-South) had nearly closed the interregional gap, particularly if we take into account the higher cost of living associated with the non-South's typically larger urban centers. On the other hand, Southern non-farm Negro families were only 60 percent, and Southern farm-operator families were only 52 percent as well off as their non-Southern equivalents. Thus, the above data make clear that, as late as 1949, the South's low-income problem was largely centered in its non-farm Negro population and in its farm population, both white and Negro. (As to the latter group, it should also be emphasized that— while a much larger percentage of Negroes than whites was in the

[16]According to preliminary data from the 1960 Census of Population, these percentages had fallen to 10.1 and 4.0 percent, respectively, during 1949-59. This undoubtedly reflects substantial improvement, even though the common $1,000 limit represented (in 1949 dollars) only $825 in 1959.

[17]According to the author's estimate from preliminary 1960 Census data, this percentage had increased to 74 percent by 1959.

low-income group—68 percent of all low-income farm families in the South were white.) While changes during 1950-60 may well have ameliorated somewhat the relatively low incomes of Southern farm families relative to those of the non-South, it probably remains true today that further Southern economic progress will largely depend upon further improvement in the South's rural sector.

Toward a Solution

If we are to find a solution for the low-income problems of the South's urban Negroes and its rural people of both races, more vigorous public policies will be required. It is largely migrants from these groups who, because of low levels of education and skills, constitute our nation's present alarmingly large "hard core" of unemployment. Among these Negroes and rural whites are additional millions who, although officially recorded as employed in agriculture or other low-productivity occupations, are seriously *under*-employed. Hence, monetary-fiscal policies to assure expanding nonfarm job opportunities and greater public outlays for general and vocational education are essential if the South is to complete its economic renaissance.

Continued efforts to industrialize low-income rural areas will also be necessary. Improvements in public job-information and job-placement services are very much needed to facilitate migration from the rural South. Finally, the resources devoted to supervised public farm credit must be greatly increased to help those who remain in Southern agriculture to reorganize their farms into larger-scale, more mechanized, more productive enterprises. Only through a three-pronged attack—directed at further industrial-urban development, even greater labor mobility, and increased farm-capital resources—can the Southern economy at last become a full partner in the nation's further economic progress.

Such a program will be costly. But, if a modest fraction of the billions of dollars being wasted by our extravagant and ill-conceived agricultural price-support program were diverted to such uses, the problems of the South's low-income rural people would be far more quickly solved. If the South's Congressional delegations were (like their constituencies) less reluctant to recognize the problems and needs of the new industrial-urban South, more satisfactory federal policies would undoubtedly be forthcoming. But few Southern Congressmen have yet abandoned the old rural traditions which have so seriously hampered the region's economic progress.

Clearly, sharp shifts in both racial customs and the rural-urban balance of political power have become essential to the South's further economic development, and are actually under way to a much greater extent than Southerners themselves yet realize. Recent Supreme Court decisions on school integration and legislative reapportionment—while roundly damned by many Southerners—will probably appear a generation hence to have been major landmarks in Southern progress. The principal support for segregating the races comes from the South's tradition-bound rural minorities. The significance of the reapportionment decision is profound, since it will at last give the South's increasingly urban-industrial majorities a voice more nearly proportional to their numbers. As a result, the forward-looking, progressive, and dynamic forces which Southern industrial-urban development has already created will rather quickly erode away the blind sectionalism, the negative and defensive states'-right doctrines, the disinterest in general social and economic betterment, and the race extremism which have so long diverted Southern energies from constructive channels.

The non-economic factors which historically have shackled the South's economic progress are at last in full retreat. The recent sound and fury emerging from the South can easily be misunderstood. It clearly represents the death throes, not the renaissance, of those Southern traditions which are inconsistent with the region's industrial-urban development. In the process, the South is finally creating the environment needed for it to achieve full economic parity with the rest of the nation. I am now confident that, if appropriate public policies are forthcoming, the South can and will achieve this goal.

SOUTHERN REGIONAL PLANNING AND DEVELOPMENT

LAWRENCE LOGAN DURISCH
Tennessee Valley Authority

T WENTY-FIVE YEARS AGO, the same year in which the first issue
of the *Journal of Politics* appeared, the National Resources
Planning Board was established by congressional action as part of
the Executive Office of the President. The primary function of the
Board as constituted in 1939 was to advise the President on matters
of long-range policy. Another function was to stimulate interest and
activity in planning, nationally and by states, regions, and local governments. The Board saw area planning as a responsibility shared by
all levels of government, and the passing of a quarter of a century
has served to make even clearer the intergovernmental character
of planning.

In 1942 the National Resources Planning Board issued as one
of a series a report on *Regional Planning in the Southeast.* The
series, which in a sense was to be the swan song of the agency,
placed great emphasis on a regional approach to the development of
American resources and gave considered emphasis to the role that
state planning must play in that process. The report for the Southeast directed attention to the activities and potential usefulness of
the Southeastern Regional Planning Commission, an agency destined
soon to disappear. It discussed also the activities of the various
state planning agencies which had recently been organized and were
functioning with assistance of various types from the National Resources Planning Board.

The state planning agencies of the 1940's were concerned with
inventorying resources and with the collection of basic data over a
wide range of subject fields. They addressed themselves also to
problems of physical planning, such as the conservation of land
and water resources, and to the formulation of public works programs. A few of the state planning agencies undertook studies of
special problems in the economic and social fields, but none produced
or even undertook to produce comprehensive state plans in an action
framework.

The state planning agencies that survived World War II and the immediate post-war period turned their attention to providing technical assistance to local planning commissions and to industrial development. Research was retained as a function, but again little or no attention was given to comprehensive state planning.

Recently, the idea of state planning has been given new emphasis. This time, moreover, an effort is being made to fit planning into the framework of state administration, and a great deal of attention is being given to the place of the planning agency in the organizational structure. The case for a central planning agency as a staff arm of the governor has made progress and at the same time the need for decentralized planning by the operating departments of state government is recognized.

Planning is still not well established as a function of state government in the South—nor for that matter in any other part of the nation. Only the state of Hawaii seems to have produced an effective and comprehensive development plan. Some progress is being made in over-all state planning by certain other states, including Alaska, Delaware, California, New Jersey, New Mexico, Maryland, Minnesota, Pennsylvania, Wisconsin, and in the South, Tennessee. Perhaps others should be added to this list for there is new concern with state planning and a growing realization that some of the most important decisions in the field of economics and social development in the next decade or two must be made at the state capitols.

The developmental needs and opportunities of the Southern region, including those relating to the conservation and better utilization of its resources, lend emphasis to the importance of state planning. This is true whether the state action called for is that of implementing Federal programs, of metropolitan area adjustment, of authorizing or participating in the multi-purpose development of small watersheds or other subregions, or of meeting the special challenge presented by the Appalachian or Piedmont regions or by other major physiographic areas. State planning becomes a necessary complement to organized efforts to promote industrial development and is inherent in the decisions called for in comprehensive resources programs, however organized. Responsibility and the legal power to decide and act in many developmental situations rests squarely with the states—accordingly, even in cases where Federal grants-in-aid are involved, most of the program planning must be state planning.

The establishment of over-all planning as a function of state government presents organizational problems that vary somewhat from state to state. However, the general considerations noted and the point of view set out in a report by a special committee of the American Institute of Planners will bear repeating here:

> To be effective state planning must meet the organizational as well as functional needs of present-day state government. This report does not lay down hard and fast rules as to how state planning should be organized. It does suggest principles of organization for state planning based on the general concept that the chief executive has the responsibility for formulating long-range policies and for directing programs to carry them out. Moreover, in many states the chief is becoming more and more the focal point for legislative leadership. The planning staff should be in a position to help him in preparing policy and program recommendations for administrative and legislative consideration.
>
> Within these general concepts, the following principles of organization for state planning are suggested:
>
> 1) State planning must be an integral part of the administrative structure of state government.
> 2) The staff concerned with over-all state planning should be advisory to the chief executive. The staff should act at his direction in its relationships with the legislature and with individual state departments.
> 3) The director of planning must be acceptable to the chief executive and should be qualified by training and experience in state and regional planning. The trained technical staff should be within the career service.
> 4) An advisory commission may or may not be needed. If such a commission is created it should be advisory to the director of planning who takes full administrative responsibility for recommendations.[1]

Planning thus is seen as a staff function designed to assist the governor in making decisions relative to policy formulation and to supply for his use the facts and analysis required in administration. State planning in the modern scheme of affairs takes its place along with budgeting, to which it is closely related. What programs the state spends money for and how much it spends along with the determination of priorities among programs and emphasis within programs are planning matters. It is in central policy formulation that the core function of state planning is executed; but it also has important responsibilities relating to general and capital improvement

---

[1]The Drafting Committee members were A. J. Gray, Chairman, Edward L. Hopkins, L. L. Durisch, and E. David Stoloff. The complete report is printed in *The Journal of American Institute of Planners,* Vol. XXV, No. 4, November, 1959. See also the provocative comment on the report by Elton R. Andrews in the same issue.

programing and to the planning and programing carried on by operating or line departments.

The importance of planning in the future of the South—and particularly that of state planning—calls for a great deal of attention to structure and organization as well as to purpose and function. Properly organized and oriented state planning agencies can be a factor in all developmental programs, whether of Federal, state, or local origin, and regardless of whether the area of operation is region-wide, confined to the limits of one state, or to a portion of a state such as a small watershed or a metropolitan region. All functional and areal programs call for identifiable state goals, established priorities, and the achievement of balance among various activities. These requisites of sound long-range development are the products of the planning process.

*   *   *   *

The Southern region is usually considered as made up of thirteen states; namely, West Virginia, Virginia, Kentucky, Tennessee, North Carolina, South Carolina, Georgia, Alabama, Mississippi, Arkansas, Louisiana, Texas, and Florida. The South is one of the major divisions of the nation set apart for purposes of study and analysis. The problems of the region have long been a matter of concern, and in 1938 President Franklin D. Roosevelt felt justified in characterizing the region as the nation's number one economic problem. Since 1938 the tempo of growth has picked up and the southern states have made considerable progress. They have, for example, made absolute gains in population, nonfarm employment, personal income, and per capita income during the period. In spite of these gains, for the South as a whole, the problems outlined in 1938 persist. They persist in terms of the uneven character of the gains, for not all parts of the South have shared in the progress that has been made. In the aggregate the region has suffered a steady decline in its share of the total population of the nation and in its share of national employment. The conclusion which emerges from a maze of statistics is that the South is one of the slow-growing parts of the nation. A key question this suggests is: Can the relationship of the people and their institutions to the natural resources of the South be altered by wise planning and by the will to action so as to move the region ahead at a faster rate? What are the strengths and weaknesses of the region's economy and how can both be taken into account in drawing up an action agenda for the South?

Fifty million people were living in the 13 southern states in mid 1962.[2] Over the 25-year period from 1937 to 1962 the population of this region increased by 43 percent—a rate equivalent to that for conterminous United States.[3] In absolute numbers the region's increase of 15 million approximated the combined 1962 population of the states of Texas, Louisiana, and Arkansas. There were extreme variations in the pattern of growth of the individual states. During this 25-year period Florida experienced an increase of 219 percent; Texas and Virginia, 62 and 61 percent respectively. In contrast, Mississippi's gain was less than 1 percent, and Arkansas and West Virginia had population losses of 4 and 2 percent respectively.

The birth rate in the South is approaching that of the nation. In 1940, births to residents of the southern states were 25.0 per 1,000 population, whereas the national rate was 19.4. By 1950 the rate for the South was 27.4 against 24.1 for the nation, but in 1960 the rate had dropped to 24.7 compared to 23.6 in the nation. The birth rates for the eight Mountain states[4] now exceed those of the South.

About one-half of the southern population live in metropolitan areas as compared to more than 65 percent in the country as a whole. Florida's Fort Lauderdale-Hollywood metropolitan area experienced the highest rate (264 percent) of in-migration during the 1950's of any of the nation's 212 metropolitan areas. Net out-migration from the southern states, however, numbered 1.4 million people in the 1950's and 2.1 million in the 1940's—combined, this number is equivalent to almost 10 percent of the 1940 population. In *Recent Southern Economic Development As Revealed by the Changing Structure of Employment*,[5] Edgar S. Dunn, Jr. states that "The time is past when we can assume that the economic opportunity hypothesis alone is adequate to explain migration behavior. There is a substantial amount of migration taking place that is primarily amenity seeking." The challenge presented by out-migration is a complex one and those who would see the South retain its natural increase in population must direct their efforts not to one but to many fronts.

[2]U. S. Bureau of the Census, *Current Population Reports,* Series P-25, No. 259.
[3]The United States excluding Hawaii and Alaska.
[4]Arizona, Colorado, Idaho, Montana, Nevada, New Mexico, Utah, and Wyoming.
[5]University of Florida Monographs, Social Sciences, No. 14, Spring 1962.

The South now has an average per capita income of around 73 percent of that for the nation, and the per capita income of the Southern region is still the lowest of any major part of the United States. Moreover, the Southern states have experienced a reduction in their share of the nation's employment. As workers move out of agriculture, many of them are not able to find employment opportunity in nonfarm jobs in the South. Manufacturing employment increased about 15 percent in the region during the last decade, but the increase in trades and service occupations lagged behind national rates (20 percent compared with more than 30 percent). Employment in mining in the South declined sharply while transportation and construction registered only modest gains. In contrast employment in government, particularly in state and local government, has added substantial numbers of new jobs to the Southern economy in recent years.

In the last two decades there has been in the South a mass migration from agriculture to public service. Between 1940 and 1960 agricultural employment lost 2.4 million (nearly 60 percent) of its workers in the 13 states. During the same period, public employment gained 1.2 million jobs (12.6 percent increase). As a result it is fair to characterize the shift as opening a new frontier in the government sector of the employment pattern.

The Manpower Report of the President, transmitted to Congress in March 1963, has this to say of the national trend in the field:

> The changing structure of employment from manufacturing production to private and public services, may be seen from the singular fact that nearly two-thirds of the new jobs added to the economy in the past five years have been in state and local government, for the most part in teaching. We cannot accept this situation.[6]

This situation may generally be quite unacceptable, but it will be noted that the new governmental jobs are predominantly in the teaching field. In a region whose educational level both in quality and in number of years in school achieved by its adult population is well below national levels, an increase in the number of teachers must be viewed as necessary and desirable.

The commitment of the South to programs designed to achieve better utilization of resources most recently finds expression in terms

---

[6]U. S. President (Kennedy), *Manpower Report of the President and Report on Manpower Requirements, Resources, Utilization, and Training by Department of Labor*. Transmitted to Congress March 1963. Washington, Government Printing Office, 1963, p. xi.

of the quest for industrial development, or more realistically economic growth. The region now looks to industrial promotion in its effort to undo the mistake attributed to the year 1828 when the leadership of the South is said to have decided that its future was in agriculture. The year 1939 can be said to mark the date of general acceptance by the leadership of the South of the importance of industrialization. An examination of the messages of southern governors to the legislative bodies over the last 25 years discloses only a few instances in which the state executive failed to emphasize the need to move the state ahead industrially. Most of the messages pledged support to efforts to industrialize and proposed public action of some form or another to encourage economic growth.

Southern states are concerned about their "state image," and in all of them there are signs that the desire for industrial growth is a factor in modifying outmoded attitudes and long-cherished but irrelevant traditions. The quest for industry has led, for example, to the re-examination of tax systems, to the redirection of educational activities along vocational lines, to state support of research, and to the rearrangement of state-local relations. The need for non-farm employment finds its way into state conservation activities. Recreation programs are most often approached in their commercial aspects. The old saying about tourists being more profitable and easier to pick than cotton has its more serious implications. A reforestation program recently conducted in a number of southern states is presented to the public with the persuasive slogan "Plant Trees—Grow Jobs." At the local level the search for industry takes many forms, including governmental subsidies sometimes involving staggering industrial bond issues (for example, Cherokee, Alabama; population 1,349—industrial bond issue $25 million).

The natural endowment of the South—its soils, climate, mineral deposits, and its water resources—gives variety both to problems and to developmental possibilities. The changing patterns of agriculture together with more adequate attention to problems of soil fertility, erosion, and other aspects of land management have increased farm production during a period when employment in farming has experienced marked decreases. The same principles of improved management have made the forests of the South a greatly improved regional asset. The better adjustment of the forest resource to agriculture and to industry is an understandable goal—a goal that is being achieved in many southern states.

Water is a regional resource of increasing importance. Like the soil and the timber, it has been used wastefully as though the supply were unlimited. Most of the South is a water abundant area, but there is now evidence that the demand for water for domestic use, for industry, for recreation, for irrigation, as well as for navigation and power means that water uses must be carefully planned and co-ordinated. Water is definitely establishing itself as a resource with uses ranging from domestic consumption to recreation.

Water technology has scored impressive gains in recent years, and the South is beginning to realize that it has a tremendous task of enlarging, conserving, and using wisely all available water re-sources. The job is one of creating public understanding and of providing the organizational arrangements—national, regional, and state—that will permit constructive action over the entire range of problems and opportunities presented by the water situation. Water adequacy in most parts of the Southern region for ages to come will involve human wisdom and institutional arrangements, including the ability to plan constructively, more than the limits nature has set for the resource.

Urbanization and industrial growth are introducing basic changes in resource use patterns. Among the new points of emphasis are space and locational requirements for industrial, commercial, resi-dential, and recreational areas. A new highway pattern is removing vast areas from other uses; at the same time it is making larger areas more accessible for recreational, residential, and industrial use.

Governmental decisions regarding resource development are in the last analysis political decisions; economic considerations may, of course, be a factor in arriving at the necessary value judgments in support of a given course of action. The planning process has an active role to play in shaping resource policy in a changing South. The planning approach can help to clarify issues, provide a basis for allocation of public funds among programs, and help in securing the unified approach to resource development called for under present conditions. If, for example, an industrial plant by inade-quate treatment of wastes will render a stream unfit for other pur-poses, the nature of the alternative uses of the flowing water and their relationship to the whole economy and to society generally should enter into the decision to tolerate or not to tolerate the con-ditions which may result from the plant location.

The South has actual and potential economic advantages which may well give it a higher relative economic position in the nation.[7] Among these are various aspects of the natural environment including abundant water and forest resources, favorable climatic conditions, and important outdoor recreational opportunities. The agricultural economy of the South has in the past not utilized these advantages effectively; but as farms and farmers decrease in numbers, southern agriculture must become more efficient and must produce higher incomes for those remaining in agriculture. The new interstate highway system along with improved waterways and extended air service, combined with advancing technology, are encouraging industrial development and with it the rapid urbanization of a traditionally agricultural South.

The increased attention being given to the orderly development of public services and facilities and to educational programs are definite developmental advantages. The abundant labor supply, which seems somewhat reluctant to migrate, becomes an attraction to industry as educational levels are raised. Although conditions in the South seem favorable for relatively rapid economic growth, such growth is not a certainty. To a considerable extent the rate of progress will depend on national decisions and national economic progress, but it will also depend on human efforts and institutional factors within the region. It will require developmental planning and programing on a state and regional basis done with skill and imagination and on a large scale.

*   *   *   *

The South provides in the Tennessee Valley program an example of area development which has attracted world-wide attention. The Act of 1933 for the first time in national experience, gave one agency, the Tennessee Valley Authority, responsibility for an entire river system in what were considered to be its principal public aspects: flood control, navigation, and hydro-electric development. TVA was also to fit the government-owned chemical plant facilities at Muscle Shoals into the needs of national defense as well as to the agricultural needs of the region. The agency was to cooperate with states and localities in studies and surveys for the "purpose of fostering an orderly and proper physical, economic, and social development" of the Tennessee Basin and adjoining territory.

[7]See *Region, Resources and Economic Growth,* Perloff, Harvey S., and others. Baltimore, The Johns Hopkins Press, 1960.

In addition to the concept of unified river improvement, the Act creating TVA reflected the idea of regional planning. President Franklin D. Roosevelt in his message to Congress called for the creation of an administrative agency ". . . charged with the broadest duty of planning for the proper use, conservation, and development of the natural resources of the Tennessee River drainage basin and its adjoining territory for the general, social, and economic welfare of the nation. This authority should be clothed with the necessary powers to carry these plans into effect."[8] There was, however, no real discussion of planning by the Congress and no precedent for the type of regional planning envisaged by the President's message.

The Valley itself is made up of parts of seven southern states. It is bound together by no common administrative ties other than those of the Federal Government including the cohesive force supplied by the regional program fashioned by TVA. As early as 1936 TVA recorded its understanding and acceptance of the framework within which its developmental effort was to proceed:

> The planning of the river's future is entrusted to the TVA. The planning of the Valley's future must be the democratic labor of many agencies and individuals, and final success is as much a matter of general initiative as of general consent[9]

The approach of TVA is regional, and its methods of relating the river improvements it constructs to the development of the entire watershed are cooperative. Most observers will agree that TVA has planned and carried out its direct activities rather well and that the unified development of the river system represents a major engineering achievement. The power program has proceeded in accordance with bold long-range plans that have correctly interpreted the growing needs for electricity. Navigation and flood control have been adequately covered in the development which has taken place. The greatest test of regionalism, as typified by TVA, centers in the cooperative procedures and programs which can be developed. It is the cooperative approach that gives the TVA experiment its distinctive character and which holds out the greatest promise of continuing regional progress.

The extent to which states, local government, and non-public entities have entered into the spirit and purpose of the program in

[8]Message of April 10, 1933 (73rd Congress, 1st Session, House Document 15, p 2).

[9]Annual Report of the Tennessee Valley Authority, 1936, p. 2.

the Tennessee Valley region is noteworthy. Nevertheless, as the fourth decade of TVA's activity begins, the need to intensify efforts to achieve cooperative planning and develpment can be clearly seen. Certain facilities, important in the growth of any region, have been supplied by the program—an improved waterway, a stabilized water supply for industrial and recreational uses, a flood-free shoreline, an adequate supply of low-cost electricity, high analysis fertilizers for building sound farm management practices, and technical assistance to states and local agencies in a score of subject fields. These activities must be supplemented by and related to a wide range of state and local governmental activity. In many cases utilization of the facilities provided by the Federal Government are dependent upon state and local action if they are to be major factors in regional progress. The responsibility for relating Federal programs and facilities to the general functions of state and local government in a comprehensive regional development effort rests mainly with the states. The future of the Tennessee Valley program, in particular, is dependent to a considerable extent upon the further development and extension of the theory and practice of sound planning and constructive action by the states in the region.[10]

The same problems of Federal-state-local relations exist in other river basins. Recently, the U. S. Study Commission, Southeast River Basins, and the U. S. Study Commission, Southwest River Basins—Texas completed the initial report phase of what, in each case, has been described as a new venture in cooperative planning to facilitate the optimum development of the land and water resources of major portions of the Southern region. While the Federal acts, which created the commissions, call for a comprehensive and coordinated plan for basin development, they do not contemplate the creation of any new permanent Federal developmental agencies of the type represented by TVA. The acts and the resulting reports rather place responsibility for coordination and integration of developmental activities with the states in their individual and collective capacities.[11] The developmental plans for the Arkansas-White

[10]See Menhinick, H. K. and Durisch, L. L., "Tennessee Valley Authority: Planning in Operation," *The Town Planning Review*, 24:116-145, July 1953.

[11]The Delaware River Basin Compact, which received Federal approval in 1961, was a precedent creating effort to solve the problems of interstate basins by creating a new agency "which is at once a part of the government of each of the affected states and the United States Government." This pooling of legal

river system, the product of a Federal inter-agency committee working with representatives of the several states directly concerned, serve also to emphasize that the states must play an important part in basin development.

While the states need planning programs to participate effectively in the development of major river basins, such programs are equally urgent in the smaller watershed areas within the several states. The program of small watershed development undertaken by the Soil Conservation Service is designed to deal with water problems and related land-use problems in the smaller watersheds of the nation. The program makes use of state and locally organized committees — essentially areal planning agencies. In its tributary area development program TVA is extending to the upper reaches of the Tennessee River system the total program of integrated development of all resources, using small watersheds as the basis of activity organizations. The TVA tributary area program begins with an inventory of resources and problems undertaken by locally organized groups. Technicians from the states and from TVA assist in the inventory and appraisal, but their role is primarily that of advice and consultation. TVA does supply a technical water plan, but it is a water plan based on locally determined needs and objectives. The plans for the watershed are essentially locally developed plans.

The states have a major role to play in the development of tributary areas—a role that goes beyond technical assistance or the perfunctory attention they have been given to date. The state, and only the state, is in a position to determine priorities in state assistance as between local watersheds—all anxious for immediate development. As programs of local water control are merged with broader considerations of area development, the state must redirect and channel its services with the larger program objectives in view. The state is in a position to relate a watershed to the larger economic area of which it is a part and to the state as a whole. Finally, the organization, legal authorizations, and financing of watershed activities require state action. Procedures for small watershed devel-

authority, administrative talent, and resources of four state governments and of the Federal Government is discussed in:

Zimmerman, F. L., and Mitchell, W., "New Horizons on the Delaware," *State Government*, 36:157-165, Summer 1963. See also Grad, Frank, "Federal-State Compact, A New Experiment in Cooperative Federalism," *Columbia Law Review*, 63:825-855, May 1963.

opment are only now being developed, and the situation presents a real challenge to the "American talent for political and administrative invention"—state government must especially respond to that challenge.[12]

*   *   *   *

In addition to watersheds and other resource-oriented areas, other economic regions emerge as planning and development units. Here again there is need to relate activities in the smaller areas to some statewide development plan. This is particularly important as the boundaries separating urban and resource areas become more and more blurred and indistinct. Furthermore, the same forces of industrialization and technological advance which are leading to the expansion of individual cities are also creating urbanizing regions made up of groups of cities. Urban and various resource areas are certain to be interdependent and should be planned together. The solution to problems arising out of resource utilization may be found in the jobs that can be developed in urbanizing areas.

The South has approximately 70 standard metropolitan areas as defined by the Bureau of the Census. Each has a core city with a population of 50,000 or more, surrounded by a fringe area in which urban type services are needed. Each metropolitan area presents a difficult and important planning and development problem—difficult due in large part to the lack of a general metropolitan government, important because it is here where almost all economic growth is taking place. The lack of a general government for metropolitan government to which service planning can be related is a serious handicap; and while attempts to remedy this situation have been made in many southern metropolitan areas, only three—Davidson County, Tennessee; Dade County, Florida; and East Baton Rouge Parish—have succeeded in their efforts to establish a form of metropolitan government. The success of metropolitan government is not yet fully established in any of these cases nor are the examples they present generally acceptable elsewhere.

In the absence of general metropolitan type government, planning becomes extremely difficult. Almost all of the southern states have enabling legislation of some type which would permit the creation of regional planning agencies. Despite such authorization, most of

[12]Durisch, L. L., and Lowry, R. E., "State Watershed Policy and Administration in Tennessee," *Public Administration Review*, 15:17-20, Winter 1955.

the metropolitan areas do not have regional planning agencies; those which are operative are dependent for the implementation of plans, not on one but on many local governments.

Planning for metropolitan areas can be strengthened by the adoption of positive state policies and programs. Such fields as transportation, recreation, water use, sanitation, education, welfare, and industrial promotion address themselves to state as well as to local action. Regional programs within a state must and should rely on state government with its complete areal coverage, broader powers, and superior financing to set the general stage for economic growth.

The national government has attempted to be helpful in encouraging regional planning by requiring certain plans and programs to be on an area-wide basis as a condition precedent to Federal grants-in-aid, Federal loans, and other assistance. The Federal Government in this connection has provided financial help and technical assistance to regional planning staffs. The Housing Act of 1954 authorizes matching funds to states to be used for community, state, and regional planning. Recent action in the field represents a growing national concern for the problems of the local areas and reflects the often expressed idea that the metropolitan regions are strong in Washington even though they may be weak in their own state capitols.

In view of the growth of cities in the South, it is important that state policies and programs be framed with the welfare of urban areas high among the factors considered. It has been too easy for the legislatures to view all cities and all urban areas with suspicion and distrust—especially has this been easy for un-reapportioned state legislative bodies in which rural areas are grossly over-represented. It is time for state programs to be devised and carried out by those who recognize the importance of cities, and perhaps even like them. The South is committed to an urban way of life and must become better adjusted to it.

Many states are giving attention to the planning and development of larger economic regions within the state, which may be made up of a number of watersheds and other resource areas and include perhaps a number of urban centers. Studies of the Carolina Piedmont, the great valley of eastern Tennessee, of eastern Kentucky, and of north Alabama are illustrative of this type of regional approach. Tennessee in particular is approaching state planning in a series of well-conceived and related studies of major subdivisions of the state.

Statewide planning also appears to be needed for the successful operation of the Area Redevelopment Act, passed by the Congress in 1961. The Act is designed primarily to cope with the problem of "depressed areas" characterized by high and persistent unemployment. The Act recognizes that, while high level economic activity nationally and for major parts of the nation is a necessary condition, it is not sufficient to assure the growth and prosperity of all areas. It is recognized that the problem of depressed areas is a long-term one and will require long-term solutions.

The Area Redevelopment Act has been criticized for the extreme localism of its point of view. Counties are used to determine eligibility for ARA assistance. Each county requesting assistance is required to file economic development plans which are approved by the state before submission to Washington. An economic plan for a county, particularly for a depressed county, needs, however, to be related to a much larger area of potential employment and development. The "community-at-a-time" approach cannot result in effective or even meaningful developmental planning. It must be noted that the Area Redevelopment Administration, within the limits of its Act, is encouraging the wider view through the factor of state participation in the formulation of county economic development plans and of state review and approval of such plans. However, to date only Mississippi has submitted to ARA a developmental plan which includes the whole state. The Mississippi example should become the standard practice.

The Southern Appalachian Region is in terms of its low income and widespread unemployment or underemployment one of the major problem areas in the United States. It includes 80,000 square miles and parts of Kentucky, Tennessee, West Virginia, Virginia, Alabama, Georgia, and North Carolina. It is inhabited by 6 million people.

In 1960 a conference of the governors concerned with a somewhat larger Appalachian region, meeting at Annapolis, Maryland, recognized that a special planning and development effort was indicated. The problem was recognized as interstate in character addressing itself to the states collectively and in their individual capacities and to the Federal Government.

To serve as a planning and coordinating agency, the President's Joint State-Federal Committee on the Appalachian Region was set

up. Franklin D. Roosevelt, Jr., Under Secretary of Commerce, is
chairman of this committee whose establishment is a recognition
that a more comprehensive approach by the Federal Government is
needed. Each of the states concerned has also been asked to review
its planning and programing for the portion of Appalachia contained within its borders. The Area Redevelopment Administration
is cooperating in the Appalachian effort, and funds from the Accelerated Public Works program and other sources are being applied
in the implementation of plans. Out of the joint effort it is hoped
that an effective plan for Appalachia will emerge—a plan which can
be quickly translated into action.

The solution to the problems of Appalachia is not yet apparent.[13] In the meantime Appalachia presents a major challenge to
planning and to the theory and practice of induced economic development. The problem of a permanent administrative agency to devote special attention to Appalachian problems is still under consideration. At the current session of Congress (88th Congress, 2d
Session) H.R. 7935, which calls for a "joint Federal-State Commission on Appalachia" to serve as a planning and development agency
for the region, is receiving careful attention. The bill provides also
for the establishment of a Federal coordinator to see that all programs of the Federal Government are consistent with the plan for
over-all economic development of the region. An Appalachian Institute would be established to conduct research designed to further
economic development and existing programs of Federal assistance
would be accelerated. Regardless of Federal action, the states already
are responsible for such a broad range of activities that comprehensive planning programs to provide a basis for state action and for cooperation with other states and with Federal agencies in the Appalachia region is a first order of business.

*   *   *   *

The Committee of the South of the National Planning Association published in 1949 a study of the activities of planning commissions of southern states. The author, Dr. Albert Lepawsky,
devoted a great deal of attention to the dual-purpose nature of the
state agencies which had evolved over a 10 or 15-year period. He

[13]Levin, Melvin R., "What Do We Do With Depressed Areas?" *Iowa Business Digest*, 31:1-3, April 1960; Sufrin, Sidney C., "A Problem Prolonged Not
Solved," *Challenge*, 11:8-10, July 1963.

then concluded that "the overriding question of organization continues to be that of associating units and personnel attempting to combine effectively the diverse duties inherent in the function of both development and planning."[14] Dr. Lepawsky identified another problem which has since become more important; namely that of the place of the planning agency in the structure of state government and its relation to other staff units, particularly the budget agency. Greatly expanded activities in industrial promotion and a better understanding of the desirability of achieving both a comprehensive and balanced approach to resource development suggest some of the reasons why it is now considered desirable to place planning in the mainstream of state administration. An independent but isolated planning board, "non-political" in outlook, is unrealistic at a time when the end objective of so much governmental action is economic development.

Its relatively low income status makes it certain that the South will have less money available for state and local governmental services than other parts of the nation—this in spite of a tax effort equal to or in excess of that made elsewhere. Furthermore, the tasks of government in terms of children to be educated, aged and indigent to be cared for, and health problems to be met are greater than those encountered in any other major region in the United States. It is essential that the South get more value for its tax dollars if the region is to compete successfully for a larger share of the national income and employment. The planning process lends itself to the establishment of administrative goals and the determination of priorities in the expenditure of scarce governmental funds. Planning is a prime means of furthering coordination among programs at all levels of government and a very essential part of public administration.

It is becoming increasingly clear that governmental activities that affect economic development encompass the whole range of state programs and relationships. Economic development takes its place as one of the goals, and an important one, of state planning. On the other hand, highly specialized advertising and promotional effort geared to the attraction and expansion of industry is not state planning. Key problems today involve the relationship of the state planning agency to the leadership role of the governor and to the

[14]Lepawsky, Albert, *State Planning and Economic Development in the South,* Committee of the South, National Planning Association, 1949, p. 173.

part the process of planning can play in decision making at the highest administrative and legislative levels.

The rapidity of change in the South gives purpose and a sense of urgency to state planning. A new pattern of population distribution is rapidly taking form and the isolation of the rural areas is giving way to new transportation and employment factors. Problems of industrialization and urbanization are making obsolete the present organization of local government and are giving rise to new demands for governmental services which are now inadequately met. The revenue structure of the local units of government, their limited legal powers and restricted areal coverage, are everywhere posing questions to which the state must find answers in a conscious or unconscious application of the planning process. The results arrived at may either be sound and constructive or ineffective and sporadic, serving to compound the problems which planning should alleviate.

The South needs planning in order to realize the economic advantages it possesses and to overcome or minimize the handicaps under which it operates. The relative gains made by the region in per capita income as workers shift out of agriculture at a time when total agricultural production is increasing gives both the basis and the opportunity to plan. The continuation of this shift is governed in large part by nonfarm opportunities, but its continuation can bring the income of the South closer to the national average. Improvement in technology and the redistribution of population among rural and urban areas are producing a "likeness" among regions which place a high premium on the quality of the governmental institutions which a given region can create. The opportunities present in every region place a premium on planning which should proceed with both caution and optimism.

The South needs to foster the theory and philosophy of state planning in order to work effectively with the Federal programs operative in the region. The initiative for cooperative programs is not, or should not be, entirely with the Federal Government in that respect. A basic problem which confronted TVA in 1933, and which still confronts every agency which works on a regional basis, is to find ways to cooperate constructively with state agencies with which it shares developmental responsibility. State planning can devote major attention to the theory and practice of shared functions in resource development and provide a basis for and an approach to the infinitely difficult tasks of intergovernmental cooperation and program coordination. In trying to weld an effective program in the resource development field, TVA recognized long ago the desirability in the Tennessee Valley of, not a *planned region,* but a region *that plans.* Properly organized and broadly oriented state and regional planning has an important role to play if the South is to utilize fully its resources in solving problems and capitalizing on opportunities.

SOUTHERN METROPOLIS: CHALLENGE TO GOVERNMENT

ROBERT H. CONNERY

AND

RICHARD H. LEACH

Duke University

I

THE RECENT DEVELOPMENT OF "the metropolis" in the South[1] is posing grave questions for all levels of government. Prior to World War I, with a few notable exceptions, the picture of a slow moving, largely agricultural economy, of small towns dozing under a benevolent sun, and cities more noted for their past than for their present, was not far from the truth in the South. By 1963, some forty years later, the entire picture had changed. Not that the old was entirely gone, but it was no longer dominant. Today an accurate picture of the South would emphasize its growing industrial strength, the diversification of its agriculture, the increased tempo of its trade and commerce, the rise in its per capita incomes, the expansion and change visible in every direction. But more than anything else, it would emphasize urban development. Nowhere is change more noticeable than in the South's rapidly expanding metropolitan areas.

As a result of all these forces, the South is coming to be much more like the rest of the nation. The factors that formerly made the South different as a region are disappearing. The trend that Maclachlan and Floyd[2] noted in 1956 is continuing. People are leaving southern farms for the cities, and rural population is declining in proportion to urban population. Not only are small towns growing as they attract new industries, but numerous southern cities are taking on the appearance of metropolitan communities. The suburbs are exploding, and sub-divisions are extending miles into the coun-

[1]The authors employ the U. S. Bureau of the Census definition of the South which includes Alabama, Arkansas, Delaware, the District of Columbia, Florida, Georgia, Kentucky, Louisiana, Maryland, Mississippi, North Carolina, Oklahoma, South Carolina, Tennessee, Texas, Virginia, and West Virginia.

[2]John M. Maclachlan and Joe S. Floyd, *This Changing South* (Gainesville, Florida, 1956).

[60]

try side. There is a demand everywhere for more and better schools, for more recreational facilities, for governmental services of all kinds. The tempo of growth is not the same throughout the region, of course, nor are the governmental problems everywhere the same. But the very fact that the tempo is uneven offers possibilities absent in other parts of the nation for meeting, at least, some of the problems of government which the growth of metropolitan areas is bringing with it.

Table I indicates the extent to which the population in southern states is urban and metropolitan and the extent of change in that direction in the decade 1950-60.[3] The definitions of urban and metropolitan as used in this table follow those of the U. S. Bureau of the Census. As one might expect, these are exact but complicated definitions which need not be discussed here.[4] It is sufficient to note that urban is used to describe in general communities of 2,500 and more inhabitants and that metropolitan in general is used to describe communities of 50,000 and more inhabitants.

The first thing that strikes one on examining Table I is the range of difference between states. While the population of Texas is 75% urban, that of Florida, 73%, and that of Maryland, 72%, the population of Mississippi is only 37% urban, West Virginia 38%, and North Carolina 39%. This variation between states within a region is not peculiar to the South but is found to a considerable degree in all four regions of the United States. There are, however, more southern states in the lower ranges. Urbanization is increasing in the South, but in 1960 six of the southern states were among the ten least urban states in the nation and only Texas was among the ten most urban.

Although the development of urbanism in the South undoubtedly has had an impact on certain governmental functions, as, for example, on water supply and waste disposal, it probably does not have as much significance nor create as many problems as the growth of the larger metropolitan communities. Much of the urban growth in the South has been in the development of small communities ranging in population from 2,500 to 50,000. It is the metropolitan

[3]The authors are indebted to Dr. John Morgan and Peter Meekison for preparing Tables I-IV and for their assistance in interpreting the data therein.
[4]For definition of "urban" see U. S. Bureau of the Census, *U. S. Census of the Population,* (1960), Vol. I, Part A, p. xii, and for definition of "Standard Metropolitan Statistical Areas" see *ibid.,* pp. xiii and xxiv.

TABLE I
PERCENT OF POPULATION IN URBAN AND METROPOLITAN AREAS IN THE SOUTH BY STATE 1960, PERCENT OF CHANGE FROM 1950 TO 1960 AND AVERAGE BY REGIONS

STATE[1]	PERCENT URBAN 1960	PERCENT CHANGE 1950-60	U. S. RANK BY PERCENT POP.URBAN 1960	PERCENT OF POP. IN S.M.S.A.	PERCENT CHANGE IN METRO POP. 1950-60
Alabama	54	33	34	45	21
Arkansas	42	21	42	19	16
Delaware	65	47	22	38	40
Florida	73	101	12	65	93
Georgia	55	39	33	46	35
Kentucky	44	24	41	34	22
Louisiana	63	40	24	50	32
Maryland	72	39	16	78	37
Mississippi	37	35	49	8	31
N. Carolina	39	31	44	24	24
Oklahoma	62	28	25	43	31
S. Carolina	41	26	43	32	34
Tennessee	52	28	37	45	21
Texas	75	48	9	63	42
Virginia	55	41	32	50	38
W. Virginia	38	2	47	30	3
Regional Average					
South	54.2	36.4		43.8	32.5
Northeast	70.9	13.8		58.2[2]	10.5[2]
Midwest	60.1	25.1		45.8	23.9
West	64.5	64.2		46.6[3]	42.8[3]

"Metropolitan areas" as used here means U. S. Census Standard Metropolitan Statistical Areas.

[1]The District of Columbia is not a state and consequently is omitted from this table.

[2]Average is derived from total of 9 states, one of which—Vermont—does not have any S.M.S.A.'s.

[3]Average is derived from total of thirteen states, three of which (Alaska, Idaho, and Wyoming) do not have any S.M.S.A.'s.

Source: Derived from U. S. Bureau of the Census, *1960 Census of Population* (Washington, 1960) Vol. I, Part A. Figures 30, 31, 36, 39, 45.

communities, however, and particularly the larger ones that create the most challenging problems for government.

While the South has a smaller percentage of its people living in the metropolitan areas than any other region, as Table I indicates, the difference is not striking except between the South and the northeastern region. Again, there is considerable difference between states in the South: but the more urbanized states—Maryland, Florida, and Texas—are also high in the percentage of population living in the metropolitan areas. At the other end of the scale, Mississippi, Arkansas, and North Carolina are low. So far as Mississippi is concerned, there is only one metropolis, Jackson, and this contains but 8% of the total population of the state.

But if the South is still behind the other regions of the nation in percentage of its population in metropolitan areas, it contains a disproportionately high number of metropolitan areas. In 1960, there were 212 S.M.S.A.'s in the continental United States and of these 78 were in the South. A good argument can be made, however, that the Census Bureau's Standard Metropolitan Statistical Area is primarily, as its name implies, a unit of statistical measurement. Communities of 50,000 are not much different as far as the functions they perform in the economic and social life of the nation from communities of 30,000 to 40,000. Sociologists have been quick to point this out. As Vance and Smith explain,[5]

"Whereas urbanization may refer to any aspect of population agglomeration, metropolitanism should be reserved for the organizational component that great cities impose upon the urbanization process. Any city with a large population is usually referred to as a metropolis, but it may be well to point out that while all metropolises are large cities, not all large cities are metropolises. Population size is a concomitant; function is the keynote."

Otis Duncan suggests that it is in communities of roughly 300,000 inhabitants that a transition point occurs where distinctively "metropolitan" characteristics first begin to appear.[6] Looking at southern metropolitan communities in these terms, one finds that the South, even excluding Washington, D. C., has twenty-five out of a total of eighty-one in the whole country. Thus, the South has slightly less than one-third of the communities that can properly be classed as metropolitan, a larger percentage of such communities than is found in any other region in the nation.

An examination of Table II indicates that there is considerable variation between these twenty-five communities. There is, for example, no correlation between size of the population and density.

[5]Rupert B. Vance and Lara Smith, "Metropolitan Dominance and Integration," in Rupert B. Vance and Nicholas J. Demerath (eds.), The Urban South (Chapel Hill, 1954), p. 115.
[6]Otis Duncan, Metropolis and Regions (Baltimore, 1960), p. 275.

The Dallas and Atlanta metropolises each have somewhat over one million inhabitants, but Dallas has a density of 295 persons per square mile while Atlanta has 590. The range for these southern communities is from Tulsa with 110 persons per square mile to Baltimore with 956 per square mile. But no southern city has the density of population that can be found in portions of what Jean Gottmann has characterized as the "megalopolis" that is the urbanized northeastern seaboard of the United States.[7] In general, the density figures indicate that southern metropolitan communities are characterized by an open-order pattern of development. Many of the southern metropolises occupy large areas, and this in turn has a relationship to the nature of government services. Moreover, it is likely that in the years to come the spread of cities over the landscape will continue and "the physical form which the urban environment assumes, will have a great deal to do with the costs of city living. . . ."[8]

There has been a good deal of research in the past decade in regard to the form that the land development of cities takes and the problems that certain patterns create.[9] Vast metropolitan belts which Charlton Chute called metropolitan regions like that extending from Boston to Washington have been identified. More localized patterns termed "sprawl," "scatter," and "nucleated" have been described. Each in its way involves physical problems that have an impact on government. As F. Stuart Chapin, Jr. states,

> "The sprawl pattern, which has come to connote an aimless overspill of the city into the country-side, frequently presents problems of overload—overtaxed highways and water systems and other inadequate community facilities and services. The scatter pattern poses the problem of providing these same facilities and services in widely separated locations. In the case of the nucleated patterns problems such as water supply, sewage disposal, or airports revolve around conflict of interest or uneconomical duplication of effort where a coordinated regional approach is indicated."[10]

Various metropolises in the South have followed each of these patterns of land development. But it will be many years before the Piedmont Crescent of North Carolina or the Gulf Coast belt, for

[7]Jean Gottmann, *Megalopolis* (New York, 1961)

[8]F. Stuart Chapin, Jr. and Shirley F. Weiss (eds.), *Urban Growth Dynamics* (New York, 1962), p. 422.

[9]See Gottmann, *op. cit.;* Kevin Lynch, *The Image of the City* (Cambridge, 1960); F. Stuart Chapin, Jr., *Urban Land Use Planning* (New York, 1957), among others.

[10]Chapin and Weiss, *op. cit.,* p. 448.

TABLE II

STANDARD METROPOLITAN STATISTICAL AREAS IN THE SOUTH WITH A POPULATION OF 300,000 OR MORE, POPULATION 1960. U. S. RANK, PERCENT OF CHANGE 1950-60, PERCENT OF CHANGE IN CENTRAL CITY AND IN URBAN FRINGE AND POPULATION DENSITY OF TOTAL SMSA.

STANDARD METROPOLITAN STATISTICAL AREA 1960	POP. (1000's) 1960	U.S. RANK OF POP. 1960	SMSA PERCENT CHANGE 1950-60	CENTRAL CITY PERCENT CHANGE 1950-60	URBAN FRINGE CHANGE 1950-60	DENSITY PER SQ. MI. TOTAL METRO
Baltimore	1727.0	12	22.9	—1.1	126.2	956
Houston	1243.2	16	54.1	57.4	93.1	727
Dallas[1]	1083.6	20	45.7	56.4	140.9	297
Atlanta	1017.2	24	39.9	47.1	59.0	590
Miami	935.0	25	88.9	17.0	168.0	455
New Orleans	868.5	27	26.7	10.0	143.7	777
Tampa-St. Petersburg[2]	772.5	31	88.8	106.1	134.9	592
Louisville	725.1	32	25.7	5.8	108.5	799
San Antonio	687.2	35	37.3	43.9	32.1	551
Birmingham	634.9	40	13.6	4.6	51.3	568
Memphis	627.0	41	30.0	25.6	368.2	835
Norfolk-Portsmouth	578.5	44	29.7	43.3	—3.7	867
Fort Worth[1]	573.2	46	46.0	27.8	297.9	358
Oklahoma City	511.8	50	30.4	33.2	232.2	240
Jacksonville[3]	455.4	58	49.8	—1.7	357.9	586
Tulsa	419.0	59	27.8	43.2	58.0	110
Richmond	408.5	60	24.5	—4.5	309.9	563
Nashville	399.7	61	24.2	—2.0	107.9	751
Knoxville	368.1	64	9.2	—10.4	160.3	258
Wilmington	366.2	65	36.4	—13.2	143.9	465
Ft. Lauderdale-Hollywood	333.9	73	297.9	134.6	—	274
Orlando	318.5	77	124.6	68.3	442.7	257
Mobile	314.3	78	36.0	57.2	21.1	253
El Paso	314.1	79	61.1	112.0	—3.1	298
Beaumont-Pt. Arthur[4]	306.0	81	29.9	22.6	110.6	235

[1]Dallas urbanized area extends outside S.M.S.A. into part of Tarrant County in Fort Worth S.M.S.A.

[2]Tampa and St. Petersburg urbanized areas in the same S.M.S.A. are treated as a single urbanized area.

[3]Jacksonville urbanized area extends outside S.M.S.A. into part of Clay County, Fla.

[4]Beaumont and Port Arthur urbanized areas in the same S.M.S.A. are treated as a single urbanized area.

[5]Washington, D. C., S.M.S.A. omitted.

Source: Tables 3 and 6, *City and County Data Book*, 1962, U.S. Dept. of Commerce, Bureau of Census (Washington, D.C., 1962). Urban fringe data from Jones, Victor, "Metropolitan and Urbanized Areas," Table II, *The Municipal Year Book,* 1962 (Chicago, International City Managers Association, 1962). Urban fringe is the urbanized area as defined by the Census Bureau minus the population of the Central City. The percent change has been calculated from the data given in these two classifications.

example, will rival the northeastern megalopolis in density of population.

When one breaks down the population between central cities and urban fringe, one finds that some central cities in the South have declined in population just as they have in other regions. Indeed, this fact is not so extraordinary as some of the amazing increases in population. The fantastic growth of suburbs in Florida and Texas is quite evident. In general, the growth of the urban fringe during the last ten years has been much higher in the South than for the rest of the country.

Most of the southern metropolises are rather old fashioned and remind one of northern communities of several decades ago. Frequently they consist of a central city surrounded by an urban fringe of satellite communities which may or may not be incorporated. True, there are parts of the Midwest and Far West where this same phenomenon exists, but it is strikingly different from the Northeast where more often than not metropolitan communities are continuous. This means that the fringe of a southern metropolis, with few exceptions, does not have much importance independent of the central city. Thus the whole is very much like the northern metropolis of fifty years ago.

There is another dimension of the southern metropolis apart from the pattern of land development that ought to be considered. The South differs markedly from the other regions in the country as far as the functions its metropolises perform in the economic and social life of the nation. Economic historians sometimes refer to the economy of the modern world as a "metropolitan economy" because of the part played by great cities in organizing and integrating a nation's manufacturing, commercial, financial, and communications arrangements. But not all metropolises play leading roles in this story, and there is a discernible hierarchy among them. Sociologists do not agree completely among themselves on the factors that should be used to measure this role, and exact quantitative data for measurement is not always available. However, using financial, employment, transportation, retailing, and wholesaling statistics, they have developed categories of metropolises based on the economic functions which each performs. Generally they agree that there are four or five metropolises like New York, Chicago, Philadelphia, Los Angeles, and Detroit which should go in the first order of importance as national metropolises. Otis Duncan uses six other categories.[11] It is significant that he lists only Atlanta and Dallas as regional metropolises in the South. The fact that the others do not duplicate the functions of long established national centers, Vance thinks, need not be an adverse finding. On the contrary, they may "support a mode of life that gives great accessibility to the open country" and provide a type of integration between farm and city that long has been sought.[12]

One may conclude, consequently, that although the South as a region contains nearly one-third of the nation's metropolises of 300,000 or more inhabitants, it has only two with major metropolitan characteristics. While other southern metropolises serve a vital purpose, their role in the national picture is still secondary to that of metropolises in other regions. While metropolitan functions of southern cities are increasing, they may never be able to overcome the lead of the northeastern and north central cities. But one should emphasize that southern cities have time to influence the way in which they will develop in the future and thus perhaps create a better balance in their economic structure than has been achieved elsewhere.

II

The problem of organizing for effective government in metropolitan communities is always a difficult one. Probably every problem encountered by governments elsewhere in the nation as metropolitan areas developed and expanded has arisen in the South as well. Problems of mass transit, water supply and water polution, housing and urban renewal, air pollution and school facilities—the list could be extended—are common in every southern metropolitan area. For the most part, however, it does not appear that there is anything unique about these problems in the South. There does not seem to be anything in the development of southern areas which

[11]Duncan, *op. cit.*, p. 271.
[12]Vance and Demerath, *op. cit.*, p. 134.

created problems different from those encountered elsewhere, even
the extent to which southern metropolises extend across state boundaries.[13] The growth of southern areas came about later, and when
it came, it came faster than it did in areas outside the region; and
both of these time factors have no doubt complicated problems of
transportation, urban housing, pollution, etc., in southern areas.
But beyond this, it is hard to demonstrate that a separate *genus
southernis* of metropolitan area problems has developed. Thus the
temptation to undertake an analysis of substantive metropolitan area
problems has been resisted (although an area by area analysis of
those problems would certainly be useful), and our attention has
been devoted instead to the major problem in all metropolitan areas,
the problem of adjusting government to meet the new metropolitan
situation. For though some substantive problems can be met at
least in part by private, voluntary action, most of those problems
will have to be solved by governments. How metropolitan areas
react in terms of bringing government into alignment with the facts
of metropolitan life may well be the key to the rest of the metropolitan puzzle, in the South as elsewhere.

Table III shows the extent of governmental fragmentation in the
twenty-five southern metropolises with a population of 300,000 or
more and the average for metropolises in the four regions of the
United States. It immediately becomes apparent that southern
metropolises are less fragmented than those in other regions. However, the spread within the region from five units in the case of
Richmond to 166 in the case of Dallas imposes certain limitations on
regional comparisons. Nevertheless, for what it may be worth, the
regional average is strikingly below that of other regions. Attention
should especially be directed to the fact that while the southern
average for special districts has increased slightly during the last five
years, the increase has been less than in any other region. It should
be emphasized, however, that while southern metropolitan areas have
fewer governmental units than other regions, they still have a sufficient number to make effective government extremely difficult.[14]

[13]See for example Daniel R. Grant, "The Government of Interstate Metropolitan Areas," *Western Political Quarterly* 8:90-107 (March, 1955); John M.
Winters, *Interstate Metropolitan Areas* (Ann Arbor, 1962).

[14]A more detailed analysis of the significance of fragmentation in metropolises of this size will be included in a forthcoming study by Robert H. Connery and others, which has been made possible by a grant from the National
Institute of Mental Health.

TABLE III

LOCAL GOVERNMENTS, INDEPENDENT SCHOOL DISTRICTS, AND NON-SCHOOL SPECIAL DISTRICTS, NUMBER IN SOUTHERN METROPOLITAN AREAS WITH 300,000 OR MORE INHABITANTS AND AVERAGES FOR METROPOLISES OF THIS POPULATION GROUPING BY REGION*

METROPOLITAN AREA OR REGION	NUMBER, OR AVERAGE NUMBER					
	LOCAL GOVERNMENTS		SCHOOL DISTRICTS		SPECIAL DISTRICTS	
	1957	1962	1957	1962	1957	1962
Baltimore	23	23	—	—	8	8
Houston	94	82	22	21	47	35
Dallas	157	166	66	60	25	28
Atlanta	71	84	9	9	15	25
Miami	31	32	1	1	4	3
New Orleans	33	20	3	3	23	9
Tampa-St. Petersburg	43	40	2	2	11	10
Louisville	97	129	18	18	17	34
San Antonio	33	43	18	16	6	11
Birmingham	39	44	5	6	6	7
Memphis	14	15	—	—	7	8
Norfolk-Portsmouth	8	9	—	—	2	3
Fort Worth	87	89	43	36	5	9
Oklahoma City	110	86	73	46	5	5
Jacksonville	11	11	1	1	4	4
Tulsa	127	124	79	75	12	13
Richmond	5	5	—	—	2	2
Nashville	11	15	—	—	6	7
Knoxville	26	28	—	—	15	16
Wilmington	47	73	17	36	4	10
Ft. Lauderdale-Hollywood	25	38	1	1	10	12
Orlando	25	41	2	2	6	19
Mobile	9	12	1	1	2	2
El Paso	15	17	7	7	5	5
Beaumont-Port Arthur	55	50	19	16	23	19
Average South	47.8	51.0	15.5	14.3	10.8	12.2
Average Northeastern	232.9	260.8	91.6	81.2	38.7	77.4
Average North Central	198.9	189.6	83.8	66.5	30.8	39.7
Average West	189.7	201.1	77.1	64.8	85.4	105.4
Average U. S. (Excluding Honolulu and Washington)	155.1	163.8	61.7	52.3	35.5	51.0

*"Metropolitan areas" as used here means the Census Bureau "Standard Metropolitan Statistical Areas" with three qualifications: 1) Figures are given for the New York-Northeastern New Jersey and the Chicago-Northwestern Indiana "Standard Consolidated Areas" rather than for the six S.M.S.A.'s included therein.

2) Honolulu, Hawaii, and Washington, D. C., are omitted due to the unique problems of comparison which they present.

3) 1957 figures have been adjusted where necessary in order to take into account redefinition of S.M.S.A.'s; consequently, the 1957 and 1962 figures are in each case for the same geographic area.

Source: *Governmental Organization* (Census of Governments: 1957, Vol.), No. 1: Table 14, No. 2: Table 3; *Governmental Organization* (Census of Governments: 1962, Vol. I), Table 15.

Perhaps one of the principal reasons why the number of governments in southern metropolitan areas has been kept down—besides of course for the historic preference in the South for the use of the county as the chief unit of local government—is that annexation has been easier to use in the South than elsewhere. As a result, there are normally more annexations per year in the South than in any other region of the country.[15] Table IV shows the number of annexation actions in the twenty-five southern metropolises, and the areas annexed over the five year period 1957-62. Only in the West is annexation used almost as much. Indeed, in the Northeast and Midwest, annexation has ceased to be important as a tool to fight fragmentation of government.[16]

Texas and Virginia have been leaders in the use of annexation. In Texas, home rule cities whose charters provide for it (not all of them do) may exercise the power unilaterally. The statistics of growth in a number of Texas communities show something of the benefits of such a policy. However, even in Texas, the use of annexation is not altogether unrestricted. In *City of Houston* vs. *City of Magnolia Park*,[17] the Texas Supreme Court ruled that a city could not annex another city of more than 5,000 people. The result has been that since 1925 there has been a proliferation of small cities adjacent to metropolitan centers in Texas. The only way cities can prevent it is to act far in advance of their rapid growth. Thus Port Arthur, a part of the Beaumont-Port Arthur S.M.S.A., recently added 25.88 square miles to still rural but developing Jefferson County and Houston moved far out into Harris County, annexing 187.63 square miles in 1956. Houston's annexations since that year have not been large, but plans are being developed to annex most of the remaining unincorporated land in Harris County.

[15]See Victor Jones, "Metropolitan Areas," *The Municipal Year Book, 1961* (Chicago, 1961), p. 40, Table IV.

[16]For a general analysis of annexation, see Frank S. Sengstock, *Annexation: A Solution to the Metropolitan Area Problem* (Ann Arbor, 1960).

[17]115 Tex. 101, 276 S. W. 685 (1925).

TABLE IV

NUMBER OF ANNEXATION ACTIONS OF ONE-FOURTH
SQUARE MILE OR MORE, LAND AREA ADDED AND POPULATION OF
ANNEXED AREA FOR CENTRAL CITIES OF SOUTHERN
METROPOLITAN AREAS. 1957-1962 INCLUSIVE.

CITY	NUMBER OF ANNEXATION ACTIONS	LAND AREA ADDED (SQ. MILES)	ESTIMATED POPULATION ADDED
Atlanta	None		
Baltimore	None		
Beaumont	None		
Birmingham	6	.41	1,130
Dallas	27	52.79	9,520*
El Paso	3	10.40	500
Ft. Lauderdale	24	8.17	16,862
Ft. Worth	28	14.93	215*
Hollywood	2	1.30	3,700
Houston	2	10.39	500
Jacksonville	None		
Knoxville	6	51.00	67,000
Louisville	32	3.33	9,200*
Memphis	1*	12.64*	20,000*
Miami	None		
Mobile	2	68.55	28,930
Nashville	20	49.72	87,593
New Orleans	None		
Norfolk	1	13.50	38,038
Oklahoma City	145*	359.43*	20,847*
Orlando	40*	30.66*	100*
Port Arthur	14	25.88	6,000
Portsmouth	1	10.00	32,300
Richmond	*	*	*
St. Petersburg	2	.51	0
San Antonio	1	5.58	250
Tampa	None		
Tulsa	36*	6.40*	15,000*
Wilmington	None		

*Information incomplete either as to number of annexations, area aded, or population added.
Source: Table derived from J. C. Bollens, "Metropolitan and Fringe Area Developments," *Municipal Year Book. op. cit.* Vols. 25, 26, 27, 28, 29, 30.

In Virginia, the method of judicial annexation has been in effect since 1904, and it is sufficiently simple to use to have by and large prevented fragmentation of government from marring the growth of such areas as Richmond, Norfolk-Portsmouth and Newport News-Hampton. Kentucky makes use of the same device, but it substitutes the judgments of a jury for that of a judge in deciding the merits of a petition for annexation. In North Carolina, annexation procedures were simplified in 1959 to permit cities of 5,000 or more to annex by council ordinance if the standards laid down by the legislature are met and if required services can be supplied to the new areas. In addition, the North Carolina Municipal Board of Control was prohibited from incorporating new municipalities within three miles of an existing city. And in Tennessee, since 1955, the land outside a city may be acquired by ordinance, subject to the condition that the governing body of the annexing municipality must adopt a plan of service if more than one-quarter of a square mile or 500 people are involved in the area to be annexed.

In the other southern states annexation is not as easy to use, requiring as it does legislative action on the one hand and approval by referendum on the other, but state legislatures have not always been reluctant to act nor the people unwilling to approve. Even in these states there have been major annexations. Oklahoma City, for example, was allowed to annex an overall total of 483 square miles in three counties, making her the largest city in area in the United States. If the Oklahoma legislature's motive in permitting it was to take the title away from Los Angeles, as it may possibly have been, it was nevertheless permitted. Nor is Oklahoma an isolated example. Generally, despite their rural domination, legislatures in the South have not sought to inhibit the use of annexation. This raises the interesting question whether there is as much conflict of interest between rural areas and big cities as there is generally thought to be or whether the conflict instead is between the big cities and their suburbs.

III

Annexation is not the only device southern metropolitan areas have brought into use in their attempt to adjust their governments to the new facts of life. As the difficulties involved in trying to meet substantive problems through the traditional units of government became more obvious, as they have particularly since 1950, southern metropolitan areas began to seek other solutions as well

It is not possible within the confines of this paper to list every move taken by every area in the South. Suffice it to say that metropolitan areas are steadily becoming more aware of the handicap fragmentation places on effective action and more and more of them have taken steps toward overcoming it. To be sure, the leadership sometimes has been taken by non-governmental persons or groups—economists, students of government and administration, groups of lay citizens—rather than by political leaders, but the number of occasions are increasing.

> Item. A Metropolitan Area Study Commision has been established in San Antonio and is already at work studying the 54 local governments in Bexar County with the object of recommending how they might best be related for the more efficient government of the entire area.

> Item. A Metropolitan Government Charter Commission has been formed in the Chattanooga area to study the feasibility of consolidating Chattanooga and Hamilton County as a partial solution to that area's problems of government.

> Item. A Baltimore Metropolitan Area Study Commission is at work preparing a report on problems of governing the Baltimore area.

> Item. The General Assembly of Georgia provided in 1962 for the creation of a Municipal Study Committee to look into the needs and problems of municipalities in general in that state.

> Item. A commission on city and county government has been appointed in Texas to study the advisability and feasibility of city-county consolidation generally.

> Item. *A Plan of Government for the Richmond Region* has been prepared by the Richmond Regional Planning and Economic Development Commission.

Other surveys and studies—the necessary preludes to action in every case—are presently underway in Arkansas, Georgia, Maryland, North Carolina, Tennessee, Texas, Virginia, and the District of Columbia.[18]

The number of southern governors who have become interested in the problem of metropolitan government is also steadily increasing. In 1963 alone Governor Terry Sanford of North Carolina, Governor J. Millard Tawes of Maryland, Governor Donald Russell of South Carolina, Governor Carl Sanders of Georgia, and Governor John Connally of Texas all drew specific attention to one aspect or another of the metropolitan area problems in their "State of the State" addresses to their respective state legislatures.

---

[18]For fairly complete reporting of such studies, consult the annual digest of metropolitan surveys in progress, published as a supplement to *Metropolitan Area News and Digest,* a publication now of the Graduate School of Public Affairs of the State University of New York.

But study and admonition are not the only responses in the South to increasing metropolitanization and its effect on the government of metropolitan areas. In several states, a good deal of legislative action has been taken as well.

Item.   In 1960, the Virginia General Assembly granted the more populous counties of the state (those with over 90,000 population) the option of forming an urban county and thus avoiding the evils of further incorporation and the resultant necessity of annexation in the future. Fairfax County in the Washington Metropolitan area at once took advantage of the option.

Item.   Kentucky adopted a law in 1960 permitting the creation of multi-purpose metropolitan districts and area-wide planning agencies.

Item.   The North Carolina General Assembly passed a law in 1962 permitting two or more local governments in a county to petition the county commissioners to create joint metropolitan sewer districts.

Item.   In 1962, Louisiana adopted a constitutional amendment authorizing parish governments to consolidate special service districts and assume their management with the consent of the municipalities involved.

The regional planning idea has also begun to be accepted in the South. Three regional planning agencies are now operating in Floride alone—in the Fort Lauderdale-Hollywood area, the Jacksonville area, and the Tampa-St. Petersburg area—and a Regional Planning Council for the Baltimore metropolitan area was established in 1963. The Atlanta Regional Metropolitan Planning Commission has been expanded from a bi-county agency to one whose jurisdiction extends to all five counties in the Atlanta metropolitan area.

In addition, ten of the sixteen southern states have provided that planning by individual municipalities may include areas beyond the corporate limits of municipalities. At least some degree of extraterritorial *zoning* is now permitted in Alabama,. Kentucky, North Carolina, Oklahoma, South Carolina, Tennessee, and West Virginia, and statutory authority for extraterritorial *subdivision control* has been granted in twelve of the sixteen Southern states.[19]

All this is indicative of an awareness in the South that sound metropolitan development is contingent upon effective government and that both are essential to the long term health of the southern states individually and of the region as a whole. Even so, however,

[19]For a general discussion of the subject, see Frank S. Sengstock, *Extraterritorial Powers in the Metropolitan Areas* (Ann Arbor, 1962).

southern states have not yet begun to act in a way commensurate with the mounting challenge metropolitanization presents to them. The Advisory Commission on Intergovernmental Relations in a 1961 report urged the states to assume vigorous leadership in meeting that challenge, to take action on problems transcending satisfactory local solutions, and to grant a number of permissive powers for selective use by metropolitan area governments themselves.[20] If some of them have paid some heed to the latter piece of advice, there is little evidence that the southern states have responded in any effective way to the first two recommendations. Perhaps such a response must await the development of a more meaningful two party system. That development seems already to be underway, paralleling the rapid urbanization of the South, and to the extent that it continues, the chances for action on metropolitan area problems may be improved as well.

Whatever the cause, the South has not made as much of the opportunity to attack the problem of government in its metropolitan areas as it might have. True, Miami has adopted a federated form of metropolitan government and Nashville a consolidated metropolitan government,[21] and both are unique in the nation. This is one way of overcoming fragmentation. But their example has not been followed elsewhere. If the voters of Nashville and Davidson County accepted metropolitan government, the voters in both Memphis and Shelby County, by heavy majorities, turned the same opportunity down. So did the voters of Knox County, Tennessee, Durham County, North Carolina, and Bibb County, Georgia, decide against consolidation with Knoxville, Durham, and Macon.

So too did the people of Georgia defeat at the polls an amendment to that state's constitution to enable county governments to engage in public mass transportation programs, an action which would have been of invaluable aid to Atlanta, Savannah, and Columbus.

[20]See Advisory Commission on Intergovernmental Relations, *Governmental Structure, Organization and Planning in Metropolitan Areas* (July, 1961); see also *ibid.*, *Factors Affecting Voter Reactions to Governmental Reorganization in Metropolitan Areas* (May, 1962).

[21]For a discussion of the differences between the two, see Daniel R. Grant, "Consolidations Compared," *National Civic Review* 52:10-p. (January, 1963). See also Edward Sofen, *The Miami Metropolitan Government* (Bloomington, 1962) and David A. Booth, *Metropolitics: The Nashville Consolidation* (East Lansing, 1963).

In some states outside the South, state governments have begun
to establish a department or agency to provide a focal point for
actions with regard to urban and metropolitan problems, but only
in North Carolina to date has the suggestion even been advanced,
and there from the tenor of Governor Sanford's remarks it is obvious
he was thinking primarily of the aid such an office could render small
cities rather than of the help it could be to North Carolina's six
metropolitan areas.

While numerous experiments in the use of the interstate compact
as a device to assist in solving problems of interstate metropolitan
areas have been made elsewhere,[22] the southern record is devoid
of accomplishment here, except for the approval by the Virginia
legislature of two compacts applying to the Washington Metropolitan
area.[23]

And although one of the paths to better metropolitan government taken with increasing frequency in recent years in non-southern areas—New York, Detroit, San Francisco, to name only three—
has been the voluntary association of the existing governmental units
in a regional council, only one such council has been created in the
South—the Washington Metropolitan Regional Council which has
had very limited success—and no others seem to be in the process
of formation.

Nor does the South seem to have given consideration to an
aspect of the problem of government in metropolitan areas which is
of special concern to the authors of this article—the problem of the
impact of the federal government on the development of its metropolitan areas. This is in spite of the fact that the impact of federal
activities has perhaps been greater on the South than on any other
region. Although none of the case studies we recommended[24] have
been made elsewhere, none have been made in the South, where the
very presence of the atomic energy center at Augusta, the rocket research facility at Huntsville, the vast armed services installations
at Newport News-Hampton and Columbus, and the NASA Manned

[22]See Winters, *op. cit.*, for a discussion of these experiments.
[23]It is perhaps possible to consider the adoption in 1955 by Virginia and
Kentucky of the compact creating the Breaks Interstate Park as being an
attempt to provide additional recreational facilities for residents of those two
states' metropolitan areas, but to do so would probably be to assign motives
which were in fact not there at the time.
[24]See Robert H. Connery and Richard H. Leach, *The Federal Government
and Metropolitan Areas* (Cambridge, 1960), ch. 7.

Space Flight Center just now being built near Houston must be acknowledged as major contributors to metropolitan growth.

In such a survey as this, it is impossible to describe the impact of federal programs on government in each metropolitan area. One area might be singled out, however, to give some idea of the missed opportunities involved. Nowhere has metropolitanization taken place more rapidly than in the 3,000 square mile area in east central Florida which has been nicknamed "Moonland," and solely because of activities of the national government. Cape Kennedy is located approximately in the middle of the area, and since the first missile was set off from there in 1950, a virtual revolution has taken place in the region. From a quiet, predominantly agricultural and recreational area, it has mushroomed into a complicated conurbation. The area around Orlando, the region's central city, grew faster than any other southern metropolitan area in the 1950-60 decade. The city itself increased 68.3% in population in those ten years, the immediate urban fringe areas grew 442.7% and the remoter outlying areas grew 71.2%.[25] Orange County, in which Orlando lies, grew 130%, while Brevard County to the east, where the NASA installation is actually located, more than quadrupled its population in the same period. Sharp, if not quite as spectacular, increases marked Volusia and Seminole Counties to the north and Osceola County to the southwest. Population statistics, however, only begin to describe the change. "Today," wrote Charles Layng in *The National Observer*, "the area looks like the world's biggest commuters' traffic jam. Hundreds of housing subdivisions have sprung up and a whole new city of 50,000 or possibly more between Orlando and Cape Canaveral [*sic*] is being planned. Traffic clogs the inadequate roads to the Cape, and . . . contractors are doing their best to meet the crushing need for convenient housing for workers at Cape Canaveral [*sic*], the Martin Missile plant in Orlando, and the proposed plants in Daytona and elsewhere . . . . new schools and elaborate shopping centers have proliferated."[26]

Here was an opportunity for all levels of government—federal, state, and local—to cooperate in planning ahead so as to avoid the problems of government which plague all metropolitan areas. Unfortunately, the opportunity was not acted upon. The Florida legis-

[25]*The Municipal Year Book, 1962, op. cit.,* p. 39.
[26]Charles Layng, "Some Growing Pains in Florida's 'Moonland,'" *The National Observer,* April 29, 1963, p. 8.

lature, traditionally responsive to Florida's citrus and cattle interests, has even refused so far to enact laws to allow zoning and subdivision controls of primarily rural lands. Nor have Orlando and the five counties involved tried to work out some joint arrangement between them to offset legislative indifference. Like Topsy, the whole area "just growed."

Mention might also be made of Houston, already one of the largest and most important metropolitan areas in the South, which missed an opportunity in 1957 to strengthen the governmental machinery of the area by accepting the recommendations of the Harris County Home Rule Commission. Established by the state legislature in 1955, the Commission recommended that the county be allowed to assume the functions necessary to provide adequate services to the residents of the metropolitan area and to consider either the eventual consolidation of the 24 municipalities in the county with the county itself or to devise such a "union of effort of municipalities as circumstance [might] dictate."[27] But the opportunity was turned down in favor of continuing the present fragmented situation. As one observer recently put it, "Houstonians are jealous of their personal liberties, suspicious of authority. . . . As a result of [their] anarchic individualism, Houston is probably the nation's most lightly governed city."[28] With such an outlook, the impact of the Manned Space Flight Center on the area will be interesting, to say the least.

IV

In the South as everywhere else in the United States, it is obvious by now that government in metropolitan areas is profoundly influenced by the action of both the states and the federal government. Every-day problems of metropolitan living—transportation, sanitation, health, water supply, and housing—are becoming more and more matters that require inter governmental action. As a result, we must ask with Victor Jones whether "local governments as traditionally organized can play a meaningful role in planning, formulating, and administering inter-governmental urban programs?"[29] In

[27]Harris County Home Rule Commission, *Metropolitan Harris County* (Houston, 1957), p. 103.
[28]*Time,* April 12, 1963, p 27.
[29]Victor Jones, "Metropolitan Reorganization: An Appraisal of Success and Failures," *Metropolitan Problems and Politics,* Division of Research, College of Business Administration, University of Denver, p. 24 (July, 1962).

the South, where the tradition of local government is still strong, the question has special pertinence. Must it, like the other regions of the country, turn to wider use of *ad hoc* agencies, special districts, and authorities in metropolitan areas, or will it be able to develop new tools of its own? What will it develop as counterparts of state and federal agencies?

The Advisory Commission on Intergovernmental Relations has urged that all future applications for federal grants, planning in-aid in metropolitan areas be reviewed by a metropolitan-agency. Should this recommendation be adopted, as it may well be in the next decade, it will pose major questions for the South's metropolitan communities. If federal programs affecting urban areas continue to proliferate, as they undoubtedly will, will the specialists who staff Washington agencies be satisfied to deal with many individual municipalities, townships, and counties in a metropolis, none of whom can speak for the whole area? Will they even be satisfied with informal understandings between the independent units of government in a metropolis? Everything points to the contrary. To quote Victor Jones again, "We have passed the point where it can be answered that the federal government has no responsibility for local government and that it should leave questions of this kind entirely to the states."[30]

Unless metropolitan communities act to put their own houses in order according to some rational plan—and this they cannot do without the active, intelligent help of the state government—there is grave danger that the *ad hoc* metropolitan agencies so often set up in response to the pressures of federal programs will be divorced from a meaningful political base. It would be most unfortunate if metropolitan planning agencies become the exclusive preserve of professional planners, with the result that national policy decisions could be reached in the guise of technical decisions. Planning should involve a representative body of local elected officials.

As we have said previously, the answer so far as the federal government is concerned lies in the conscious recognition of the fact that federal programs have a tremendous impact on local government.[31] This is true not only in regard to individual programs but whole groups of programs which frequently have an accumulative effect as well. This situation demands personnel on the staff of fed-

[30]*Ibid.*, p. 28.
[31]Connery and Leach, *op. cit.*

eral agencies which make grants to local government who are knowledgeable about the impact that their program may have on local communities. This consciousness must be broad and take into account values ranging far beyond their immediate activities. On the other hand, if local governments are to remain democratic institutions for self government and not merely conduits for the carrying out of political decisions made in Washington, metropolitan areas must devise ways of organizing themselves for effective metropolitan planning, decision making, and administration. Each metropolitan area will have to find its own best way to tackle its problems of government. A number of avenues have been opened up,[32] and one or more of them will probably lead any southern metropolitan community which makes the effort to use it to a more rational way of governing itself.

Southern metropolitan areas have perhaps the best opportunity of any in the nation to move ahead because so many of them are new and the layers of government do not lie so heavily upon them. If the South fails to grasp the opportunity, it will be because of its own inertia, not because there are no paths to follow out of chaos. This inertia to change one might regard almost as a southern tradition. Several years ago the economist William H. Nicholls wrote a book entitled *Southern Tradition and Regional Progress*,[33] in which he concluded that southern progress generally depended to a large extent on the degree to which the South could overcome the handicap imposed by its peculiar regional culture. Certainly those traditions need no discussion here. But it is beyond argument that southern states have habitually been less concerned with accepting social responsibility than have states outside the region. Solution of the problem of government in metropolitan areas necessarily involves departure from that pattern. Indeed, to look for early solution in any of the states which have not cut their ties with the past is probably to look in vain.

In the last analysis, however, what will probably retard a good many southern metropolitan areas from making the governmental adjustments they require as soon as they otherwise might will be the

[32]See Roscoe Martin, "Action in Metropolis," *National Civic Review* 52:302-7, 316 (June, 1963); and 52:363-7, 71 (July, 1963). Both parts of the article are well worth reading. Some fifteen suggestions are made for improving government in metropolitan areas.
[33]Chapel Hill, 1960.

race question, which will be examined in other articles in this series. What V. O. Key had to say in his *Southern Politics* years ago is still valid:

> In its grand outlines the politics of the South revolves around the position of the Negro . . . Whatever phase of the southern political process one seeks to understand, sooner or later the trail of inquiry leads to the Negro.[34]

The adjustment of metropolitan government in the South is a political matter, and here too the trail leads back to the Negro. There can be little doubt that the race problem dominates the political arena. Those who seek metropolitan reform, however compelling their case, must take the back seat to the primary issue of race.

Thus the picture in the South is a mixed one. On the one hand, there are signs of real progress on the road toward governmental adjustment to urbanization and metropolitan development. On the other, the South has not taken advantage of all the opportunities it might have. On balance, it is probably not very different from any of the other sections of the nation. The South has an opportunity to avoid the mistakes of the past, however, and thus the challenge is a greater one.

---

[34] V. O. Key, *Southern Politics* (New York, 1949), p. 5.

SOUTHERN IMAGES OF POLITICAL PARTIES:
AN ANALYSIS OF WHITE AND NEGRO
ATTITUDES*

DONALD R. MATTHEWS
JAMES W. PROTHRO
University of North Carolina

"I THINK IF YOU'D put them in a sack and shake them up," a
white mail carrier in rural Georgia said while attempting to
define the difference between the Democratic and Republican parties,
"you wouldn't know which . . . jump(ed) out first." A retired car-
penter living nearby disagreed. "They's a difference, Lawd yes. The
main difference is the Republicans believe in a lot of hard, harsh
things and the Democrats in good living, good jobs, and good times."
Others were less certain of the distinction. A 70 year old dowager
in Florida said, "The name (Republican) offends my sensibilities
but actually in some ways it is more like the old Democratic party
I once believed in." In Little Rock, Arkansas, a 60 year old woman
also was puzzled. "I was always raised a Democrat. I used to think
Republicans made depressions, but Eisenhower didn't make one.
But I don't believe he was a real Republican."

Southern Negroes are equally perplexed. "The southern Democrats fight Civil Rights," according to a Negro college student in
North Carolina. A Negro share-cropper in Georgia looked at the
parties differently. He was a Republican until ". . . President Roosevelt brought us out, the Negro out in the world. I figured I should
be what my daddy was. (But) President Roosevelt did a miracle,
put bread in our mouths. Hoover put money in his own pocket and
nobody else's." A Negro brick maker in Florida said that he liked
the Republican party ". . . because I am an old man and I believe
in old things. And to my weak judgment the Republicans always did
more for the colored people than the Democratic people." But another elderly Negro, this one a Democrat in Tennessee, replied,
". . . I know they say the Republicans freed the slaves, . . . (but)
. . . to me they are not free yet."

These are some responses of southern voters when asked about
the Democratic and Republican parties. Obviously, the politics of

the 1950's has left them puzzled, confused, and of several minds about the Democratic and Republican parties. In this paper, we shall describe the attitudes of white and Negro southerners toward the American political parties, and examine the relationships between these attitudes and their party affiliation, voting, and other attitudes. Finally, we shall examine the social and economic correlates of the different party images held by southerners and draw some tentative conclusions about the future.

This endeavor could throw light on several problems that have concerned political scientists. First of all, there is considerable interest in the possibility of a party realignment in the region. That the South is no longer "solid" in presidential elections is clear, yet the kind of party politics which is replacing one-partyism apparently is not the normal sort of two-party system. If the party system of the region continues to change, it will be in response to the attitudes and feelings of southern voters. But—and this is our second point—the behavior of southern voters has yet to be studied systematically. Most academic studies of voting behavior either have been conducted in the North or have been based on national samples in which the southern segment is too small to permit detailed analysis. Many widely accepted generalizations about the voting behavior of Americans may not fit the southern political landscape. Third, the growth of Negro voting in the South has added to the region's electorate a new element which may respond to quite different pressures and felt needs than those of other groups. Finally, by studying the southern electorate in some detail, we may be able better to understand the attitudes and behavior of voters in general, as well as to develop a deeper understanding of southern politics in particular.

Our findings are based on interviews with Negroes and whites chosen by strict probability methods from all citizens of voting age living in private households in the eleven former confederate states. These two samples, which consisted of 618 Negro and 694 white

*This study has been supported by a grant from the Rockefeller Foundation to the Institute for Research in Social Science of the University of North Carolina and by awards from the Social Science Research Council to each of the authors. We wish to express our gratitude to these organizations for providing the resources needed to engage in this analysis, but they should not be held responsible for the contents of this paper.

This is a revised version of a paper presented at the Annual Meeting of the Southern Political Science Association, November 8-10, 1962, at Gatlinburg, Tennessee.

respondents, are the largest **ever** interviewed in the South for a political study. The interviews were conducted between March and August, 1961, by professional interviewers of the same race as the respondent.[1] The questions in the interview schedules of particular importance to this analysis are standard ones on party identification, party voting, and political attitudes which have been successfully employed by the Survey Research Center at the University of Michigan for a decade.

PARTY IDENTIFICATION AND REGISTRATION OF SOUTHERNERS

"Belonging" to a political party in America is a casual affair. As a result, no universally recognized and accepted way exists to determine who is a Democrat and who is a Republican.

The most general and useful approach is to define as Democrats or Republicans those who *think* of themselves as Democrats or Republicans. Rather than slicing the electorate in two, this approach encourages us to think of the electorate as ranging along a continuum from those most strongly identified with the Democratic party; through decreasing states of emotional commitment to those who identify with neither party; and then, in gradually increasing degrees, to those who identify strongly with the Republican party.[2] Southern whites and Negroes are so arranged in Table 1. Despite heavy defections to the Republicans in recent presidential elections, it is evident at once that southerners are still very heavily Democratic in their party identification. A little over 60 per cent of the southern whites think of themselves as either "strong" or "not so strong" Democrats, compared to about 14 per cent who think of themselves as Republican in some degree. Southern Negroes show equal disdain for the party of Lincoln (and Earl Warren). Only about 10 per cent of the voting age Negroes call themselves strong or weak Republicans, while slightly over half consider themselves to be Democrats. The small differences in party preferences between Negroes and whites result primarily from the fact that 20 per cent

[1]For a description of the field phase of the study see M. Axelrod, D. R. Matthews, and J. W. Prothro, "Recruitment for Survey Research on Race Problems in the South," *Public Opinion Quarterly*, XXVI (Summer 1962), pp. 254-262.

[2]This approach has been pioneered by the Survey Research Center. See A. Campbell, P. E. Converse, W. E. Miller, and D. E. Stokes, *The American Voter* (N. Y., John Wiley and Sons, Inc., 1960), ch. 6.

TABLE 1

PARTY IDENTIFICATION OF SOUTHERNERS, BY RACE

PARTY IDENTIFICATION	TOTAL DISTRIBUTION		DISTRIBUTION, ELIMINATING APOLITICALS, MINOR PARTY IDENTIFIERS, DK'S, ETC.	
	WHITES	NEGROES	WHITES	NEGROES
Strong Democrat	29%	28%	31%	36%
Weak Democrat	32	23	34	29
Independent, closer to Democrats	7	8	8	10
Independent	7	5	7	7
Independent, closer to Republicans	5	4	5	5
Weak Republican	6	7	7	9
Strong Republican	8	3	8	4
Apolitical	5	20	—	----
Other, Minor Party	*	0	—	—
Don't know, Refusal, No answer	1	2	—	—
Total	100%	100%	100%	100%
N	(694)	(618)	(655)	(480)
P	<.001		.02>P>.01	

NOTES: Party identification was determined by response to the following standard questions:

"Generally speaking, do you usually think of yourself as a Republican, a Democrat, an Independent or what?"

"Would you call yourself a strong Democrat (Republican) or a not very strong Democrat (Republican)?"

IF "INDEPENDENT," "OTHER," "DON'T KNOW":

"Do you think of yourself as closer to the Republican or Democratic party?"

The chi-square test of statistical significance was used in this and all other tables and figures for which P is reported.

* = less than 0.5%

of the Negroes were unable to classify themselves along the partisan continuum, while only 5 per cent of the whites were equally "apolitical." When these respondents—for whom politics has almost no psychological reality anyway—are eliminated, the differences between the two races in the distribution of party identification are greatly reduced.

Ignoring strength of identification, exactly the same proportion (65 per cent) of Negro and white party identifiers call themselves Democrats. This consensus between southern Negroes and whites is amazing, even to those hardened to the vagaries of American politics. The sharpest and most divisive conflict in American politics exists between these same southern Negroes and whites.[3] About

[3] A fuller development of this point may be found in D. R. Matthews and J. W. Prothro, "Southern Racial Attitudes: Conflict, Awareness, and Political Change," *The Annals of the American Academy of Political and Social Science,* CCCXXXXIV (November, 1962), pp. 108-121.

70 per cent of the white Democrats say that they believe in "strict segregation" of the races, a belief that is concurred in by only about 14 per cent of their Negro fellow Democrats (Figure 1).[4] Or, focusing on those who believe in integration, only 6 per cent of the white Democrats agree with almost 80 per cent of Negro Democrats who say that integration is desirable. A majority of whites in the South,

[4] Segregation-integration attitudes of whites were determined by responses to the following question: "What about you? Are you in favor of strict segregation, integration, or something in between?" The attitudes of Negroes were determined by responses to the same question with the order of choices changed to ". . . integration, strict segregation, or something in between?" The relationship between party identification and racial attitudes of whites is significant at the .01 > P > .001 level. Among Negroes, P < .001. For purposes of presentation, the "strong" and "weak" Democrats and Republicans have been collapsed into Democratic and Republican categories, and the three types of independents have been treated as a single group in this and several other figures and tables in this article.

Figure I

RELATIONSHIPS BETWEEN PARTY IDENTIFICATION
AND OTHER ATTITUDES OF SOUTHERNERS, BY RACE

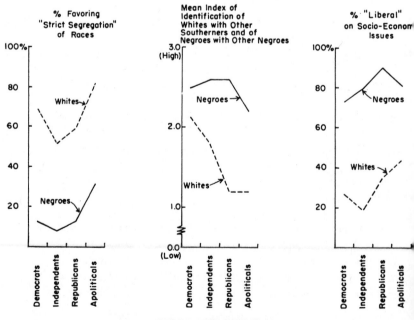

PARTY IDENTIFICATION

TABLE 2

PARTY REGISTRATION OF SOUTHERNERS, BY PARTY IDENTIFICATION AND RACE

PARTY IDENTIFICATION	WHITES					NEGROES				
	% REGISTERED TO VOTE	DEMOCRAT	INDE-PENDENT	REPUB-LICAN	TOTAL AND N	% REGISTERED TO VOTE	DEM.	IND.	REP.	TOTAL AND N
Strong Democrat	87.5%	96%	0	4%	100% (176)	52%	97%	0	3%	100% (99)
Weak Democrat	77%	96	1	3	100% (169)	32%	96	0	4	100% (44)
Independent, Closer to Democrat	55%	71	18	11	100% (28)	35%	82	6	12	100% (17)
Independent	44%	62	33	5	100% (21)	27%	33	45	22	100% (9)
Independent, Closer to Republican	67.5%	39	26	35	100% (23)	23%	40	20	40	100% (5)
Weak Republican	76%	21	3	76	100% (34)	36%	25	6	69	100% (16)
Strong Republican	92.5%	14	2	84	100% (51)	30%	50	17	33	100% (6)
Apolitical	12%	100	0	0	100% (4)	2%	67	33	0	100% (3)
Total (includes DK, NA, RA, other on party identification question)	73%	78%	18%	4%	100%	33%	83%	12%	5%	100%
N	(694)	(393)	(93)	(21)	(507)	(618)	(167)	(25)	(9)	(201)

NOTE: The differences in the proportion of whites and Negroes registered as Democrats or Republicans, by party identication, are not statistically significant. There are too few registered independents to permit the computation of chi-square.

whatever their party identification, prefer strict segregation, but the size of the majorities varies. Next to the white "apoliticals," the white Democrats are the most segregationist group in the electorate, while the Negro Democrats are as strongly in favor of racial integration as are other Negroes.

This anomaly is underscored by other findings. Among whites, identification with the Democratic party is positively associated with identification with the South as a region.[5] Indeed, white Democrats are almost twice as likely as white Republicans to "feel close to" other southerners. Negroes, regardless of party identification, feel much closer to fellow Negroes than to other people, and are an even more self-conscious group than white southerners. Thus the southern Negroes' overwhelming identification with a party which in their region consists predominantly of southern-oriented, white strict segregationists cannot be explained by indifference to the fortunes of their own race.

Perhaps this massive political miscegenation can be accounted for on the basis of perceived common interest in "bread-and-butter" social welfare issues. The data summarized in Figure 1 do not point in this direction.[6] In both races, the Republicans are, on the average, a little more "liberal" than the Democrats. But these differences are small enough that it is safer to conclude that party identification is not strongly and consistently linked with social welfare liberalism among either whites or Negroes in the former confederate

[5]White identification with other southerners and Negro identification with other Negroes were determined by responses to the following questions:

"Some people in the South [some Negroes] feel they have a lot in common with other southerners [Negroes]; but others we talk to don't feel this way so much. How about you? Would you say you feel *pretty close* to southerners [Negroes] in general or that you don't *feel much closer* to them than you do to other people?" "How much interest would you say you have in how southerners [Negroes] as a whole are getting along in this country? Do you have a *good deal* of interest in it, *some* interest, or *not much* interest at all?"

The mean scores reported in Figure 1 are based on an index that measures strength of identification from 0 to 3, with a score of 3 given to respondents who gave the most positive response to both items and a score of 0 to those who gave the most negative response to both items. The relationship between party identification and identification with other southerners is significant at the .001 level for whites; between party identification and identification with other Negroes, $.01 > P > .001$.

[6]The social welfare liberalism scale was based on expressions of agreement or disagreement ("agree quite a bit," "agree a little," "disagree a little," "disagree quite a bit") with the following statements:

states. Southern Negroes, regardless of their party identification, tend to be "liberal" while southern whites, regardless of their party identification, tend to be relatively conservative. The Negroes are so much more liberal than the whites that the most conservative partisan grouping of Negroes contains twice the proportion of liberals as the most liberal partisan group of whites. Perhaps nowhere is the cliché about bedfellows in politics more true than in the South today.

Party identification is one thing, party *registration* is another. Only one-third of our sample of Negro potential voters were actually registered to vote, compared to about three-quarters of the whites (Table 2). But of those Negroes registered to vote, 83 per cent were registered Democrats while only 78 per cent of the whites were on the voting lists as Democrats.[7] When it is remembered that the two races contained similar divisions of party identifiers, it seems as if the Negroes take their Democratic identification more seriously than the whites do. But a closer examination of Table 2 shows that this is not really the case, so far as party registration is concerned. Ninety-six or -seven per cent of the registered voters in both races who think of themselves as Democrats are also registered as Democrats. The Negroes who call themselves independents are more likely to be registered as independents than is true among whites. But among the Republican identifiers and the independents who feel closer to one party than the other, the Negroes are more likely than the whites to be registered as Democrats. Thus, for example, 50 per cent of the Negroes who call themselves strong Republicans are

"The government should leave things like electric power and housing for private businessmen to handle." "The government in Washington ought to see to it that everybody who wants to work can find a job." "If cities and towns around the country need help to build more schools, the government in Washington ought to give them the money they need." "The government ought to help people get doctors and hospital care at low cost."

Disagreement with the first item and agreement with the other three items were counted as "liberal" responses. Responses were scaled according to Gutte-mann procedures, with the following coefficients of reproducibility: white scale, .92; Negro scale, .96; southern scale (combining white interviews with the Negro interviews that were part of the southwide sample without regard to race), .93. Scale types I and II were classified as "liberal." The relationship between party identification and "liberalism" for whites is significant at the $.02 > P > .01$ level; for Negroes, at the $.05 > P > .02$ level.

[7] All southern states do not require registration by party; these data are based on respondents' statements as to the party affiliation they gave in registering.

registered Democrats compared to only 14 per cent of the white strong Republicans. When one also notes the sharp drop-off in rates of registration among Negro Republicans and independents, it is clear that the Republicans have done a far poorer job than the Democrats in enrolling potential supporters among Negroes.

One possible explanation for the tendency of Negro Republicans to register as Democrats in the South is the greater vulnerability of

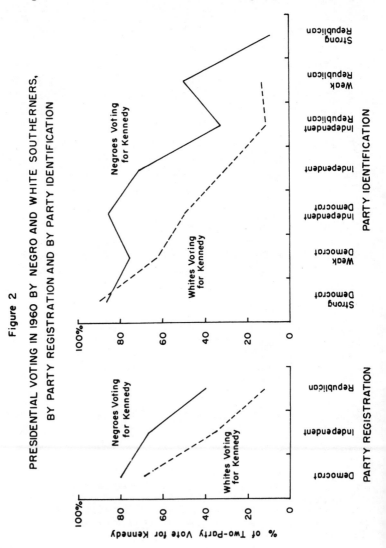

Figure 2

PRESIDENTIAL VOTING IN 1960 BY NEGRO AND WHITE SOUTHERNERS, BY PARTY REGISTRATION AND BY PARTY IDENTIFICATION

Negroes to community pressure in general and to the blandishments of white voter registration officials in particular. One could easily imagine that a Negro Republican might in some areas be afraid to violate local norms by registering as anything other than a Democrat. While this explanation appears plausible, it is not supported by other findings. If it were valid, we could expect a heavier Republican vote from Negroes than from whites registered as Democrats. But when we consider the 1960 presidential vote, we discover that Negro Republicans were more likely than whites with the same party registration to vote for Kennedy.

In Figure 2, the proportion of the two-party vote polled by Kennedy in 1960 is plotted, by race and party registration. It can be seen that Kennedy carried the registered Democrats of both races quite handily, gaining about 80 per cent of the Negro Democrats' votes and almost 70 per cent of the votes of the white Democrats. But Nixon carried the white independents with a great many votes to spare while Kennedy was carrying the Negro independents with almost as lopsided a margin as he carried the white Democrats. Even among the Negro Republicans, Kennedy did well, polling 40 per cent of the vote while doing miserably among the white Republicans.

Party identification is somewhat more closely linked than party registration to presidential voting in 1960. Kennedy carried both the strong and weak Democrats of both races and, among whites, split the independents leaning toward the Democratic party with Nixon. In every other white partisan grouping he was badly defeated. But he carried the Negro independents by almost as large a margin as he did the Democrats and did quite well among the Negro Republicans.

Two central conclusions emerge from these figures. First of all, neither party identification nor party registration is a perfect indicator of the voting preferences of southerners in presidential elections. Second, Negroes tend to vote Democratic far more overwhelmingly than whites even when controls are introduced for party identification and party registration. We shall argue that the concept of "party image" helps explain both these phenomena.

THE CONCEPT OF "PARTY IMAGE"

American political parties speak with many voices. Not only are the national Democratic and Republican parties loose confederations of state and local organizations, but they are normally divided into competing "wings" and "factions" at each level of government. The tendency for all these party groups to avoid clear-cut or extreme policy stands contributes to the confusion. Confronted with this ambiguity, voters can have quite different pictures of what the parties are like. Either party might be thought "liberal" or "conservative," honest or venal, internationalist or isolationist, and so forth, depending upon which aspects of the party the voter chooses to see and evaluate. It is the voter's picture of the party which we call the "party image."

Party image is not the same thing as party identification. While the two concepts are related to one another, two people may identify with the same party but have very different mental pictures of it and evaluate these pictures in different ways. Party identification is no doubt the more basic and less changeful of the two variables— the evidence is overwhelming that it is formed early in life and does not easily or often change.[8] But while party image is not as deeply-rooted or as stable as party identification, it is likely to be less ephemeral than voter attitudes toward the issues and candidates of specific campaigns.

Most studies of attitudes toward political parties are carried out during election campaigns, and this circumstance of timing may be expected to maximize the extent to which respondents comment on the parties in terms of the transient and particular issues and personalities that are most visible during the campaign. Indeed, so great is this tendency that attitudes toward parties as such are treated separately from attitudes toward candidates and issues. Since these studies generally have the purpose of accounting for the outcome of a particular election, the maximization of campaign-related responses is entirely appropriate. For a study of relatively stable images of political parties, however, data collection during a non-campaign period appears to offer distinct advantages. Granted that attitudes toward specific issues and party leaders will still be an important component of party images, they can be built into the over-all concept of the party as an enduring organization.[9]

[8]H. Hyman, *Political Socialization* (Glencoe, Illinois: The Free Press, 1959); H. McClosky and H. E. Dahlgren, "Primary Group Influence on Party Loyalty," *American Political Science Review,* LIII (September 1959), pp. 757-776.

[9]While the Survey Research Center does not specifically utilize the concept of party image, their analysis of perceptions of parties and partisan attitudes is similar. See Campbell *et al., op. cit.,* ch. 3-4.

Since our interviews were conducted months after the most recent national election, we are able to concentrate on and to spell out the relatively stable and enduring party attitudes of southerners. In order to ascertain these, respondents were asked in a series of open-ended questions to indicate what they "like" and "don't like" about both parties. About one-third of both races (31% for whites, 33%

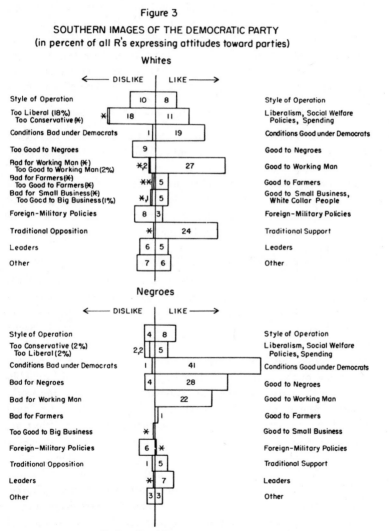

Figure 3

SOUTHERN IMAGES OF THE DEMOCRATIC PARTY
(in percent of all R's expressing attitudes toward parties)

Whites

← DISLIKE | LIKE →

	DISLIKE	LIKE	
Style of Operation	10	8	Style of Operation
Too Liberal (18%) / Too Conservative (✱)	18	11	Liberalism, Social Welfare Policies, Spending
Conditions Bad under Democrats	1	19	Conditions Good under Democrats
Too Good to Negroes	9		Good to Negroes
Bad for Working Man (✱) / Too Good to Working Man (2%)	✱,2	27	Good to Working Man
Bad for Farmers (✱) / Too Good to Farmers (✱)	✱✱	5	Good to Farmers
Bad for Small Business (✱) / Too Good to Big Business (1%)	✱,1	5	Good to Small Business, White Collar People
Foreign-Military Policies	8	3	Foreign-Military Policies
Traditional Opposition	✱	24	Traditional Support
Leaders	6	5	Leaders
Other	7	6	Other

Negroes

← DISLIKE | LIKE →

	DISLIKE	LIKE	
Style of Operation	4	8	Style of Operation
Too Conservative (2%) / Too Liberal (2%)	2,2	5	Liberalism, Social Welfare Policies, Spending
Conditions Bad under Democrats	1	41	Conditions Good under Democrats
Bad for Negroes	4	28	Good to Negroes
Bad for Working Man		22	Good to Working Man
Bad for Farmers		1	Good to Farmers
Too Good to Big Business	✱		Good to Small Business
Foreign-Military Policies	6	✱	Foreign-Military Policies
Traditional Opposition	1	5	Traditional Support
Leaders	✱	7	Leaders
Other	3	3	Other

✱ = Less than 0.5%

for Negroes) could not name a single thing they liked or disliked about either party. For this group, party politics either does not exist, or is entirely devoid of content. Forty-seven per cent of the whites and 43 per cent of the Negroes, however, could say something good or bad about *both* parties, while almost 20 per cent of both races expressed images of the Democratic party but were unable to say anything about the Republican; and about 5 per cent of both races had likes or dislikes about the Republican party but said nothing about the Democratic party. Perhaps the most surprising fact here is that the Negroes have as fully developed images of the two parties as do the whites, despite their lower educational level and the fact that most of them are not registered voters.

Southern Images of the Democratic Party

Both races have essentially favorable attitudes toward the Democratic party. The white respondents liked almost twice as many things as they disliked about the Democrats and disliked almost twice as many things as they liked about the Republican party. The Negroes were even more favorably inclined toward the Democratic party: they mentioned more than six favorable attitudes toward the Democrats for every unfavorable reference, while taking a somewhat dimmer view of the GOP than the whites.

The most popular aspect of the Democratic party's image among white southerners is that the party is good to (or better for) the common people and the working man (Figure 3). Twenty-seven per cent of the white respondents with any image of the parties mentioned this as something they liked about the Democratic party. Moreover, this is the favorable attitude most often mentioned by strong-, weak-, and independent Democrats and by the apoliticals. A very few of the whites—less than 2.5 per cent and mostly Republicans—see the party is being "too good to" or "bad for" the workers and common man. But the Democratic party, more than anything else, is viewed and praised as the champion of the little man. Almost as many whites—19 per cent of those with party images—said that "conditions are good (or better) under the Democrats," and that the Democratic party brings higher wages, more jobs, and the like. Less than one per cent of the whites volunteered disagreement with this point of view and most who did were Republicans. These two points, plus traditional support for the party—"I'm just a Democrat," "I've always been a Democrat," a view expressed by

24 per cent of the whites—provide the overwhelmingly favorable portion of the Democratic party's white image in the South.

The party's perceived liberalism and dedication to social welfare policies and government spending was a much more controversial aspect of the Democratic image. Eleven per cent of the whites approved of this "liberalism," while 18 per cent complained that the party was too liberal, and less than 0.5 per cent said the party was too conservative. The Democrats' liberalism on economic issues is not particularly important, among the many other party appeals, to the strong and weak Democrats, but it is more popular among the relatively few independents, Republicans, and apoliticals who can find anything to like about the Democrats. These same groups, however, are those most likely to criticize the party as being too liberal. All things considered, the net loss of party popularity from the Democrats' association with economic liberalism is substantial.

The "style" of the Democratic party—the *way* in which it runs the government and manages its own internal affairs—is also more frequently a negative (10%) than a positive (8%) factor. Here the independents seem to be the most impressed with the view that the Democrats are inefficient, dishonest, and undignified. Democratic leaders—the ones most frequently mentioned were recent presidents and almost all were national rather than regional or local figures— were a little more often disliked (6%) than liked (5%). Democratic foreign policy also was, on balance, a source of unpopularity among the few whites mentioning it at all. But the most negative element in the Democratic image held by white southerners is that it is "too good to Negroes"; 9 per cent of the whites with party images mentioned this facet of the party while not one mentioned that he approved of the party's racial policies. Moreover, this is the thing most disliked by strong Democrats, and is the second most unpopular aspect of the party among weak Democrats. While mentioned by surprisingly few white respondents, the Democrats' reputation for being pro-Negro has the largest negative impact on the white Democratic image, followed closely by the belief that it is too liberal. The party's foreign and military policies are the third most unpopular aspect of the image, with the party "style" far behind in fourth place.

The Negro image of the Democratic party has many similarities to that of the whites, along with significant differences. Forty-one per cent of Negroes agree with the whites that "conditions are good" under the Democrats. Not much of an argument is possible on this point among Negro southerners; Negro Republicans no less than Democrats believe that conditions are good under the Democrats. Negroes mention that the party is "good to workers" almost as often as whites (22 per cent compared to 27 per cent). The overwhelming view is that the party is "good to Negroes"; 28 per cent mentioned this belief while only 4 per cent (mostly independents and Republicans) disagreed. The relatively few whites mentioning the party's racial policies agree that Democrats are pro-Negro, but unanimously deplored rather than applauded the fact. A second major difference between the two races should be pointed out. The Negro image of the Democratic party is far less ambivalent than that of the southern whites. The Negroes like almost everything about the party as they see it. Only in two categories of issues— foreign policy and relationships with big business—is the Negro image predominantly negative and in neither case is the number of respondents mentioning the point large or the surplus of dislikes over likes substantial.

SOUTHERN IMAGES OF THE REPUBLICAN PARTY

Attitudes of southern whites toward the Republican party mirror in neat reversal their views of the Democratic party—the same grounds for liking and disliking are brought into play, with each party seen as good where the other is bad. Granted that the net view of the Democrats is favorable, the net view of the Republicans emerges as unfavorable. (See Figure 4.) The most frequently mentioned factor, good or bad, is the charge that the Republicans are "too good to big business" (21 per cent). Associated dislikes—that conditions are bad under the Republicans (8%), that the Republican party is bad for workers (6%) and farmers (2%), and it is too conservative (6%)—add further to the image of the Republican party as favorable to big business and opposed to the "common man." As would be expected, Democrats are the source of most of these dislikes, both numerically and proportionately.

Several of the unfavorable elements in the southern whites' image of the Republican party are not offset by any appreciable favorable comment—bad "conditions," favoritism toward big business and Negroes, and unfavorable treatment of workers and farmers stand as overwhelmingly unfavorable aspects in the image of the party. All of the favorable elements in the Republican party's image are weakened by some unfavorable reactions to the same elements. The conservatism of the party on social welfare questions supplies more favorable comment (13%) than any other feature of the party, but Democrats and independents cite the same feature as one of the objectionable aspects of Republicanism (11%). And if we count negative comments on related subjects—such as the alleged big business orientation of the Republicans (21 per cent) — the specific manifestations of its conservatism may be a disadvantage to the Republican party. Favorable comments on the foreign-military policies of the Republicans (9 per cent) more clearly outweigh unfavorable reactions (5%) on the same point. This is not only the second most emphasized attraction of the Republican party for the white population as a whole but it is also the factor most emphasized by those Democrats able to express any liking for the Republican party. Republican leaders are liked (7%) more than they are disliked (5%) but their style of operation receives more unfavorable (9%) than favorable (8%) comment.

Although southern Negroes are no more Democratic than southern whites by subjective party identification, Figure 4 shows that they are even more overwhelmingly unfavorable than southern whites in their view of the Republican party. While this would not have been expected from party identification alone, it is perfectly consistent with southern Negroes' greater Democratic registration, heavier vote for Kennedy, and more clearly favorable view of the Democratic party. Although lower levels of education are generally associated with reluctance to give critical responses, 39 per cent of the Negro respondents (as great a proportion as for the whites) offered criticisms of the Republican party.[10] These criticisms almost completely overshadow the favorable comment. The best thing about the Republican party as seen by the southern Negro is its policy toward Negroes. But even here, the ratio of favorable comment is much smaller than for the Democratic party. Only one aspect of the Republican party—its foreign-military policies—gives it a clear net advantage with southern Negroes, and only 6 per cent of the Negroes mention foreign policy at all. The "party of Lincoln" is now seen as the party of depression, big business favoritism, and mistreatment of workers.

[10]This finding offers reassurance on the troublesome problem of "response set." Granted their lower educational levels, southern Negroes might be thought to be disposed toward positive rather than negative comment in general.

Figure 4

SOUTHERN IMAGES OF THE REPUBLICAN PARTY
(in percent of all R's expressing attitudes toward parties)

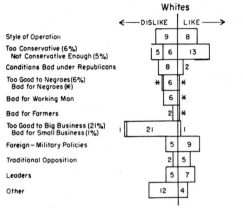

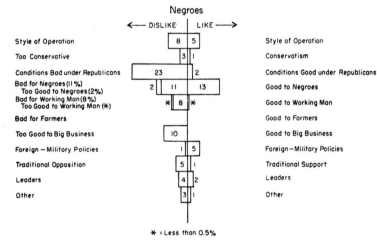

✳ = Less than 0.5%

PARTY IDENTIFICATION, PARTY IMAGE AND THE VOTE

A description of southern images of political parties has, we hope, an intrinsic interest for students of public opinion and political parties. But, if the findings are to be more than simply "interesting," we must be able to demonstrate the relationship between party images and other political attitudes and behavior.

In order to explore this question, an index of party image was devised by counting each favorable attitude toward the Democratic party or unfavorable attitude toward the Republican party as $+1.0$, while each unfavorable Democratic or favorable Republican reference was counted as -1.0. Since as many as four "likes" and four "dislikes" were coded for each party, this provides an overall index of party attitudes for each respondent ranging from $+8.0$ (most pro-Democratic) to -8.0 (most pro-Republican).

The mean index of party image by party identification and race is presented in Table 3. It is apparent, not surprisingly, that party image is closely related to party identification in both races. The Democrats see more good things about the Democratic party (or more bad things about the Republicans) while Republicans tend to see the parties in the opposite light. But party identification and party image are not identical; the index of party image varies a good deal *within* each party identification category. Moreover, Negroes have more pro-Democratic images than the whites even after controlling the party identification. At every level of party identification save that of strong Democrat, the Negroes have higher scores than the whites. Could this help account for the greater proportion of Negroes voting for Kennedy in 1960 despite the very similar distribution of party identification within the two races?

Table 4 suggests that the answer is yes—at least in part. The table shows that a favorable Democratic image is associated with a

TABLE 3

MEAN AND RANGE OF PARTY IMAGE SCORES OF SOUTHERNERS,
BY PARTY IDENTIFICATION AND RACE

PARTY IDENTIFICATION	MEAN SCORE		RANGE OF SCORES		N	
	WHITES	NEGROES	WHITES	NEGROES	WHITES	NEGROES
Strong Democrat	+2.3	+2.2	—5.0 to +6.0	—1.0 to +6.0	175	152
Weak Democrat	+1.0	+1.8	—7.0 to +5.0	—1.0 to +6.0	145	115
Independent Democrat	+0.3	+1.9	—5.0 to +3.0	—1.0 to +6.0	28	44
Independent	—0.6	+1.1	—6.0 to +3.0	—1.0 to +4.0	22	16
Independent Republican	—1.6	+0.4	—5.0 to +1.0	—2.0 to +2.0	23	14
Weak Republican	—0.7	—0.5	—3.0 to +2.0	—4.0 to +3.0	28	25
Strong Republican	—1.8	—0.3	—4.0 to +3.0	—4.0 to +2.0	49	19
Apolitical	+0.1	+0.3	—3.0 to +3.0	—3.0 to +3.0	7	24

vote for Kennedy even after controlling for party identification. Thus the mean party image score of white strong Democrats who voted for Kennedy is +2.4, while the white strong Democrats voting for Nixon had a mean party image score of only +1.0. In every case and within both races the Kennedy voters had higher party image scores (*i.e.*, had more pro-Democratic attitudes) than the Nixon voters. *Thus party image would appear to have an effect on voting over and above that of party identification.*

The index of party image admittedly is a crude measure of party attitude. Each expression of attitude is counted equally, despite the fact that some may be much more important than others, so far as influencing the vote is concerned.

Table 4

Mean Party Images Scores of Kennedy and Nixon Voters
in the South, by Party Identification and Race

Party Identification	Whites		Negroes	
	Kennedy Voters	Nixon Voters	Kennedy Voters	Nixon Voters
Strong Democrat	+2.4 (119)	+1.0 (12)	+2.3 (73)	+1.6 (9)
Weak Democrat	+1.8 (57)	—0.4 (34)	+2.2 (33)	+0.9 (7)
Independent	—0.1 (10)	—1.4 (42)	+1.6 (18)	+1.1 (10)
Republican	—0.3 (3)	—1.5 (62)	0.0 (3)	—0.7 (15)

Note: Independent Democrats, Independents, and Independent Republicans were combined as "Independents"; strong Republicans and weak Republicans were combined as "Republicans" because of small numbers. Too few apoliticals voted to permit computation of means. The figures in parentheses are the number of cases upon which the means have been computed.

In order to estimate the relative importance of the various aspects of party image, we have examined the group of respondents who mentioned each attitude toward the parties and how their votes divided between Kennedy and Nixon in 1960. The percentage point deviation of the Kennedy vote above and below the normal division for each race indicates the extent to which people holding a particular attitude voted abnormally in 1960. A large deviation—plus deviations indicate a surplus of Kennedy votes while minus deviations indicate more votes than normal for Nixon—does not prove a causal connection between party image and the vote. But it does show that those with a stipulated party image voted, for a variety of reasons, more heavily for one candidate or the other than did other members of their own race.

The picture for southern whites is contained in the first column of Table 5. Those whites who said that the Democrats were better for farmers or that they liked the Democrats' style were most over-whelmingly Democratic in the 1960 presidential voting. Viewing the electoral consequences of party images simply in terms of raw percentage point deviations, however, may be misleading. Much larger groups of whites said, for example, that the Democrats were good for workers or that conditions were better under Democrats. While the voters holding these party images did not deviate as far in voting for Kennedy as did those who liked the Democrats' style or treatment of farmers, their greater numbers rendered the deviation more consequential for the outcome of the election. Accordingly, we calculated an "index of electoral deviation" (column 2) which reflects the *proportion of voters* holding each party image as well as the *magnitude of their deviation* in voting. (See the notes to Table 5 for a complete explanation of the calculation of this measure.)

As a combined measure of distinctiveness in voting and of the fre-quency with which an image is held, the index of electoral deviation permits a more meaningful appraisal of the relative importance of different aspects of party image. In terms of Democratic voting strength, the most important components of party image are the views that the Democrats are better for workers and promote better conditions, traditional support for Democracy, and three anti-Repub-lican attitudes—that Republicans favor "big business," have objec-tionable leaders, and are the party of depression. At the opposite extreme, liking Republican conservatism and disliking Democrats' liberalism were by far the most important images associated with pro-Republican vote deviations. These heavily pro-Republican images were followed by "style" reactions unfavorable to the Demo-crat and favorable to the Republican. Significantly, traditional sup-port for the Republican party, which would appear as the strongest pro-Republican image in terms of raw deviation, is found of minor importance when the frequency of attitudes is taken into account.

In terms of voting, the aspects of the party images with the big-gest apparent pay-offs for the Democrats are the "gut" and group issues—that the party is good to workers and little people while the Republicans are heartless lackies of Wall Street and General Motors. For the Republicans, the most productive images are its conservatism and style and dislike of Democratic liberalism, style, and national leaders.

Table 5

ELEMENTS OF PARTY IMAGES AND DEVIATIONS FROM
VOTING NORMS AMONG WHITE SOUTHERNERS

Elements of Party Image	Percentage Point Deviation*	Index of Electoral Deviation**
Democrats better for workers	+25	+12.4
Conditions better under Democrats	+27	+10.7
Traditional Democratic supporter	+22	+ 8.4
Republicans too good to big business	+22	+ 7.8
Dislike Republican leaders	+17	+ 6.1
Conditions bad under Republicans	+31	+ 4.3
Like Democrats' style	+32	+ 3.7
Republicans bad for workers	+28	+ 3.2
Democrats better for small business	+25	+ 2.5
Democrats better for farmers	+32	+ 2.4
Republicans too conservative	+14	+ 2.0
Democrats too good to Negroes	+ 6	+ 0.8
Dislike Republican foreign-military policies	+ 5	+ 0.6
Republicans too good to Negroes	+ 5	+ 0.5
Like Democrats' liberalism	0	0.0
Like Democratic leaders	— 8	— 0.5
Like Democratic foreign-military policies	—15	— 0.9
Dislike Republican style	—17	— 2.7
Like Republican leaders	—23	— 2.9
Traditional Republican supporter	—49	— 3.6
Dislike Democratic foreign-military policies	—29	— 3.7
Like Republican foreign-military policies	—31	— 3.7
Dislike Democratic leaders	—42	— 4.0
Like Republican style	—33	— 5.0
Dislike Democrats' style	—36	— 6.9
Democrats too liberal	—37	—12.8
Like Republican conservatism	—48	—14.1

* Percentage point deviation is the difference, in percentage points, between the 1960 per cent for Kennedy for the group holding the specific image and for the entire white electorate. A plus deviation indicates a Kennedy surplus, a minus deviation, a Nixon surplus. All party image groups with less than 10 cases omitted.

** The index of electoral deviation is the *actual* per cent of the *maximum possible* deviation from white voting norms. The formula is as follows:

$$\left(\frac{d}{D}\right) \times \left(\frac{f}{N}\right) \times 100$$

where

    d = the percentage point deviation from the racial norm (above or below 55% for Kennedy in this case).

    D = the maximum possible percentage point deviation (+45 or —55 percentage points in this case).

    f = number of white respondents mentioning the element of party image.

    N = number of white voters in the sample.

The measure corrects simple percentage point deviations both for the differing electoral divisions (55-45 for Kennedy among whites, 75-25 for Kennedy among Negroes) and for the size of the group with the image. It ranges from 0 (no apparent impact) to 100 (the actual deviation is the maximum possible deviation and all respondents mentioned the view).

The overwhelming (75%) preference of Negro voters in the South for Kennedy left little room for pro-Kennedy deviation by party image. Hence the division of Negro votes appears to vary much less in response to party image than was the case for whites (Table 6, column 1). But when account is taken of the maximum possible pro-Kennedy and pro-Nixon deviations, as in column 2 of Table 6, we see that electoral deviation in terms of party image among Negroes is almost as great as among whites. Indeed, it is greater in the pro-Democratic direction.

The greatest raw deviation among Negro attitudinal groups comes from those who feel that the Republicans are better for Negroes, but the small number of Negroes holding this view renders its electoral significance less than that of four opposite images—that conditions are bad under the Republicans, that the Democrats are better for workers and for Negroes, and that the Republicans favor "big business." Again, the "gut" and group images favor the Democrats.

TABLE 6

ELEMENTS OF PARTY IMAGES AND DEVIATIONS
FROM VOTING NORMS AMONG NEGRO SOUTHERNERS

ELEMENTS OF PARTY IMAGE	PERCENTAGE POINT DEVIATION	INDEX OF ELECTORAL DEVIATION
Conditions bad under Republicans	+15	+14.3
Democrats better for workers	+13	+11.4
Democrats better for Negroes	+ 9	+ 8.9
Republicans too good to businessmen	+16	+ 7.0
Conditions better under Democrats	+ 2	+ 3.2
Dislike Republicans' style	+11	+ 3.1
Like Democrats' style	+ 7	+ 3.0
Republicans bad for workers	+ 8	+ 2.9
Like Democrats' liberalism	+ 6	+ 1.9
Republicans bad for Negroes	+ 5	+ 1.5
Traditional Democratic supporter	− 2	− 0.1
Like Democratic leaders	− 7	− 0.9
Republicans better for Negroes	−40	− 6.9

Note: See notes to Table 5.

Rather than viewing the components of party image for each party separately, a more general view of the electoral importance of party images may be obtained by combining all references to a common component. Subsuming all attitudes under ten categories, and again scoring each pro-Democratic or anti-Republican reference as positive and each anti-Democratic or pro-Republican reference as negative, we get the summary index of electoral deviation presented in Table 7. For Negroes, only one object of attitudes—foreign-military policies—is associated with pro-Republican deviation, and this net deviation is very small. For whites, on the other hand, the issue of liberalism-conservatism, party style, and foreign-military policies are all linked to heavy pro-Republican deviation. For both Negroes and whites, the "hard" issues of economic conditions and policies toward specific groups have net scores that heavily favor the Democrats.

TABLE 7

NET INDEX OF ELECTORAL DEVIATION BY RACE
AND ELEMENTS OF PARTY IMAGES

ELEMENTS OF PARTY IMAGE	WHITES	NEGROES
Conditions under parties' rule	+20.8	+17.2
Parties' policies toward workers	+14.2	+14.3
Parties' policies toward business	+ 9.6	+ 7.5
Traditional support of party	+ 7.3	+ 1.9
Other, unclassified	+ 6.3	+ 0.5
Parties' policies toward farmers	+ 1.9	0.0
Parties' policies toward Negroes	+ 1.3	+ 1.9
Parties' leaders	+ 0.9	+ 0.8
Parties' foreign-military policies	− 7.8	− 2.7
Parties' style of operation	−11.1	+ 3.9
Parties' ideology	−26.0	+ 1.8

Note: See notes to Table 5.

CONCLUSIONS: PARTY IMAGES AND PARTY REALIGNMENT

The party identification of southerners has changed little in recent years. Only 15 per cent of the white and 14 per cent of the Negro respondents report *ever* having changed their party identification. Of those who have changed, about 14 per cent of the whites changed from Democratic to Republican and 17 per cent from Republican to Democratic (Table 8). Another 15 per cent of the

whites have wavered—starting out their political lives as Democrats, switching to the Republicans and then back again to the
Democratic party. The small net effects of these changes among
southern whites is in sharp contrast to the massive shifts in party
identification that some have read into recent presidential election
returns. Moreover, among Negro changers the Democrats enjoy a
net advantage of over two converts for every one lost to the GOP.
Among those who have changed from a party identification to self-
classification as an independent or apolitical, on the other hand, the
Democrats are the heavy losers among both whites and Negroes.
If this net movement from Democratic to independent is viewed as
a transitional stage enroute to identification with the Republicans,
then the long-run prospects for the Republican party appear somewhat brighter. This, in fact, would seem likely to be the case among
the whites. The whites who have changed from Democratic to independent have a mean party image score of —1.1, almost as pro-
Republican an image as those who have been Republicans all their
lives (mean score, —1.4). And the white Republicans who have
changed to independent are more favorably inclined toward the
Republicans than the Democrats. Among Negroes, however, a shift
toward independent status is not associated with a favorable picture
of the GOP. The Negro ex-Democrats who are now independents
have a mean party image score of +1.9, almost as pro-Democratic
as the Negro Democrats who have never changed (+2.0). Thus
while the Democrats have lost about half as many southern Negroes
to political independence as they have gained from the Republicans,
the first group seems almost as likely to vote Democratic as the second.

It should be remembered, however, that these are changes in
party identification which have occured over the *entire lifetime* of
the respondents. This plus the very small percentage of southerners
who have ever changed their party identification means that the net
movement would make only small and slow changes in the overwhelmingly pro-Democratic distribution of southern party loyalties[11]
On this level, the Republican tide is sweeping over Dixie at glacial
speed.

[11]See also P. E. Converse, "On the Possibility of Major Political Realignment in the South," a paper presented at the Duke University Conference on
"The Impact of Political and Legal Changes in the Postwar South," July 12-14,
1962.

Despite these indications of stability in party loyalties, Republicans have enjoyed a substantial increase in presidential voting along with modest gains at lower levels of the ballot[12] This anomaly could be the result of such transitory factors as the nature of the candidates and the issues of specific campaigns which temporarily diverted many southern Democrats from their normal ways. Once Eisenhower, the Korean War, and the Catholic issue pass from the scene, the straying Democrats may return unchanged to the welcoming arms of Democracy. Or, despite the apparently stable Democratic attachment of most southerners, the rise in Republican voting may indicate the beginning of more basic and permanent change which could lead to massive changes in party loyalties over the long haul.

TABLE 8

CHANGES IN PARTY IDENTIFICATION OF SOUTHERNERS, BY RACE, AND MEAN PARTY IMAGE SCORES OF TYPES OF CHANGES

| | WHITES | | NEGROES | |
PATTERN OF CHANGE IN IDENTIFICATION	%	MEAN SCORE	%	MEAN SCORE
Republican to Democrat	17%	+1.7	42%	+2.0
Democrat to Republican to Democrat	15%	+0.8	0	—
Republican to Independent	11%	—0.6	11%	+0.4
Independent to Republican to Independent	1%	*	0	—
Republican to Apolitical	0	—	1%	*
Democrat to Apolitical	2%	*	6%	+1.0
Independent to Democrat to Independent	1%	*	0	—
Democrat to Independent	39%	—1.1	21%	+1.9
Republican to Democrat to Republican	0	—	1%	*
Democrat to Republican	14%	—1.6	18%	—0.1
Total	100%		100%	
N	(100)		(81)	

* = too few cases for computing mean Party Image Score.

Our analysis of the party images of white and Negro southerners throws at least some light on this question.

[12]See A. Heard, *A Two-Party South?* (Chapel Hill, N. C.: University of North Carolina Press, 1952); D. S. Strong, *The 1952 Presidential Election in the South* (University, Alabama: University of Alabama Bureau of Public Administration, 1955); D. S. Strong, *Urban Republicanism in the South* (University, Ala.: University of Alabama Bureau of Public Administration, 1960).

In Table 9, the mean party image scores of Democratic identifiers are given by their presidential vote in 1956 and 1960. The Negro Democrats who shifted to the Republican column in either 1956 or 1960 have retained their favorable attitudes towards the Democratic party despite their defections. Only if the Republican party is somehow able to improve its image among southern Negroes will

Table 9

Mean Party Image Scores of White and Negro Southern Democrats, By Presidential Vote in 1956 and 1960

1956 Vote	1960 Vote	Mean Party Image Scores Whites	Negroes
Stevenson	Kennedy	+2.1 (108)	+2.2 (65)
Eisenhower	Kennedy	+2.0 (45)	+1.9 (39)
Stevenson	Nixon	+1.1 (14)	+2.2 (4)
Eisenhower	Nixon	—0.5 (31)	+0.2 (39)

Note: The numbers in parentheses are the base upon which the means were computed. "Strong" and "weak" Democrats were classified as Democrats.

these occasional defections solidify into Republican identification and a "normal" Republican vote. Given the congruence of the Negroes' pro-Democratic views on civil rights with their other attitudes about the parties, the other groups to which the Republican party seeks to appeal, and the party's gradually increasing strength among white southerners, the Republicans do not seem likely to capture Negro support on a continuing basis. A more likely possibility would be a growing independence among southern Negroes. A slight trend in this direction is already discernible (Table 8), but even these new Negro independents are far more favorably inclined toward the Democratic than the Republican party

Among whites, those who voted for both Stevenson and Kennedy have the most favorable image of the Democratic party. Those who broke away from the Democratic party in 1956 to vote for Eisenhower and then returned to the fold with Kennedy in 1960 have almost as favorable an image of their own party, a fact which suggests that many southerners agree with the lady quoted at the beginning of this article who said that Ike was not a "real" Republican. A vote for Nixon by a white Democrat who supported Stevenson is associated with a low pro-Democratic party image score, while those who voted for both Eisenhower and Nixon actually have a slightly more favorable image of the Republican party than they do of the one with which they identify.

The low party image scores of white Democrats for Nixon suggest that anti-Catholicism was not the only factor in the wholesale desertion of the Democratic party in favor of a man who clearly was a "real" Republican. Other studies have shown that the more frequently a southern Protestant attended church, the more seriously he took the threat from Rome and the more likely he was to vote for Nixon over Kennedy.[13] Our data show some tendency for images of the Democratic party to become less favorable as church attendance becomes more regular.[14] These relationships may reflect an enduring suspicion among churchgoing Protestants about the role of minority religious groups in the Democratic party, a suspicion that was merely heightened during the 1960 campaign. Or they may represent nothing more than the lingering effects of the singular importance of religion in the 1960 campaign, in which case the relevance of Protestant church-attendance for party image may gradually diminish.

Assuming that most Democratic identifiers once had a pro-Democratic image, we can say that changes in party images are associated with changes in party voting, regardless of party identification. While we cannot say which of these changes is "cause" and which is "effect," we can say that they go together. Perhaps eventually change will occur in party identification as well, since party image and party identification are normally consistent with one another.

Without earlier survey data we cannot say that the relative ambivalence of southern white party images in 1961 represented a change from the past. However, we can look at the kinds of people in the South who have pro-Democratic, ambivalent, and pro-Republican images and then, on the basis of what is known about the probable growth or decline of these groups, draw some speculative inferences about the future. Among whites, immigration from outside the region is a major source of pro-Republican image. The more southern—in a cultural and political sense—the area in which white southern residents grew up, the more favorable their views of the Democratic party are likely to be. The same is true of present place

[13]P. F. Converse, A. Campbell, W. E. Miller and D. Stokes, "Stability and Change in 1960: A Reinstating Election," *American Political Science Review,* LV (June, 1961), pp. 269-280.

[14]White Protestants attending church "regularly" had a mean party image score of +0.7; "often," +0.7; "seldom," +1.3; "never," +0.7.

of residence: white residents in the Deep South have twice as many favorable attitudes toward the Democratic party (or unfavorable attitudes toward the Republicans) as those living on the periphery of the region. We can confidently predict that white in-migration will continue and that the white electorate of the peripheral South will increase at a faster rate than that of the Deep South. Southern whites living in rural areas are twice as favorable to the Democrats as southern suburbanites, with city dwellers falling between the two extremes. Urbanization and suburbanization of the region will certainly continue. A college education is associated with relatively pro-Republican images, and the proportion of southern whites attending college is on the increase. Southerners who think of themselves as belonging to the middle class are much less Democratic in their sentiments than those who think of themselves as belonging to the working class; it is fairly safe to assume that an increasing proportion of white southerners, as well as other Americans, will think of themselves as middle class in the future. The only datum which we have examined which does not suggest that social and economic change will lead to increasingly pro-Republican images among white southerners in the years ahead is that on age. Young white southerners tend to have more pro-Democratic images than older ones. Yet save for the group over 70, the differences are not large and may well be obliterated by the conservative effects of aging.

While the net impact of anticipated demographic changes in the South points to a growing Republicanism among whites, the same trends suggest the opposite conclusion for southern Negroes. The Negroes who grew up or live on the periphery of the region, reside in urban and suburban areas, and obtained a high school education have more pro-Democratic images of the parties than other Negroes, and these groups can be expected to grow in the future among Negroes no less than among whites.

Nonetheless, all things considered, the thrust of history seems to be on the Republicans' side. But this can be a very slow process, depending upon rates of social and economic change, the expected and off-setting increase in Negro voting, and other unforeseen and largely unpredictable events. If party realignment is to come to the South more suddenly, the Negro problem will probably serve as the catalyst.

The combination of southern whites and Negroes in the same party seems to be a potentially explosive alliance. But our analysis of Negro and white images of the two parties suggests a number of things which contribute to the stability of this arrangement. In the first place, almost 40 per cent of each race has no image of the Democratic party and a large number of others have only the most rudimentary picture. This widespread ignorance facilitates the peaceable coexistence of clashing racial groups within the same party. In the second place, the amorphous nature of American parties permits the two races to perceive the same party somewhat differently. The whites do not identify with the Democrats on the state and local levels while the Negroes identify on the national level—neither set of respondents made such neat distinctions and both groups responded to our questions primarily in national terms.[15] But the southern and congressional wings of the party no doubt loomed as a larger portion of the total party among whites than among Negroes. Third, the white strong Democrats include a large share of those whites most likely to be repelled by the party on racial grounds. Since identification with the Democratic party is viewed by these people as a reaffirmation of faith in the southern way life, it is difficult for these southern-oriented whites to break away from it even when the party may be, in fact, undermining southern traditions. (In this connection, it is interesting to note that those southern whites who complained that the Democratic party was "too good to Negroes" voted six percentage points more heavily for Kennedy than did the other southern whites!) Fourth, southern Negroes and whites are in substantial agreement about the Democratic party. True, on racial matters they are sharply divided. But on domestic economic issues many Negroes and whites in the South agree that the Democratic party is the party of prosperity, jobs, and government spending. They approve—the Negroes even more than the whites—of this kind of a party. And neither race is particularly happy about the alternative to the Democrats, the Republican party.

" 'Course neither party likes us much," a 74 year old Negro Democrat said, "but we here and they have to do something." So far, the Democrats have done enough to please most southern Negroes without alienating too many whites. Thus a 71 year old white Democrat, a strict segregationist, remembers, "When I was little the Republicans was called Radicals, and they weren't much thought

[15]This point will be developed at further length in a paper by the authors in Kent Jennings and Harmon Zeigler (eds.), *The Electoral System,* forthcoming book to be published by Prentice-Hall, Inc.

of in the neighborhood." The Democrats are sufficiently successful in maintaining support from this unlikely coalition to dim the short-run prospects of the Republicans. But the average age of this pair is 72 years, and their average schooling is 6 years. As they, their political memories, and their demographic attributes fade from the southern scene, the Republicans can anticipate a brighter future.

THE MANIPULATED NEGRO VOTE:
SOME PRE-CONDITIONS AND CONSEQUENCES*

ALFRED B. CLUBOK, JOHN M. DE GROVE AND CHARLES D. FARRIS
University of Florida

THE SUBJECT OF THIS PAPER is one aspect of our recently completed field research on political leadership in the "face-to-face" community. We selected six small Florida towns for interviewing, ranging in population from approximately 4,000 to 15,000. Two towns were selected in each of three major geographical areas of the State: the old South agricultural and pine tree area of northern Florida; the citrus, cattle, vegetable area of the central portion of the peninsula; and the light industry, tourism, retirement area of southern coastal Florida. The towns in the northern tier of counties are still little different from their counterparts in neighboring Southern states. On the other hand, the dynamic economic and population growth in peninsular Florida afforded an excellent opportunity for assessing political leadership and Negro political participation in a wide variety of economic, political, and cultural settings.

A research team of two professors spent approximately six weeks in each town, and from 40 to 60 individuals, both white and Negro, were interviewed.[1] Interviewing began with present public office holders and was then expanded to include other white political influentials as they were identified. The purpose of these interviews was to develop a picture of the political structure of the white community from the end of World War II to the time of interviewing. The interview guide was also designed to obtain white conceptions of the political structure of the Negro community and to uncover the relationship between these two structures. During the white interviews a partial list of Negro leaders was developed which was later expanded during the Negro interviews. The Negro interview guide was designed to obtain information concerning the leadership structure of the Negro community, factionalism within this com-

*We gratefully acknowledge a grant from the Rockefeller Foundation which made this research possible. Of course, we accept full responsibility for all interpretations.
[1]Interview schedules were open-ended, and their construction represented a blending of the "attribution" and "issue" techniques.

munity, and the relationship of the Negro community to the white political structure over a 15-year time period.

The findings reported in this paper are consistent, we think, with the Matthews-Prothro findings on Negro political participation in the South.[2] Using multiple correlation and regression analysis these two authors found that 21 selected socio-economic variables "statistically 'explain' about 28 per cent (R^2) of the variation in Negro registration rates."[3] Adding to the 21 variables ten explicitly "political variables," the research team found that they could explain, in a statistical sense, about 50 per cent of the Southwide variance in Negro voting registration. In the social sciences a statistical explanation of approximately 50 per cent of the variance of a dependent variable is by no means a negligible accomplishment.

On the basis of our recent field research, we suggest that an examination of the political relationship of the white and Negro communities at the local level might have high explanatory value, vis-à-vis Negro registration and turnout, in the more rural towns and counties of the South and, therefore, might significantly reduce the unexplained variance of the Matthews and Prothro analysis. Data of this type are, of course, time consuming to gather since the conceptual framework underlying the analysis requires a field investigation, not only of the structure of the Negro political community, but of the white as well.

We conceive of five possible relationships between the two political communities—the Non-Voting town; the Low Voting, Unorganized town; the Manipulative town; the Independent Bargaining town; and the Office Holding town.[4]

Negroes do not register and vote in the Non-Voting town, normally because of active hostility on the part of the white political structure. However, we can conceive of a possible variant of this type where active hostility has disappeared but, out of fear, indifference, or inertia, Negroes do not register.

In the Low Voting, Unorganized town, either because of a policy of the white political structure which permits only a few selected

---

[2]Donald R. Matthews and James W. Prothro, "Political Factors and Negro Voter Registration in the South," *American Political Science Review*, Vol. LVII (1963), pp. 355-367.

[3]Matthews and Prothro, *op. cit.*, p. 355.

[4]Three major concepts were used in constructing this typology: (1) voting or non-voting as a characteristic of the Negro community, (2) the degree of political organization of the Negro community, and (3) the bargaining or manipulative nature of the relationship between the two communities.

and presumably "safe" Negroes to vote or because of fear and/or indifference, only a relatively small number of Negroes register and vote. No attempt is made either by the whites or Negroes to organize politically a significant proportion of the Negro community.

Towns in which the Negro community has been politically organized and controlled to a large degree by white political leadership we conceive of as Manipulative towns. In the Manipulative town the electoral activists—those responsible for turning out the Negro vote—are primarily the agents of members of the white political structure, and the preponderance of voting Negroes are responsive to the activists as agents of the whites.

We distinguish the Independent Bargaining town from the Manipulative town. In the Independent Bargaining town electoral activists in the Negro community tend to be independent of the white political structure and bargain with white politicians for gains, either for the Negro activists or for the Negro Community as a whole. The Negro voter tends to respond either to the activist as an individual or to the activist as a representative of the Negro community interests.

Our final category, the Office Holding town, is similar to the Independent Bargaining town in all respects except that Negro gains through independent organization and bargaining have resulted in Negroes' appointment or election to public offices.

We conceive of a town undergoing a transformation when the pattern of structural relationships change. For instance, in Prospect Bluff, a white political clique which had organized and manipulated a sizeable number of Negro votes ceased to function in the town. The Negro community remained unorganized for several years, after which Negro leadership, rather than white, emerged to reorganize the Negro political community. In this case, then, we would speak of transformations from "Manipulation" to "Low Voting, Unorganized" to "Independent Bargaining."

The following tables summarize the characteristics of the six towns.[5]

[5]In the following tables under the category of "Style of White Politics" we note two types of politics. "*Monopoly,* according to our definition, prevails when one leadership clique regularly wins all, or practically all council seats regardless of the changing identity of candidates backed by the clique and when there is no continuing opposition from a rival leadership clique that regularly sponsors candidates or coopts successful candidates. A monopoly style of politics, indeed, can prevail under the following conditions: no opposition;

TOBACCO HILL

LOCATION—North Florida (Roth County)

Population

1940	6337
1950	8072
1960	9966

Percentage Non-White

1940	32
1950	34
1960	32

Economic Base............Service, trade, and county seat

Style of White Politics

1945-47	no data
1947-51	competition
1952-56	monopoly
1956 to date	competition

Negro Community:

Structural relations with white community

1945-47	Non-Voting
1947 to date	Manipulative

Percentage white 20 years + registered (1959) 85
Percentage Negro 20 years + registered (1959) 54
Negro percentage total registered vote (1959) 22

PROSPECT BLUFF

LOCATION—North Florida (Hawkins County)

Population

1940	7641
1950	9677
1960	11529

Percentage Non-White

1940	49
1950	45
1960	43

Economic Base............Manufacturing, service, trade, county seat

Style of White Politics

1945-57	monopoly
1957 to date	competition

Negro Community:

Structural relations with white community

pre-1945	Manipulative
1945-48	Low Voting, Unorganized
1948 to date	Independent Bargaining, low level importance

Percentage white 21 years + registered (1960) 65
Percentage Negro 21 years + registered (1960) 21
Negro percentage: total registered vote (1960) 18

'personal' opposition by candidates not affiliated with a clique; or formation of a temporary opposition group constituted for a particular election and either dissolved upon its defeat or disintegrated by cooptation of its successful candidates into the ruling leadership clique. . . . *Competition*, as a style of politics, exists when at least two leadership cliques compete on a continuing basis for elective office. We do not require an alteration in the political control of the community. One clique could consistently win control of the city council, but, as long as the opposition clique exists and challenges in elections, we use the term 'competition' to describe the communities' style of politics." See Gladys M. Kammerer, Charles D. Farris, John M. De Grove, and Alfred B. Clubok, *The Urban Political Community* (Boston, 1963), p. 6.

ANGUSVILLE

LOCATION—Central Peninsula (Call County)

Population		Percentage Non-White	
1940	3726	1940	23
1950	4801	1950	24
1960	7346	1960	19

Economic Base............Service, trade, retirement, county seat

Style of White politics

1945-48..............monopoly
1948-54..............competition
1955-60..............monopoly
1961 to date....competition

Negro Community:
Structural relations with white community

1945-mid 1950s....Low Voting, Unorganized
mid 1950s to date... Manipulative, low level of importance and organization

Percentage white 20 years + registered (1962)   65
Percentage Negro 20 years + registered (1962)   33
Negro percentage: total registered vote (1962)   9

HAMLIN

LOCATION—Central Peninsula (Ward County)

Population		Percentage Non-White	
1940	3062	1940	35
1950	4307	1950	34
1960	5260	1960	29

Economic Base..............Citrus, manufacturing, service, trade, county seat

Style of White Politics

1945-55 ....monopoly
1956 to date....competition

Negro Community:
Structural relations with white community

1945-46....Low Voting, Unorganized
1946 to date....manipulative

Percentage white 20 years + registered (1959)   51
Percentage Negro 20 years + registered (1959)   20
Negro percentage: total registered vote (1959)   14

LISA CITY

LOCATION—South Florida (Reid County)

Population		Percentage Non-White	
1940	2482	1940	24
1950	4566	1950	23
1960	13046	1960	43

Economic Base........... Suburb (heavy Negro); Retirement (heavy trailer court)

Style of White Politics

1947-49..............competition
1949-59..............monopoly
1959 to date—competition

Negro Community:
Structural relations with white community

1945-48 .... Non-Voting
1948-61....Independent Bargaining
1961 to date—Office Holding

Percentage white 21 years + registered (1961)   79
Percentage Negro 21 years + registered (1961)   60
Percentage Negro: total registered vote (1961)   28

BOUGAINVILLE

LOCATION—South Florida (Reid County)

Population		Percentage Non-White
1940	4238	1940........44
1950	6813	1950........45
1960	12731	1960........44

Economic Base............Retirement, winter tourism

Style of White Politics

1945-53..............competition
1954-55..............monopoly
1956 to date—competition

Negro Community:
Structural relations with white community

1945-50............Manipulative
1950 to date............Independent
                                    Bargaining

Percentage white 21 years + registered (1962)   57
Percentage Negro 21 years + registered (1962)   22
Negro Percentage: total registered vote (1962)   22

Because of obvious space limitations we will treat only the Manipulative town in this paper and, in particular, the relationship of law enforcement agencies to the Negro vote in the Manipulative town.

II

In five of the six towns in which we interviewed, Negro registration and voting was or had been encouraged, facilitated, and, to varying degrees, organized by members of the white political structure. In four of these five Manipulative towns the agencies of the law played key roles in the relationship between the white and the Negro political structure. White encouragement of Negro voting in these towns did not stem from abstract concepts of civil liberties, nor from fears of racial disturbances. Direct contact with the United States Civil Rights Commission or concern over its activities was entirely lacking in these towns. The attitude of the white political structure in Tobacco Hill towards the activities of the Civil Rights Commission was summarized when a county judge stated: "Hell, the Federals are interested only when you try to keep the colored from voting, and we're voting them to the hilt." Our data suggests that the white politicians' encouragement of Negro registration was based either on actual or anticipated competition for public office. Organization and manipulation of a Negro vote was conceived of as a means of either obtaining or retaining control of public policy-making positions.

That the agencies of the law should be interested in election returns and, therefore, actively engaged in obtaining a "proper" outcome by securing votes should surprise very few. However, law enforcement as a political tool is often far removed from the life experience of a member of the American middle class—whether the individual is an insurance salesman or a political scientist. If we were to judge the state of knowledge within the discipline by the textbooks, then we would have to conclude that political considerations are at most aberrations in the law enforcement process. We must admit that few law enforcement officers were as openly political as a Tobacco Hill judge when he stated: "In my type of operation [he is describing the office of county judge] you have to politic every day. Favors get votes, and you have to do favors." Even so, we find the judge's position far closer to "reality" than the textbooks are.

We define law enforcement agencies broadly by including not only the police and sheriff's departments but also the courts and lawyers of the town. The political role of sheriffs, judges, or lawyers needs little further comment at this point. Lawyers traditionally have been part of the American political scene. Sheriffs and local judges run for office and, periodically at least, they must appeal to the voter. The law enforcers' membership in political parties, factions, cliques, or crowds and the attendant protection of various interests—whether they be low taxes, the office itself, or the rackets —are part of the informational backlog of any student of politics. The political ties and activities of a police chief are often hidden behind the appointive rather than the elective nature of the office; yet, in our experience, chiefs are usually members of political cliques either because the chief is indebted to the clique for his appointment and support or because the clique is beholden to the chief for favors and votes.

III

Varied techniques are used to turn out the Negro vote in the Manipulated town. In Hamlin the city judge and sheriff, along with the police chief who is recognized as a subordinate of the sheriff, handle the actual organization of the Negro vote. Before an election barbecues are held for the Negro voters on the ranch of the city judge. Negroes are driven to the ranch in trucks, and barbecue, fish, liquor, and beer are apparently in plentiful supply at this type of election meeting. On the day of the election the organization swings into high gear. A hired crew of Negro "street walkers" canvasses in the Negro community as agents for the whites.[6] The street walkers are provided with a list of registered Negro voters, and it is their job to produce the voters at the polls. The street walker is usually provided with money, some of which may be passed on to voters, but it was our impression that the money was used to defray the cost of mobilizing the vote and, of course, for the street walker's own commission.

The middle class Negro in Hamlin deplores the barbecue-liquor-street-walker complex but often finds himself in the same voting camp as the manipulated Negro. At the suggestion of the white manipulative leadership, middle class Negroes formed a Negro Civic Association and, by means of registration campaigns, increased the proportion of registered middle class and lower class Negroes. The Association does not ordinarily hold meetings with candidates prior to an election, since the contact of the middle class Negro with the white politician is still at the level of individual personal contact. Some members of the Civic Association expressed the feeling that they had been "used" by the whites simply to increase the size of the manipulated vote and yet, although they expressed bitterness, they have so far remained loyal to the manipulative camp.

In Tobacco Hill similar techniques are used. Barbecues and fish fries are held before elections. Taxis are hired to take Negroes to the polls, and city owned cars have been used on occasion for the same purpose. The police and the sheriff's deputies openly campaign. Many of the credit groceries in the Negro section of the town are tied to the manipulative camp in the town, and these are used to remind the Negro patrons of their civic duty to vote and, most important, for whom to vote. An election meeting is normally held in one of Tobacco Hill's Negro churches prior to the local election. Candidates are invited to speak before the group and usually do so. A substantial sum of money is normally spent during a Tobacco Hill election. Apparently, some of the money makes its way to the voter—there appears to be a semi-professional group of vote-sellers in the town, both Negro and white—but most of what is spent is used to defray the cost of mobilizing the vote.

In Angusville where the Negro vote is relatively small and

<hr />

[6]These people are not female prostitutes. We were surprised to find this term used in several towns.

where the organization of the Negro vote has been far less thorough than in either Hamlin or Tobacco Hill, white leadership has, nevertheless, given some thought to the mechanics of manipulation. The primary white political contact with the Negro community is made through a law firm. A lawyer in this firm divides the Negroes into four groups. The first are the more successful old line Negro families of the community. Although they are small in number and formally unorganized, they do have recognized leadership. The leadership of this segment of the community is approached and, according to the lawyer: "You ask them to go your way and more than likely they will." The second group is the Negro "working class." The approach to this segment of the Negro community is made through those in the Negro community who have partaken of the services of the law firm and also through the activities of the third group, that is, those who are involved in bolita, moonshine, and other rackets.[7] This lawyer believes, and we think correctly, that the people involved in the rackets are probably the best organized segment of the Negro community in Angusville. The fourth group contacted are the so-called transients—those who work as hands in the pulpwood industry or as citrus and vegetable pickers. Negroes in this category are difficult to organize because of the transient nature of their work, but a few votes can be obtained by contacting their employers and/or foremen. Little money is spent, as far as we can tell, in organizing the vote. Although taxis are hired on election day to take Negro voters to the polls and some private white cars are used, the machinery to turn out the Negro vote is not elaborate. Even though some effort is made to turn out the Negro vote, it is not considered to be a crucial factor in Angusville elections.

IV

Although the actual techniques of organization and manipulation of the Negro vote by law enforcement agencies were varied, law enforcement in the Manipulative town shared certain characteristics which we conceive of as *preconditions for manipulation*. Their existence promotes an atmosphere which makes the Negro susceptible to manipulation and control. In no case did we find that violence or hostility was characteristic of law enforcement in the Manipulative town. Rather, it was the absence of such stereotyped white behavior

[7]Bolita is a Spanish word used widely in Florida to indicate the numbers racket.

which we believe provided a favorable climate for manipulation by law enforcement agencies. In Tobacco Hill and Hamlin, the two towns where manipulation of the Negro vote was most evident, the agents of the law had the reputation among the Negroes of being "good men," of treating the "colored man just as they would treat a white man." Negro prisoners were not mistreated nor were they intimidated. The fair and decent treatment accorded Negroes by these manipulative law enforcement agencies was in direct contrast with the behavior of previous regimes. In both towns the memory of brutality by previous police chiefs and sheriffs was still strong among our Negro respondents. A middle class Negro respondent in Tobacco Hill described the change in law enforcement when he stated that "there are many things that happen in town between the colored and white that 20 years ago would have seen Negroes being run out of town, but this doesn't happen any more." The sheriff stopped his deputies from "beating up" Negroes when he took office in 1945, just as the mayor stopped police brutality when he took office in 1947.

The memory of a shift in the treatment of the Negro was accomplished in these two towns by what we would label a "dramatic event." Following an incident in the mid-1940's in Tobacco Hill when Mayor Nobb, with the police standing by, horsewhipped a group of Negroes including several women, he was defeated for re-election by Sam Turner, who immediately replaced the chief of police and instituted a continuing period of fair and decent treatment of Negroes by the police of the town.

Similarly, a "dramatic event" occurred in the late 1940's in Hamlin when the "High Sheriff" very firmly intervened in a rape case by refusing to allow a Negro to be "framed" for the offense of a white man. These dramatic events, combined with relatively decent treatment of Negro prisoners, have left lasting impressions on the Negroes in these towns. While we are not suggesting that fair and decent treatment of Negroes by itself provides a law enforcement agency with significant manipulative leverage, we do suggest that it is an important, and probably necessary, precondition for manipulation.

The favorable response of the Negro to fair law enforcement does not appear to be limited to those Negroes who have had direct experience with officers of the law nor to those whose behavior might lead to such an encounter. The middle class Negro in the

Manipulative town, whose chances of a hostile encounter with the law are probably no greater than his counterpart in the white community, also appears to be favorably impressed and responsive to fair and decent law enforcement. It is our impression that middle class Negroes tend to view fair law enforcement from an abstract racial standpoint. We think, then, that the middle class Negroes' racial commitment leads them to converge with the poorer, less educated Negro in supporting the manipulative white politicians.

Just as decent treatment of prisoners makes an impression on Negroes, a friendly attitude on the part of law enforcement officers when dealing with Negroes in a non-official capacity appears to have a significant impact upon a number of Negroes. For instance, middle class Negro respondents in Hamlin appeared to be impressed by the friendly behavior of the "High Sheriff" who would lean out of his car window, wave and call to them by name as he drove by, or stop and talk to them for an hour on a street corner. The friendliness of the sheriff had been affirmed on several occasions when he voiced his support for Negro requests to use city recreational facilities. The Negro middle class in Hamlin, as far as we can ascertain, supports the sheriff in his own campaigns and, at a minimum, listens sympathetically when he approaches them as individuals on behalf of other candidates.

Negroes in Tobacco Hill also were responsive to friendly behavior. Not only did Mayor Turner keep the police under control, he was considered to be the Negroes' friend—they could bring their problems to him and be treated "almost as equals." Mayor Turner had solid Negro support, not only for himself, but for other candidates as well.

The support given a sheriff or mayor by middle class Negroes appears incongruous during a period of militant Negro action on a nationwide scale. Yet we would speculate that there are many small towns in the South where Negroes are still convinced that this really is a "white man's world." In this particular type of environment, friendly behavior can easily elicit political support.

Aside from fair and friendly treatment, law enforcement agencies can provide another "service" for at least part of the Negro community which we conceive of as a precondition for manipulation. Following Dollard, we label this particular service "impulse freedom."[8] The freedoms to which we refer are in the realm of sexual

[8]John Dollard, *Caste and Class in a Southern Town* (Garden City, 1949), pp. 390-433.

behavior, public drunkenness, gambling, and aggressive behavior *within* the Negro community. Of course, freedom in the expression of impulse is judged by an idealized white middle class norm.

Impulse freedom is difficult to discuss in 1964 without offending the sensibilities of the national Negro movement—which tends to reflect, in large measure, middle class values and aspirations—or without providing ammunition for the Southern segregationist. However, for whatever historical or sociological reasons, the normative system, as well as the external behavior, of the lower class Negro diverges sharply from the idealized code of the white middle class.

The enforcement of white middle class values is, to a degree, placed in the hands of the law enforcement agencies of the town, but the agencies have, within limits, a "choice" as to how rigorously the law shall be enforced. This particular choice can be expressed, from the Negro standpoint, by the distinction between a "hard police chief" and a "good man" as police chief. The "hard police chief," from the Negroes' point of view, "goes out of his way" to discover infringements of the law and, once infringements are discovered, they are not overlooked. The hard law enforcement agency patrols the Negro community "laying for drunks." However, the "hard chief" should be distinguished from the "brutal chief." The "hard chief" is fair to the Negro once he is apprehended and, accordingly, not brutal, but he is considered "hard" because he interferes with the Negroes' freedom. In a town which has a "good man" as the police chief or sheriff, the Negroes are left alone. Law enforcement is lax—gambling, moonshine, other rackets, and aggression *within* the Negro community are tolerated. The police do not "pick on" the Negro.

The acceptance of the rackets as part of the way of life of a town is well illustrated by a story, probably apocryphal, but revealing, about the bolita racket. According to an interviewee, for a number of years in Tobacco Hill a major bolita operation was housed in Joe's Bar. On Friday afternoon when a large number of phone calls were made to the Bar to learn the winning number, the line to the Bar was often busy. Prior to the installation of a dial telephone system, the operator would inform the caller that the line was busy and then continue by saying "but the number for today is xxx."

In a town which tolerates a high degree of impulse freedom the courts, as well as the police, can be involved. Negroes before the courts, given this particular environment, might tend to receive shorter sentences than a white in similar circumstances. Lax law enforcement tends to be rationalized by the phrase "after all it's only a nigger." We by no means intend to imply that the set of attitudes which calls forth this particular rationalization is confined to manipulative law enforcement agencies. We found this attitude evident among many of our white interviewees. However, we are implying that the level of law enforcement, vis-à-vis the Negro community, is, at times, the product of a calculated choice based on strategic consideration of the Negro vote. An interesting example of this type of calculation can be found in Tobacco Hill. When Sam Turner, after having served 14 years as Mayor of Tobacco Hill, was defeated by Lewis Alger in the 1961 mayoralty election, Alger inherited a community in which, for a number of years, the rackets and police corruption were prevalent and, we might add, readily discussed by many of our interviewees.

The Negro vote in Tobacco Hill is sizeable. In 1959 it comprised 22 per cent of the registered voters in the town, and in the mayoralty election that year 21 per cent of the voters were Negroes. When Turner became mayor in 1947, Tobacco Hill was a Non-Voting town although the sheriff elected in 1944 had already begun to organize the registered Negroes for county elections. However, it was the Turner administration which openly encouraged and organized Negro registration and voting in the town. The advent of the Turner administration brought an end to police brutality in Tobacco Hill and, from the lower class Negroes' point of view, to police interference in the life of the Negro community. Asked why Negroes voted for Turner, a Negro answered "we're just satisfied. . . . Nobody bothers us and we just ain't going to have a change, 'cause we don't know what it might be like."

When Turner was defeated in 1961 the new mayor was faced with a strategic problem; to curtail the impulse freedom of the Negro would mean the probable alienation of a large number of Negroes whose friendship and votes he might need at the next election. After interviews with the new mayor and his political allies and enemies, we are convinced that he made a calculated decision to minimally increase the level of law enforcement—just enough to impress his white middle class supporters but not enough to alienate the Negro vote.

A decision of this sort, of course, must take into account the political strength and attitude of the Negro middle class in the town.

In both Tobacco Hill and Hamlin we found members of the Negro middle class who were quite concerned about the low level of law enforcement in the Negro community. Moreover, their concern was not simply at the abstract level of Negro middle class morality; they were concerned about the physical safety of their family and themselves within the Negro community. A Negro middle class respondent in Tobacco Hill stated that it was dangerous to complain of the activities of ones' neighbors to the police because, although the police might talk to the individual, they would also tell him who had registered the complaint and, accordingly, reprisals might occur. While we have some evidence which indicates that middle class Negroes are concerned about the low level of law enforcement within the Negro community, we also have evidence indicating that many middle class Negroes whom we interviewed tend to interpret strict law enforcement as discriminatory from a racial standpoint. The middle class Negro, then, may be caught in the conflict of two value systems. His middle class morality and desires for personal safety clash with his racial ideology.

Segments of the Negro middle class are often tied to law enforcement agencies by their particular economic interest. In the small town, independent Negro businesses, if they exist, often are limited to taxi service, funeral homes (which often include ambulance service), and the ownership of bars and "juke joints."[9] Each of these businesses is, to a varying degree, vulnerable to decisions made by the law enforcement agencies of the town. The bar and juke joint operators are, perhaps, most vulnerable since strict law enforcement in the immediate vicinity of their establishment would substantially reduce trade. Taxi operators are, of course, susceptible to strict enforcement of traffic regulations and to licensing procedues. Undertaking and ambulance services are less vulnerable to the activities of law enforcement agencies than the other businesses listed. However, the sheriff and the police do control a lucrative trade in ambulance service for accident victims, and the proprietors of such a service, as was the case in Tobacco Hill, can be tied economically to these law agencies. Astute and manipulative white politicians under these circumstances are likely to ignore the prob-

---

[9] A "juke joint" is an establishment which sells beer and/or whiskey, legally or illegally, and often has a coin-operated record player (juke box) on the premises used for dancing or listening. In our towns, juke joints were segregated, some for whites and others for Negroes.

lems of middle class Negroes. They are economically vulnerable, their value orientations toward whites are not completely consistent, and they are not numerous.

A Negro minister in Tobacco Hill who was bitter and disturbed by what he called the "immorality and disorganization" of the Negro community estimated the "immoral vote"—that is the vote directly controllable by the police and other agents of the white political structure by means of whiskey, fish fries, money and other techniques—at about 75 per cent of the voting Negroes. The county attorney, a member of the court house clique of Roth County, and, in our view, an astute professional politician, also estimated the "riff raff" Negro vote—the directly controllable Negro vote—at 75 per cent of the voting Negroes. There was agreement among most of our interviewees in Tobacco Hill that the directly manipulated Negro vote ran somewhere in the range of 75 per cent. In Hamlin there was less agreement over actual percentages. Estimates of the "immoral" vote ran from 90 per cent down to 60 per cent. Whatever the actual distribution of these two populations is, the strategy of the law enforcement agencies appears to be to ignore the potential problems of middle class Negroes while still remaining on friendly terms with them.

While we have mentioned the rackets previously, we will deal with them briefly here. Some testimony concerning bolita, moonshine, and prostitution was forthcoming in every town in which we interviewed. However, in only three of the six towns do we have enough data to warrant our judgment that the agencies of the law were directly connected to the rackets, either through payoff or by ownership. All three of these towns were or had been Manipulative towns. In Bougainville the police chief protected the bolita operation and controlled Negro voting in large measure until the early 1950's when Negro veterans re-organized the Civic League and began to bargain with members of the white political structure. The chief later made several attempts to elect "bolita men" to the board of the Civic League but failed. In Tobacco Hill the law enforcement agencies protected the bolita operation, while in Hamlin the data point to ownership of the rackets by the law enforcement officers. We tend to think that the significance of the rackets lies not so much in the actual number of votes which, for instance, a bolita peddler or moonshine distributor can influence as an individual, but rather in the complex we labeled impulse freedom—that is, the voter is responsive to the lawman because the latter facilitates activity desired by segments of the Negro community, and, in order that the rackets may flourish, law enforcement agencies are willing to permit a wide range of impulse freedom.

To the unsophisticated, lower class Negro in the small town the law is complicated and, usually, something to be feared. When he is in trouble he often needs someone to explain, defend, and, hopefully, extricate him from his difficulties. Help from a sophisticated member of the Negro middle class, preferably a Negro lawyer, would be desirable. However, such help is, in our experience, often unobtainable. The Negro community in most of the towns in which we interviewed is too small and probably too poor to support a Negro attorney so that the Negro in need of legal aid is forced to turn to a white lawyer. Moreover, we speculate, based on interview materials, that many Negroes, whether with reason or not, believe that a Negro attorney would be in a disadvantageous position compared to his white counterpart in local courts.

In Angusville where the Negro community is politically disorganized as compared to other Manipulative towns, the attempt to organize and direct the Negro vote by the whites originated in the family law office of a member of the political clique which had controlled that town's elected offices for a number of years. The firm handles most of the legal problems of the Negroes in the town. The senior partner is the trial lawyer of the firm and his performance in court is geared to a Florida cracker audience and jury. Amidst shouting, whispering, crying, and statements of "after all the defendant is only a nigger," the Clarence Darrow of Angusville is able to retrieve a number of Negroes from the clutches of the law.[10]

The law firm has gained in a number of ways from its endeavors for the Negro. First, it has acquired the property of some Negroes in lieu of payment of legal fees. Second, since many of its Negro clients cannot pay the fees for services rendered, the firm has "allowed" them to work off their indebtedness on the family farm. Third, the most important from our standpoint, the lawyers of the firm are looked upon by many Negroes as friends and possible saviors. Therefore, when the time of a local election approaches a series of letters and personal contacts flow from the law office to

[10]The statement "after all the defendant is only a nigger" implies that if the damaged party were white, "what would you expect from a Negro"; or if the damaged party were another Negro, "what difference does it make."

the Negro community suggesting who the firm feels is best qualified to hold public office and, apparently, many are responsive. A white lawyer, then, willing to handle Negro cases, and with the added attraction of a reputation as a winner in court, can have manipulative value at the time of an election.

V

On the basis of our case studies of various towns in their Manipulative phase, it seems clear to us that manipulation of the Negro vote by white politicians as a structural feature of a town's politics helps to account for part of the unexplained variance in the Matthews and Prothro study. Given usual abstract conceptions of civil rights, it is ironical that in our case study towns Negro registration and voting were usually initiated by the white political structure.

What has the Negro in Manipulative towns, such as Tobacco Hill or Hamlin, gained after more than 10 years of voting? Police harassment and brutality have disappeared. The Negro community in these towns is, in a relative sense, "let alone." From the standpoint of integration there were no gains. When freedom riders passed through Tobacco Hill the signs in the bus station were removed and the riders were served, but once the freedom riders were satisfied and continued their journey, signs were replaced. No Tobacco Hill or Hamlin Negro has enjoyed integrated service. The schools, restaurants, motels, and public recreational facilities all remain segregated in both towns. From the standpoint of municipal services Negroes received occasional promises but little fulfillment. In Tobacco Hill a few blocks of streets were paved in the Negro section. In Hamlin Negroes have not been able to obtain paving on the streets leading to the Negro schools. From an economic standpoint, also, gains have been minimal. In Tobacco Hill the Turner administration hired some Negroes for unskilled city work, and two Negro policemen were put on the force. In Hamlin economic gains have been even fewer than in Tobacco Hill.

Why have the Negro communities gained so little? We would suggest that the weakness of the Negro middle class in these towns prevents effective Negro leadership from emerging which might have organized the Negro community to bargain with the white political structure. In Hamlin and Tobacco Hill the Negro middle class is small and, to a degree, economically dependent upon the whites. The largest numerical segment of the Negro middle class — the school teachers—provide little or no leadership. Although the teachers are theoretically protected by a state merit system, they are still vulnerable to action by local white leadership. Furthermore, political leadership implies skills in bargaining and coalition-making which are *learned*. There are few ways that the Negro can obtain the requisite training in a small town. What political training the local Negro obtains usually has been given by whites, but this is training only in taking orders and, perhaps in a limited fashion, in individual bargaining. Negroes who acquire skills in the outside world and, therefore, would be potential leaders of the Negro community seldom return to towns like Tobacco Hill or Hamlin because of the limited number of job opportunities.

For the Negro community to successfully bargain its votes for gains, a coalition is probably necessary between the educated Negro middle class and the uneducated, but numerically larger, lower class. But as we have indicated previously, the values, life patterns, and goals of the two strata diverge. To bring them together, then, is not a simple task. The gains from Negro voting in the Manipulative town might be small from the viewpoint of the white liberal or race-conscious middle class Negro, but the uneducated, unsophisticated Negro in the Manipulative towns tends to view his gains from a different frame of reference. The voting situation in the Manipulative town, from a racial standpoint, contains a number of ambiguous elements which, we believe, makes the transformation from a Manipulative to an Independent Bargaining situation difficult. Obviously, we are not arguing that a transformation from Manipulation to Independent Bargaining is impossible, for we do have evidence of such a transformation in some of the towns we studied.[11] However, we do believe that the difficulty of effecting such a transformation helps to explain the success of the street demonstration technique as a device for bringing the two sections of the Negro community together as an effective Independent Bargaining unit. To build a voting coalition requires skill, time, and patience. Demonstrations are immediate, dramatic, and, from a racial standpoint, unambiguous. Moreover, demonstration or the threat of demonstration occurs in a situation which, unlike voting, is not structured by the white political community and, therefore, is not easily controlled or manipulated by the whites.

[11]In a forthcoming book, we will examine not only the politics of the Manipulative town, but also the other elements of the typology which we developed at the beginning of our paper—the Non-Voting town; the Low Voting, unorganized town; the Independent Bargaining town; and the Office Holding town.

POLITICAL MOVEMENTS AND ORGANIZATIONS

Samuel DuBois Cook
Atlanta University

POLITICAL MOVEMENTS may be in defense of, as well as in opposition to, the *status quo*. Just as discontent with the established order may generate movements of reform, threats to the existing balance of forces and pattern of arrangements may foster movements of stability and preservation. Events of the fifties threatened traditional Southern values and hence mothered several movements aimed at the preservation of the traditional framework. The forces of conservatism and reaction took a variety of forms: massive resistance, nullification, interposition, open defiance of federal law, and perpetuation of the Dixiecratic legacy in terms of states' rights candidates, independent electors, the formation of the National States Rights party, development of White Citizens Councils, revival of Klans, overnight conversion to Republicanism as a method of protest. The heart of the story here is the failure of Southern leadership in a crisis situation. The chief countermovement was the attempt to increase Negro political power *via* mass registration and voting.

The 1950's spawned a serious Republican effort to invade and conquer Dixie and establish a two-party system. Indeed, the surge of Republicanism is the most revolutionary wave in the drama of Southern politics since Populism. Even so, much of the GOP thrust was motivated and informed by the *status quo* mentality except in reference to the occupancy of the seats of power—that is, the chief question seemed to have been who could better preserve the non-party established order. One looks in vain for a major progressive, creative, liberal, or reformist movement, offering genuine policy alternatives, in Southern politics.

I. POLITICAL TRADITIONALISM VS. REVOLUTIONARY HISTORIC CHANGE

The most striking characteristic of the Southern political process in the revolutionary 1950's was the absence of, and the vigorous and persistent opposition to, social change. During that decade, change was, to use Morris R. Cohen's phrase "multidimensional." The region experienced great social, technological, industrial, and economic changes. But the heart of change involved the nerve center of Southern life: race relations. The story of Southern political movements in the fifties is the story of great tension between the forces of change and stability, the future and the past. The region's politics was that of defense, opposition, conservatism, stability, continuity, and traditionalism. Preservation of "the Southern way of life" against Negro aspirations was the clarion call, frame of reference, and rallying point. Political movements and organizations operated within the framework of traditional patterns of life and culture. Instead of serious and imaginative attempts to translate the inevitable consequences of vast technological, economic, legal, educational, industrial, and human innovations into the realities of political life, Southern politicians sought desperately to isolate and freeze the political process and to erect permanent bulwarks against the invading tides of change. "It is remarkable," observes Douglas Cater, "how static the politics of most of the South has been in the face of postwar economic changes."[1] The consequence of the absence of a genuine confrontation of politics and revolutionary historic change was all the brooding reality of Greek tragedy.

Political movements and organizations of the South in the 1950's were amazingly expressive of the dominant motif of the past. Southern politics, it is true, is the product of a stream of historical forces and sequences: plantation agrarianism, slavery, one-party politics, cultural isolation, a profound sense of self-consciousness and national alienation, a penchant for conformity and intolerance, the scars of the Civil War and Reconstruction, a nativist mentality, and excessive poverty and illiteracy. But the chief animation of the broad framework of southern politics has been the Negro as an object of action, manipulation, exploitation, and control. Although, in the main, voteless, the Negro has been, strangely, the prime mover in the politics of Dixie. Memories and anticipations, fears and anxieties, plans and counter-plans, programs and policies, and systems and processes in the South have often been based on the presence of the Negro.

Somehow, the Negro unwittingly has exercised a tyranny over the mind of the white South, which has found continuous expression in the politics of the region. V. O. Key comments,

[1]"Static Politics in a Changing South," *The Reporter*, March 31, 1960, p. 15.

> In its grand outlines the politics of the South revolves around the
> position of the Negro . . . in the last analysis the major peculiari-
> ties of southern politics go back to the Negro. Whatever phase of the
> southern political process one seeks to understand, sooner or later the
> trail of inquiry leads to the Negro.[2]

Indeed, Alexander Heard asserts that "Southern concern over the
Negro is the most deeply rooted source of political contention in
American politics."[3]

The ultimate tragedy of Southern political history is racism. It
has presided over every major aspects of the political life of the
region. This has been true not merely in the pre-Civil War era, the
Civil War itself, Reconstruction, the Democratic split in 1860, and
the establishment of various restrictive voting laws, but also in the
rise and perpetuation of the one-party system,[4] the birth and death
of Populism,[5] the Dixiecrat movement of 1948,[6] and many other
routine and episodic dimensions of the South's political odyssey.
Southern politics in the fifties was a faithful continuation of the
tradition of racial orthodoxy.

The decade of the 1950's was epochal for the South. In non-
political sectors, it was the most revolutionary since the Civil War
and Reconstruction. Industries expanded. Rural populations sharply declined. Cities grew. Education progressed. Technology and
research increased. Hopes soared. The Negro became more active
and restive. But politicians sought to insulate the political process
from the stunning impact of revolutionary times.

The Supreme Court's desegregation decision of May 17, 1954,
was the turning point, the dramatic pivot. As Francis Pickens Miller
noted, "the most painful experience for the South since Appomattox
and Reconstruction was the aftermath of the Supreme Court decision
of 1954."[7] A leading segregationist, Tom Brady, a Mississippi Cir-
cuit Judge, symbolized extremist contempt for the decision in his
crude little book, *Black Monday*.

[2]*Southern Politics* (New York, 1949), p. 5.

[3]*A Two-Party South?* (Chapel Hill, 1952), p. 27.

[4]See *Ibid.*, pp. 9, 145-46; J. B. Shannon, *Toward a New Politics in the
South* (Knoxville, 1949), pp. 8-9, and Harry Ashmore, *An Epitaph for Dixie*
(New York, 1957), p. 15.

[5]See Tom Watson's tragic and bitter comment in T. Harry Williams, *Ro-
mance and Realism in Southern Politics* (Athens, Georgia, 1960), p. 55.

[6]Heard, *op. cit.*, pp. 26-7, 251-53; Emile B. Ader, *The Dixiecrat Movement*
(Washington, 1955), esp. pp. 4, 10, and Ralph McGill, *The South and the
Southerner* (Boston, 1963), p. 187.

[7]"Dawn in the South," in Hoke Norris (ed.), *We Dissent* (New York,
1962), p. 124.

Let us first deal with pro-segregationist political movements and organizations.

II. PRO-SEGREGRATIONIST MOVEMENTS AND ORGANIZATIONS

Political Leadership. The movement of opposition to, and protest against, the landmark decision of 1954 was, of course, led by politicians. Sometimes in the dreadful demagogic spirit of "Pitchfork" Ben Tillman, Gene Talmadge, Tom Watson, James K. Vardaman, and Theodore Bilbo, many political leaders, in inflammatory language, railed against the Supreme Court—accusing it of "lawmaking," "judicial tyranny,," invading states' rights and subverting constitutional government. Once the darling of the South and indeed once worshiped as though it were the immortal arm and guardian angel of the Confederacy, the Court found itself bitterly denounced and desecrated. Defiance rather than compliance was the political prescription. Governors, mayors, and councilmen shouted "segregation today, segregation tomorrow, segregation forever" and proclaimed "never."

State legislatures, sometimes called into long, expensive, and noisy special sessions fought desperately to defeat the inevitable. In the four years succeeding the school decision, they passed 196 segregation laws. "Of the eleven states of the Old Confederacy . . . all have enacted interposition, nullification, or protest resolutions—in effect, claims that the segregation decision has no effect within their boundaries."[8] Various laws covered the gamut of the controversy.[9] As Harry Ashmore properly observed, the country has not witnessed such a mass of restrictive legislation "since the days of the Know Nothings."[10] Watchdog states' rights sovereignty commissions were created in almost every state to guarantee the preservation of the

[8]William Peters, *The Southern Temper* (Garden City, New York, 1959), p. 32.

[9]"By mid-1958 nine of these states had enacted pupil placement 'or assignment laws, while seven had provided for the possible abolition of public schools. Eight states had repealed or modified compulsory attendance requirements, and five had repealed or modified teacher employment laws. Four states had provided for grants for private education, for the sale or lease of school facilities, and four for the use of public funds for segregated schools only. And in a legislative lashing but at the presumed sources of their irritation eight of the eleven states had enacted laws restricting or providing for probes of both segregationist and desegregationist groups, which, in practice, have worked chiefly to the disadvantage of the desegregationists, notably the NAACP." *Ibid.* Also see Thomas D. Clark, *The Emerging South* (New York, 1961), ch. 13.

[10]Ashmore, *op. cit.*, pp. 29-30.

"Southern way of life." Impeachment of the justices of the Supreme Court was demanded by some legislative resolutions.

The nadir of the folly of Southern leadership was the issuance, on March 11, 1956, of the "Southern Manifesto." In that "Declaration of Constitutional Principles," 81 members of the House and 19 of the Senate, with all their power, eloquence, prestige, and influence, marched confidently and simultaneously in the opposing direction of law and lawlessness, order and chaos, constitutionalism and defiance.

The collective degradation of responsible leadership was the supreme tragedy of the South in the face of the Supreme Court's mandate. Political leaders provided the ideology, encouragement, respectability, and climate for the dreadful consequences that followed —and still follow.

> So it was before the winter of 1954-1955 was done, that the hoodlums were fired up by the hot defiance from state capitols, city halls, the House and Senate office buildings. If 'they,' the power structure, could damn the courts and describe their actions as illegal, then the man who wished to dynamite or burn a church or school felt himself approved. He had been given a pat on the back. If the governor was telling the courts to go to hell, why that was all he, the criminal fanatic, needed. He had a license.[11]

The inevitable consequence of the default of leadership was the encouragement and stimulation of extremist movements and organizations. After all, the region's most influential spokesmen had given them an atmosphere of acceptance and respectability—and a sense of urgency. The abdication of imaginative and responsible leadership created a vacuum. Here one realizes the awesome truth of the assertion of the former executive editor of the *Arkansas Gazette:*

> It would seem that those who resolutely turn away from the future would at least be able to read the first lesson of the South's past: When responsible men default, irresponsible men take power.[12]

In the wake of leadership's flight from reality and responsibility, White Citizens Councils, the Ku Klux Klan, the National States Rights party, bearers of the Dixiecratic legacy and other extremist groups entered the stage. The chickens of the tragic failure of Southern leadership are still coming home to roost.

---

[11]McGill, *op. cit.,* p. 248. Also see the same author's *A Church, A School* (New York, 1959). "It is not possible to preach lawlessness and restrict it. . . . When leadership in high places in any degree fails to support constituted authority, it opens the gates to all those who wish to take the law into their hands." Pp. 9-10.

[12]Ashmore, *op. cit.,* p. 14.

White Citizens Councils. White supremacist movements and organizations proliferated in the aftermath of the decision of 1954. "Not even reconstruction itself brought about the formation of so many defensive groups."[13] But White Citizens Councils were the most significant and influential. The first of these Councils was organized on July 11, 1954, in Indianola, Mississippi, in the heart of the Delta section.[14] Within a matter of weeks, White Citizens Councils had mushroomed not only in Mississippi but throughout the South as well —and in some border states. In Mississippi, a statewide association was formed, October, 1954, claiming a membership of 80,000. This was followed two years later by a regional organization: the Association of Citizens' Councils of America. This group claimed a membership of 300,000.[15] The sole article of faith of White Citizens Council is, of course, white supremacy and hence the command to preserve segregation.

Composition and leadership make Councils somewhat unique. Respectability is a precious value in American culture. In the relentless and calculated pursuit of their objectives, White Citizens Councils sought, first of all, respectability, a good public "image." To a significant degree, they were successful. Composed of prominent and responsible citizens—bankers, businessmen, public officials and other politicians, doctors, lawyers, and other members of upper and middle classes as well as farmers, laborers, and similar "God-fearing" ordinary people, Councils represent the "power structure" or "establishment" of local communities and states. Indeed, membership was a "status symbol." The "local organization's president is invariably a prominent citizen, and the board of directors is drawn from the community's Who's Who. When meetings are held, which isn't often, the same rough form of Robert's Rules of Order followed in most civic clubs is observed. The chairman begins by calling on a minister—most often a Baptist—for prayer."[16]

Hodding Carter notes,

Council leadership is drawn not from the pool room but from the country club. Its membership generally exhibits the attitude of the mid-

[13]Clark, *op. cit.*, p. 228.
[14]James G. Cook, *The Segregationists* (New York, 1962), p. 53, and Peters, *op. cit.*, pp. 40-44.
[15]Peters, *op. cit.*, p. 53.
[16]Hodding Carter, "Meanwhile, In Mississippi—Solidarity Forever," in Norris *op. cit.*, p. 93. Also see Arnold S. Rice, *The Ku Klux Klan in American Politics* (Washington, 1962), p. 121.

> dle and upper classes rather than of the poor white. And its aims are
> not couched in violent language but in the careful embroidery of
> states' rights and constitutionalism. In fact, when the first Council
> was formed . . ., one central purpose was to retain control of re-
> sistance to desegregation in the hands of the 'better people.' Then it
> was a semisecret society. Today, membership in the Citizens' Councils
> has come to be akin to membership in the Rotary or Lions Club. It is
> such an accepted mark of distinction, in fact, that many candidates
> for public or organizatonal office carefully add their participation in
> the Council to their listings of civic enterprises in which they have
> been engaged.[17]

Respectability was a key factor in the success of Councils.[18] Although they tried desperately to avoid any kind of association with
the discredited Klan mentality and character, critics labeled them
"white collar," "uptown," or "country club" Klan.

White Citizens Councils, employing the powerful weapons of
economic reprisal, political pressure, psychological and emotional
terror, and social ostracism, sought to frighten and to silence not
only Negroes but moderate and liberal whites as well and to keep
them from participating in desegregation activities, and, indeed,
from any sympathy with, or discussion of, the issue.[19] Negro allies
or potential and suspected sympathizers were as much the object
of abuse, retaliation, and intimidation as Negroes themselves.

Perhaps the basic evil of Councils was their social methodology
with its tyranny over the mind and spirit. Since the 1830's and
1840's, the South, in reaction to the Abolition movement, has been
the victim of the dreadful pressures of orthodoxy, intolerance, conformity of thought, and oppressive restraints on freedom of inquiry,
dissent, and discussion wherever the race issue is involved.[20] This
authoritarian and totalitarian technique of trying to create a single
mind and monolithic solidarity is a primary attribute of Councils.
Ashmore calls it the New Know Nothingism. The implications are
grave and far-reaching for a free and open society. Indeed, Coun-

[17]Carter, op. cit., p. 91.

[18]Cook, op. cit., p. 34.

[19]"White Citizens' Councils have been organized not only to frighten Negroes from filing local school suits but to silence potential dissenters among
the white population as well. In effect what these white-supremacy councils
are trying to do is to kill off any hopes of gradual, evolutionary change by
hammering Southern opinion into an embattled, unified state of feeling which
will brook no compromise." Samuel Lubell, *Revolt of the Moderates* (New
York, 1956), p. 197.

[20]On this problem, see Williams, op. cit., p. 18, and Ashmore, op, cit., ch. 13.

cils demand more than silence; they demand the public adoption and proclamation of their particular view.[21]

In the savage crusade for uniformity of thought (which is the same as the absence of thought), Councils tried to force the minds of scholars, thoughtful political leaders, journalists, ministers, public school teachers, businessmen, and others into a straightjacket. This pattern of thought-control, which is the legacy of what Cash called the "taboo on criticism of slavery," does havoc with freedom of the mind and spirit and precludes the very possibility of that progress which is the product of freedom of inquiry, discussion, and dissent and the handmaiden of the creative tension between the *status quo* and visions of higher possibilities and alternatives. The whole intellectual and political process of the South has been shackled and stultified by the deadening effect of the power and mentality of Citizens Councils. "What we have to fear in the South, and the world, today is not dispute—but silence. In the twilight of nondiscussion, minds do not grow tough; they do not even grow."[22] Exploiting ancient fears and old ghosts and employing effective economic and political techniques, Councils, in some states, had no difficulty exercising tyranny over the mind and spirit.

Capture and control of the political process was, from the beginning, a primary objective of Councils. In many situations, private and public power were integrally linked. Councils in about three states formed a powerful alliance with public officials and exerted controlling influence over the decision-making process—both legislative and executive. Mississippi, Louisiana, and Alabama are perhaps the best examples. Although private associations, Councils in Mississippi receive a generous subsidy from public funds.

Councils screen, endorse, support, oppose and denounce candidates and public officials and advocate restrictive legislation and administrative action to preserve segregation.[23] They participate enthusiastically in political campaigns as well as serve as pressure groups. Curtailing Negro registration and voting is a special objec-

---

[21]". . . everywhere in the South the mildest public questioning of the sanctity of segregation brings some degree of abuse and condemnation. Today . . . even silence does not afford protection against fanatics and their uninhibited party press; unless a man goes the whole way with fervid denunciation of the United States Supreme Court and all its works, he is subject to charges of disloyalty and heresy." Ashmore, *op. cit.*, p. 159.

[22]Wilma Dykeman and James Stokely, "Our Changing South: A Challenge," in Norris, *op. cit.*, p. 8.

[23]See Cook, *op. cit.*, pp. 60-7.

tive of Councils. Challenging and intimidating Negro voters and potential registrants, they are chiefly responsible for stricter voting requirements in some states, and purging of Negro registrants, and the rejection of numerous Negro applicants for the ballot.[24]

Councils have not had uniform success throughout the South—even the Deep South. In Georgia, for example, they never had wide appeal and extended success. The Georgia States Rights Council, headed by discredited politicians, was short-lived. In Mississippi, Alabama, Louisiana, and South Carolina, these organizations achieved their greatest power. Mississippi was the fountainhead.[25] In that state, Councils were somewhat held in check with reference to the governing process by former Gov. J. P. Coleman, but with the election of Gov. Ross Barnett in August of 1959, they achieved ascendancy and captured control of the machinery of the state.[26] Barnett, reputedly a member, is the darling of the Councils. Councils support Barnett and the legislature and they, in turn, support the Councils. Since Barnett's election, "the Council has all but completed the construction of a political machine whose power is publicly unchallenged by any major state official."[27] In 1960, Councils succeeded in the election of a slate of unpledged presidential electors.

> Far more important to the Council's purposes, however, and better illustrative of its grip on the state government, was the decision by the State Sovereignty Commission in late 1960 to donate $5,000 a month from tax money to support the Council's radio and television program, Citizens Council Forum. . . . The grant, combined with a

[24] ". . The editor of the Colfax *Chronicle,* of Grant Parish, Louisiana, on October 12, 1956, made a rather astonishing observation. He said that members of the local Citizens Councils had re-examined the voter rolls and had removed the names of many Negro voters. The president of the local Council, W. J. B. Jones, was reported to have said that his group voted unanimously to purge Negro voters and an estimate was made that 90 per cent of the Negro registrants were challenged. The *Chronicle's* editor checked the first one hundred white registrants' cards and found only one that would meet the exacting standards set for Negroes. He reported that not a single member of the Citizens Council Committee had filled out his card correctly by the Council's standards." Clark, *op. cit.,* p. 215. Also see the Report of the U. S. Civil Rights Commission, *Voting* (Washington, 1961), pp. 45-8, 71-2. "The citizens councils interest in voting was expressed not merely in pamphlets but in affirmative action to remove Negroes from voting rolls." p. 48.

[25] Mississippi not only provided the leadership and inspiration but "contained more than one-fourth of the membership of the Council." Rice, *op. cit.,* p. 121.

[26] See McGill, *The South and the Southerner, op. cit.,* p. 264, and the same writer's column in the *Atlanta Constitution,* August 10, 1963, as well as the relevant editorial in the *Atlanta Journal,* March 28, 1963.

[27] Carter, *op. cit.,* p. 91.

lump-sum donation of $20,000, had brought the Council over $100,000
from the public treasury by 1962. There are many other examples of
the Council's influence in state government. . . . During the regular
session of the legislature in 1960, that body acted as little more than
a rubber stamp for bills that had Council endorsement.[28]

By late-summer, 1963, the Councils had received more than $160,-
000 from public funds.[29]

That the Councils are still master of Mississippi politics is demonstrated by Lt. Gov. Paul B. Johnson's landslide victory over former Governor J. P. Coleman in the recent gubernatorial contest. As
governor, Coleman had refused to dance to the Councils' tune, and
they buried him in his political comeback attempt.[30]

Ku Klux Klan.   After its great influence of the 1920's, the Ku Klux
Klan sharply declined. Its membership and political influence waned
—except in isolated situations of state and local politics.[31] The Klan
lost respectability and since its endorsement in many situations
meant the kiss of political death, politicians shunned it.

But in the wake of the Supreme Court's school decision, there
was a resurgence of the Klan to exploit racial fears and anxieties.
It popped up in Alabama, Mississippi, Georgia, Florida. Arkansas,
and other states.

> Quite suddenly . . . in 1954, the order took a new lease on life. For
> the next few years rapid growth was the keynote of Klanism. In the
> South thousands of fiery crosses lighted up the sky. By 1958 there
> were well over 100,000 new Knights and more than 500 new chapters
> of various Klans.[32]

But the Klan, despite desperate efforts, has not regained its past
glories and respectability. Except in rare instances, public support
by the Klan is more of a curse than a blessing to aspirants for pub-

---

[28]*Ibid.*, pp. 91-2.

[29]Kenneth Toler, "Johnson's Anti-Kennedy Victory Demolishes GOP," *Atlanta Journal* and *Constitution* (combined Sunday ed.), September 1, 1963.

[30]"Mr. Johnson's win was considered a victory for the top leadership of the
prosegregation Citizens Councils, many of whom were high in his campaign
strategy. It will strengthen the already powerful hand of the councils in shaping Mississippi's policies for the four years commencing in January. Former
Gov. Coleman during his administration refused to recognize the Citizens Council leaders and was responsible for the sovereignty commission, the state's
segregation watchdog agency created under him, refusing to 'donate' public
funds to the private organization." *Ibid.*

[31]See Rice, *op. cit.*, p. 121; McGill, *The South and the Southerner, op. cit.*,
ch. 10, and Cook, *op. cit.*, p. 117.

[32]Rice, *op. cit.*, p. 118.

lic office.[33] Three forces militate against the return of the Klan to real political power: the lack of respectability rooted in a "bad" historic image, White Citizens Councils, and a vast number of competing, warring, splinter Klan groups.[34]

The most interesting aspects of present-day Klanism is its amazing attempt to create a new image or look. While clinging to its ancient articles of faith, the Klan nowadays, curiously more like the Negro protest movement than its historic identity, insists that it is peaceful, non-violent, and law-abiding.[35] At a recent cross-burning ceremony at Stone Mountain, Georgia, a Klan official proclaimed the new dispensation: "We have two great weapons, the boycott and the ballot box."

Fragmentation of the Democratic Legacy. After the Democratic split over the issue of slavery in 1860, the Democratic party and the "Solid South" carried on a love affair for nearly 80 years. The Democratic party became the Southern voice in national councils; the South became the bulwark of Democratic strength in presidential elections. But, ironically, at the very time that the Democratic party became less dependent on the South—during the Roosevelt years— the South became more and more irritated with Democratic national policies, especially in the field of civil rights. Murmurs of dissatisfaction were heard as early as 1936 and 1940. Rumblings of discontent found expression in a rudimentary organization in 1944.[36] But Truman's civil rights program generated a genuine revolt in the form of the Dixiecrat or States' Rights party.

Despite all the glib talk about states' rights, constitutional government, tidelands oil, conservatism, and anti-centralization, the Dixiecrat party of 1948, under the leadership of Strom Thurmond and Fielding Wright, was primarily an anti-Negro movement.[37] Anti-civil rights legislation was its heart and soul. Its greatest appeal—as the election returns indicate—was to racial fears and frustrations.[38] As Ralph McGill observes,

[33]Cf. Clark, in Norris, *op. cit.,* p. 49, and Cook, *op. cit.,* pp. 146-47.

[34]See McGill, *The South and the Southerner, op. cit.,* p. 143, and Rice, *op. cit.,* p. 128.

[35]On the "new look" of the Klan, see Karl Fleming, "Ku Klux Klan: Button-Down Bed Sheets," *Newsweek,* August 26, 1963.

[36]See Heard, *op. cit.,* pp. 158-60; Key, *op. cit.,* pp. 256-58, 279, 330, and Emile B. Ader, *The Dixiecrat Movement* (Washington, 1955), esp. p. 8.

[37]*Ibid.,* pp. 4, 8-13; Heard *op. cit.,* pp. 26-7, 251-53, and Key, *op. cit.,* pp. 330-36.

[38]See Heard, *op. cit.,* pp. 26-7, 251-53.

> The Dixiecratic party was, at heart, the most infamously hypocritical and intellectually dishonest political organization ever created. While it sought tto conceal its real motives with the cynical old shibboleth of states' rights, its real principles were those later espoused and practiced by the worst of the White Citizens Councils.[39]

The abiding significance of the Dixiecrat party was in the realm of strategy and policy. A sectional party based on historic regional values, capture of the White House was out of the question. The Dixiecrats hoped to pick up enough votes to throw the election of the president into the House of Representatives and, by means of electoral hocus-pocus, bargain and secure a president more favorable to their point of view. The experiment not only failed of its purpose, but boomeranged to do great harm to Southern prestige and power. The 1948 election revealed a new alignment in national politics. Its painful lesson—yet to be learned by certain disgruntled politicians—for the South is simply this: the power and prestige of the region in Democratic councils and national politics have sharply declined. The Dixiecrats, therefore, had the ironic fate of proving the very opposite of their intentions.

Yet Dixiecratic strategy, thinking, and efforts presided over a significant portion of the South in the 1950's and continue in the present decade. The fifties witnessed the fragmentation and splintering of the Dixiecratic legacy. Dispersion took a variety of forms. First, ghostly remains of the party waged token campaigns in a handful of states in 1952 and 1956, behind the names of T. Coleman Andrews and Sen. Harry Byrd, respectively. Second, efforts were made at Democratic national conventions to "win" the nomination for a states' rights candidate. Third, Dixiecratic energies were frittered away on a series of insignificant conferences, conventions, and organizations.

Fourth, elements of the Dixiecratic legacy joined the ranks of rising Republicanism in the South, as a matter of protest against the Democratic party and on the assumption that, contrary to the past, the GOP is more sympathetic to "states' rights," "conservatism," and "constitutional government." Herein lies part of the explanation of Eisenhower's invasion of Dixie's electoral riches. Fifth, some Dixiecrats hitched their wagon to the conservative and reactionary forces of White Citizens Councils.[40]

---

[39]*The South and the Southerner,* p. 187.

[40]"Indeed, many of the Dixiecrat leaders became the chief organizers and supporters of these councils," McGill, *The South and the Southerner, op. cit.,* p. 187.

Two aspects of the Dixiecratic heritage require special comment: the National States Rights party and the "free," "independent," "unpledged," or "uninstructed" electors movement.

National States Rights Party. The National States Rights (NSRP), headquartered in Birmingham, is a noisy activist group. It engages in direct action, such as anti-integration picketing, demonstrations, and boycotts, as well as pressure and electoral politics. Rowdyism and militant racism are its hallmarks. Formed in Knoxville in 1957 from the remnants of the short-lived United White party, the NSRP merged in 1962 with the National White American Party. It is a pro-Nazi totalitarian group, whose creed insists on authoritarian discipline and the infallibility of the leader—"the leader is always right. . . ." A California Senate subcommittee on un-American activities said that the NSRP is "more potentially dangerous than any of the American Nazi groups, as it is interested in activities far more vigorous than picketing" and many of its spokesmen advocate using "immediate physical violence."[41] Ultra-rightist, the NSRP advocates not the impeachment but the execution of the justices of the Supreme Court.[42]

The NSRP is Negro-hating and Jew-baiting. "Most of the key leaders of the party are rather young men; nevertheless, they are long-experienced in behalf of anti-Semitism."[43] "From the party's fountain in Birmingham flows a stream of anti-Jewish propaganda even more turbulent than the roiling polemics of Gerald K. Smith and Conde McKinley."[44]

Although the NSRP refuses to disclose its total membership, it calls itself "America's third largest party" and claims units in 37 states. But clearly the membership is small and the party has made no significant political impression.[45] In 1960, the NSRP nominated Gov. Faubus for president and Rear Admiral John Crommelin, an oft-defeated candidate in Alabama politics, for president. Faubus

[41]Quoted by Jerry Rankin, "Birch Society Found No Peril," *Atlanta Constitution*, June 13, 1963.

[42]*Ibid.*

[43]Cook, *op. cit.*, p. 170.

[44]*Ibid.*, p. 167.

[45]James G. Cook estimates that the total membership of the party is "perhaps only a few hundred persons." *Ibid.* According to another observer, "some police sources place its active membership at about 150." Fred Powledge, "Rightists Active in Alabama Fight," *New York Times*, September 6, 1963, p. 14.

declined the nomination. "Despite Faubus' withdrawal, the National States Rights party polled 28,952 votes in Arkansas—by far the best showing among all the states where the party was able to get on the ballot."[46] (Arkansas cast 428,509 votes in the presidential election of 1960). Although the party contends that it attracted 250,000 votes, it received in five states, a total of 214,549 votes, with Louisiana casting 169,572, which is by far the party's best electoral record.[47]

According to Dr. Edward R. Fields, a chiropractor, high party official, and editor of the party's paper, *The Thunderbold*, the organization would like to draft the Dixiecrat candidate of 1948, Sen. Thurmond, as its standard-bearer in 1964.[48]

Independent Electors Movement.   Echoing the Dixiecratic strategy of trying to deadlock the Electoral College and force election of the president by the House of Representatives, certain states' righters, prior to every presidential contest, engaged in what the *Atlanta Journal* called a "battered old crutch" and the "slickest confidence game going." The electoral game is called independent or "free" electors. This movement is based on a theory of the balance of power and electoral juggling. The assumption is that the South, in order to force a stalemate in the Electoral College and thereby compel House selection of the president, should withhold its electoral votes from both Democratic and Republican nominees. The hope is that, through some kind of political chemistry, the South will be able to secure a states' rights sympathizer, if not a states' rights president, in the White House. This fantasy expressed itself in Mississippi as early as 1944.

Following this strategy, Mississippi in 1960 cast its 8 electoral votes for Sen. Byrd, and Alabama cast 6 of its 11 votes for the same person.

An independent electors movement, led by Governors Barnett of Mississippi and Wallace of Alabama, is afoot today. It is also enthusiastically supported by Leander Perez, a Louisiana political kingpin, certain important forces in South Carolina and a scattering of politicians in other Deep South states. Barnett has proclaimed that the "South can positively elect the next president." Opposition

---

[46]Cook, *op cit.*, p. 170.

[47]In addition to Louisiana and Arkansas, the NSRP polled 4,367 votes in Alabama, 354 in Delaware, and 11,304 in Tennessee. Harry Hansen, ed., *The World Almanac and Book of Facts* (New York, 1963), p. 417.

[48]Powledge, *op. cit.*, p. 14.

to the Administration, motivated by and rooted in the President's civil rights program, is the creed of the unpledged electors movement.

But apart from Alabama, Mississippi, Louisiana, and South Carolina, the independent electors movement is lacking in serious interest, momentum, and leadership in Dixie. Most of the region's political leaders recognize the movement for what it is: a self-defeating exercise in futility and frustration. Georgia no longer has an independent electors law. Unpledged electors bills died in the legislatures of Virginia, Florida, and Louisiana.[49] At present, it is reasonable to say that the independent electors movement will be seriously active in the 1964 presidential election only in the above-mentioned four states, with emphasis on Mississippi and Alabama.[50] There is also a strong possibility that the sentiments and interest generated by the movement will give rise to a third or splinter party led by Governor Wallace, who seeks revenge against Kennedy and Johnson, and who might develop, out of a crusading and martyrdom complex, the frustrating illusion that he is a serious presidential contender.

III. Negro Registration and Voter Movement

In the context of the conservative and reactionary forces and organizations discussed in the previous section, the drive to increase Negro political power is a significant counter-movement. The crowning irony of Southern politics is that, despite the universality and centrality of the race issue in the legacy of the region, there has never been, with the magnificent exception of the short-lived period of Reconstruction, any meaningful Negro participation in the Southern political process.

In the wake of the Supreme Court's nullification of the white primary, Negro registration, spurred by organizational drives and individual efforts, soared. "The estimated number qualified to vote in the eleven southern states rose from 151,000 in 1940 to 595,000

[49]However, in early September, segregationist-conservative forces, under the leadership of Perez, forced the Democratic Central Committee of Louisiana—by a vote of 53-42—to accept a resolution calling for two slates of presidential electors in 1964, one pledged to the national party, the other unpledged.

[50]In an Association Press release, Jack Bell concluded: "An unpledged elector movement . . . appears to be withering on the political vine in Dixie. An Associated Press survey of 11 Southern states indicates that in only three states—Mississippi, Alabama and South Carolina—does there appear to be any significant possibility that major nominees might be denied electoral votes." *Atlanta Journal*, July 18, 1963.

in 1947 and to 900,000 in 1950."[51] The number increased to 1,008,-
614 in 1952 to 1,238,038 in 1956 and to 1,303,827 in 1958."[52]
Meantime, "the number of Negro registrants dropped slightly between 1956 and 1958."[53]

In the mid-fifties—the aftermath of the school decision—there
was a vigorous and sustained movement to restrict Negro political
participation. Several states tightened voter registration laws.[54]
In Georgia, for example, a 1957 law made a test for illiterates so
tough that even the then political editor of the *Atlanta. Constitution*
and a professor of political science conceded that, without serious
homework and luck, they would flunk it. Challenges, wholesale
purges, gerrymandering, stricter administration of voting laws and
various pressures—including coercion—were rampant in some areas
of the South.[55]

However, Congress passed Civil Rights Acts in 1957 and 1960,
dealing primarily with protecting the right to vote. In 1957, the
NAACP and other organizations launched a drive to add Negroes
to the voting rolls. But even with that intense drive and more
meaningful support from the federal government, the increase was
only slight. In 1960, the estimated number of Negro registrants was
1,414,052, about one-fourth the potential.[56]

In the spring of 1962, a comprehensive, all-out drive was set in
motion to increase Negro registration. Under the leadership of the
Voter Education Project of the Southern Regional Council, several
organizations participated: the NAACP, the Southern Christian
Leadership Conference, the Urban League, the Student Non-violent
Coordinating Committee, the Congress of Racial Equality, and numerous "independent" state and local groups. Various "citizenship
schools" and "voter clinics" were established. A grass-roots campaign was initiated throughout the South.

[51]Heard, *op. cit.,* p. 181.
[52]Margaret Price, *The Negro and the Ballot in the South* (Atlanta, 1959),
p. 9. Also see the report of the Civil Rights Commission, *Voting, op. cit.,* pp.
21-2.
[53]Price, *op. cit.,* p. 6.
[54]See, for example, Joseph L. Bernd and Lynwood M. Holland, "Recent
Restrictions Upon Negro Suffrage: The Case of Georgia," in this *Journal,* XXI
(August, 1959), 487-513.
[55]See Price, *op. cit.,* pp. 15-21, 34-46, 54-62, and *Voting, op. cit.,* pp. 23-72.
85-97.
[56]Donald R. Matthews and James W. Prothro, "Social and Economic Factors and Negro Voter Registration in the South," *American Political Science
Review,* LVIII (March, 1963), 27.

The voter registration movement is still in progress. Results thus far are not striking. The increase is substantially the same as that of the white community. Increases, for a variety of reasons, are slow and difficult and mainly in urban areas.[57]

Indeed, the total number of Negro registrants appears to have declined between 1960 and 1963. In the mid-summer of 1963, of the estimated total of 5,045,000 voting-age Negroes in the eleven Southern states, only an estimated 1,344,000, about one-fourth, were registered. Of the 17,539,000 whites of voting age in the region, an estimated 10,566,000 were registered.[58] Figures on Negro voting are hard to come by. But the best available statistics—those of the Southern Regional Council—suggest a dramatic fact. In spite of the massive and intensive Negro voter registration movement, the number of Negro registrants declined between 1960 and mid-summer, 1963. The decrease appears to be about 70,000.

IV. SOUTHERN REPUBLICANISM

A political revolution is taking place in the South. The best evidence of the changing political mind of the South is the surge of Republicanism. Republican advancement constitutes, perhaps, the greatest innovation in Southern politics since the establishment of the one-party system nearly a century ago—certainly since Populism. The GOP is discovering the wonders and infinite possibilities of leadership, organization, grass-roots contact, research, primaries, permanent headquarters, attractive candidates, contested elections on every level, the exploitation of dissatisfaction with Democratic one-party politics, issues, all-out, all-weather and all-year efforts, and grasping the impact of vast changes on traditional habits, loyalties, and images of the South.

Long in the doldrums of competitive party politics, the Old Confederacy is riding high in that area. The changing political landscape is striking. *The New York Times* caught the drama of political revolution when it remarked that, "interestingly enough, the South, long forbidden territory of the Republicans, is now the principal area of attention among the claimants for the Republican nomination. Backers of each man measure his potential in terms

[57]*Ibid.*, 24-44, and also see the authors' article in the June issue of the same publication.

[58]These figures from the Southern Regional Council were reported by Relman Morin, "The Deepening Crisis: Voting is a New Negro Symbol of Citizenship," *Atlanta Journal*, August 1, 1963.

of his ability to overturn the Democrats' historic supremacy there."[59] Perhaps the chief argument of the Goldwater supporters is that he can carry the South. To see the South as "doubtful," "strategic," or "pivotal" territory is to witness a radical discontinuity between the South's past and future. "There has been a realignment of voters since 1948," asserts Howard Penniman, "so that presidential elections are nearly as exciting in the South as in the two-party states of the North."[60] Indeed, political analyst Louis Harris contends that, "in all likelihood, as things stand now, the GOP will carry the South."[61] Although, in view of the flux and cross-currents of the region, Harris' prediction is premature, it is a magnificent reminder of the changing political face of the South. Ostrogorski's prediction, made more than a half a century ago, that the " 'Solid South' is breaking" is finally appearing on the stage of reality.

Southern Republicanism is distinct from what it was prior to the fifties.[62] In image and reality, it is something new. Republican growth in the South began with Eisenhower who gave the party respectability—at least in presidential encounters. In fact, the label "Eisenhower Republican" was something of a status symbol in 1952 and 1956.

GOP growth is indicated by several factors: victories and near-victories on various levels, total popular votes, the number of primaries and contested elections, the seriousness of campaigns, the proliferation of organizations, the number of permanent headquarters with full-time staffs, the quality of leaders and converts, etc. Let us summarize GOP gains in presidential and congressional elections.

Between 1928 and 1952, no Southern state went Republican and indeed the GOP popular vote was insignificant. Dewey, in 1948, polled more than 30 per cent of the vote only in Florida, North Carolina, Tennessee and Virginia. He received only 1,361,742 votes —26.4 per cent of the total. But the 1950's saw the erosion of Democratic solidarity. Eisenhower transformed the Democratic

[59] June 16, 1963, p. 4E.
[60] "The Republican Problem in Dealing with the South," a paper delivered at the meeting of the Southern Political Science Association, November, 1962, p. 2.
[61] " '64: The GOP Could Win—If," *Newsweek,* August 26, 1963, p. 26.
[62] On the GOP in the South historically, see Key. *op, cit.,* ch. 13, and Heard, *op. cit.,* esp. sections 2 and 3.

stronghold into a GOP beachhead. The war hero, in 1952, not only carried Florida, Tennessee, Texas, and Virginia but polled about 48 per cent of the votes of the region. He did even better four years later, when he added, by a landslide, Louisiana to his victory column, and polled 50.5 per cent of Dixie's votes.

Nixon carried only Florida, Tennessee, and Virginia, but he got nearly 49 per cent of the votes in Texas and South Carolina and almost 48 per cent of North Carolina's. South Carolina is perhaps the best example of the growth of Southern Republicanism in presidential elections. In 1948, Dewey received less than 4 per cent of the votes in that state; Nixon, however, lost South Carolina by only about 10,000 votes. It is significant that in popular vote Nixon surpassed Eisenhower's percentage in Tennessee, Georgia, Alabama, Mississippi, and South Carolina. He collected approximately 48 per cent of the Southern popular vote.

Theodore H. White summarizes Nixon's impressive vote-getting performance in Dixie:

> There, in the Old Confederacy, Richard M. Nixon made his greatest gains. It was felt by Democrats, hopefully, in 1952 and 1956 that only the glamor and fame of Eisenhower—coupled with the true affection he has in American hearts—carried the South from its traditional loyalties to the Republican column in his two elections. Yet Nixon managed to *increase* the Republican vote and *outrun* Eisenhower in no less than four states of the Deep South . . . and carried two others (Virginia and Florida) by margins almost equal to that of the war hero. All in all, in the eleven states of the old Confederacy he polled 4,723,981 votes as against 5,179,550 votes for Kennedy, to score 47.8 per cent; in 1952, Eisenhower had polled only 4,113,525, or 48.1 per cent; and in 1956, 4,218,468, or 50.5 per cent..[63]

A great task for Southern Republicans is the translation of support in presidential elections to congressional, state, and local engagements. A two-party system requires more than competitive politics in presidential races. The schizophrenia of voting GOP in presidential elections and Democratic in other contests has caused certain commentators to predict a "three-party" South.[64] "These presidential Republican voters are sometimes passionately partisan Democrats between national elections, sponsoring state and local Democratic candidates, raising money for them, and even master-minding strategy as delegates to Democratic national conventions."[65] There

[63]*The Making of the President, 1960* (New York, 1962), p. 359.

[64]Ashmore, *op. cit.*, p. 147, and Lubell, *op. cit.*, ch. 8.

[65]Jack Spalding, "Organization Can Produce a Two-Party System," *Atlanta Journal*, September 12, 1963.

are two obvious reasons for this. First, presidential Republicans are often disgruntled *national* Democrats and have no gripe with the conservatism of state and local Democrats. Second, state and local Republicans do not have the "respectability" of presidential Republicans. Of course, even some presidential Republicans have difficulty in this connection, as "Democrats-for-Eisenhower," "Democrats-for-Nixon and Lodge," and the curious present group, "Democrats-for-Goldwater" disclose.

There are, in the South, traditional congressional Republicans just as there are traditional presidential Republicans. Indeed, two districts in Tennessee (the 1st and 2nd) and one in North Carolina (the old 10th) have consistently sent Republicans to Washington. Of late, however, Republicans have begun to take seriously the task of electing solons in the South. Real progress was made in 1960 and 1962. In 1960, Republicans entered candidates in 41 of the 96 congressional districts and in 5 of the 10 senatorial encounters. No candidate for the Senate won, but the aspirant in North Carolina received over 40 per cent of the vote and John Tower laid the foundation for his startling victory in the special election of 1961. Tower's election, of course, was the high tide of Southern Republicanism in non-presidential politics. Republicans won 7 of the 41 contests for the House, and in 10 other districts GOP condidates received about 40 per cent of the vote. North Carolina was particularly impressive; although only the incumbent won, 5 others collected about 40 per cent of the vote there.

The GOP fared better in the 1962 elections. Contesting 56 seats, the GOP picked up new congressmen in Florida, North Carolina, Texas, and Tennessee. (Kentucky, which also elected a new GOP congressman, is not defined as Southern within the meaning of this paper). In 8 other congressional districts, GOP candidates polled about 45 per cent of the vote. Even in Georgia—the most consistently and thoroughly Democratic state—, a GOP candidate garnered almost 45 per cent of the vote; though in the other contest in that state, the Republican aspirant polled only about 29 per cent. While in the Old Confederacy the total GOP congressional vote in 1958 was only 606,108, in 1962 the total was 2,083,971. For the first time, the GOP plans to contest all congressional seats in 1964.[66]

[66]The GOP National Committee explains the gains this way: Between 1958 and 1962, Republican growth was 244 per cent while Democratic growth was only 41 per cent. "Major Republican gains were made in every Southern state with the single exception of Mississippi where there were no Republican candi-

In 1962, the GOP contested Senate seats in Alabama, Arkansas, Florida, Louisiana, and the Carolinas. Indeed, only Talmadge of Georgia missed opposition in the country's senatorial contests. The GOP won no seats in the Senate, but almost toppled veteran Sen. Lister Hill, when a relatively unknown candidate came within 7,000 votes of winning, gaining 49.1 per cent of the votes. Another surprise was South Carolina, where the GOP candidate polled slightly more than 42 per cent of the votes in an engagement against Olin Johnston. In that state, the GOP had not contested a Senate seat since 1956, when its candidate polled only 17.8 per cent of the vote.

In state and local elections, the heart of competitive party life, the GOP has won a scattering of offices—mayors, councilmen, state legislators, and lesser officials. In the region, GOP gains, though somewhat dramatic, have not been uniform and great.

The South does not yet have a two-party system, but one is a-borning. Although the region nearly has a two-party system in presidential elections, on the congressional, state, and local levels, effective competitive party politics is a good distance away. Only a handful of Southern states—Tennessee, North Carolina, Virginia, Florida, and Texas—are well on their way to a truly two-party system. Only Florida, Tennessee, and North Carolina have meaningful GOP representation in legislatures. The GOP has not had any significant success in statewide elections—with a few isolated exceptions. However, in a handful of states, GOP statewide prospects are excellent—including gubernatorial offices in North Carolina, Texas, Florida, Virginia, and Tennessee.

A "new breed" of leadership is the key factor in GOP successes in Dixie. Unlike the historic emphasis on patronage and the building of empires of personal prestige and power, the new "organization men" of Southern Republicanism are equally concerned with ideology and the establishment of an effective opposition party. Considerable stress is on youth. Young business executives on the go are the typical GOP leaders.[67] Also young ambitious lawyers

dates. These gains range from a 9.2 percentage point increase in the Republican percentage of the vote in Florida to 32.0 points in Texas. In three Southern states—North Carolina, Texas, and Virginia—Republicans won 40% or more of the total vote. In three additional states—Alabama, Florida, and Tennessee—the Republican percentage exceeded 33%." *The 1962 Election: A Summary Report with Supporting Tables,* mimeo. (Washington, 1963), p. 9. Also see *Newsweek,* May 20, 1962, p. 29.

[67]See Virginius Dabney, "What the GOP Is Doing in the South," *Harper's* May, 1943, p. 87, *Time,* July 13, 1962, p. 12, and William Morris, "Texas Politics in turmoil," *Harper's,* September, 1962, p. 82.

are conspicuous in the ranks of the party. The new breed of GOP leadership in North Carolina, comments Jay Jenkins, "is a hustler and a doorbell ringer." In some situations, the new type of GOP leadership is partly motivated by strange idealistic elements. Goldwater is the darling of Southern Republicanism.

The GOP no longer depends for its strength on traditional Republicans in the hills and mountains—the bearers of the legacy of Unionist sentiments. Modern Southern Republicanism is a creature of the regions growing industrialization and urbanization. The cities and suburban areas provide the chief sources of strength.[68] Paradoxically, Southern Republicanism, which stresses the philosophy of conservatism, is the product of revolutionary industrial and technological change. In the cities and suburbs are the rising middle classes—as well as the region's big business leadership and corporate industrial interests—which are increasingly dissatisfied with the liberalism of the national Democratic party. The influx of executive newcomers adds to GOP strength. The main appeal of the GOP to urban and suburban voters is economic. Another great source of surging Republican strength is racial discontent. Much of the GOP appeal is to those groups which are angry with the national Democratic party and the strong Kennedy-Johnson civil rights program.[69] In Mississippi, Alabama, Louisiana, and South Carolina, the GOP has sometimes made outright racist appeals. But, on the whole, the GOP has been the beneficiary of segregationist support either because of the strategy of silence or because of the ideological camouflage of states' rights and conservatism. In many situations, conservatism and states' rights are masks for racism. Racism and segregationist sentiment are a basic part of the current "Goldwater movement."[70]

The future of Southern Republicanism may well depend—apart from problems of mechanics—upon how it responds to two crucial issues: racial extremism and ultra-conservatism. The GOP is going to be under increasing pressure and temptation to exploit racial fears, tensions, and frustrations. But an effective and enduring party cannot be largely built on anti-Negro individuals and groups who, overnight, become GOP converts—trying to use the party of Lin-

[68]See Lubell, *op. cit.*, pp. 179-99; White, *op. cit.*, p. 360; Dabney, *op. cit.*, p. 88, and Miller, *op. cit.*, pp. 127-28.
[69]Lubell, *op. cit.*, ch. 8, and White, *op. cit.*, p. 360.
[70]See McGill's column in the *Atlanta Constitution,* May 5 and August 26, 1963.

coln for cynical and opportunistic purposes. The second major GOP problem is that of ultra-conservatism. How can challengers of the party *status quo* be more conservative than most Southern Democrats? How can they get to the right of men like Byrd and Thurmond? What can the GOP offer the *status quo* to compensate for the commanding influence of the Southern bloc in Congress—especially when it is recalled that 10 of the 16 standing committee chairmanships of the Senate and 11 of the 20 in the House are held by Southern Democrats? Moreover, in view of the increasing problems of burgeoning Southern cities—rapid transit, slum clearance, urban renewal and redevelopment, unemployment, education, etc.—the conservative motif of the GOP may pose this dilemma: abandon or be abandoned. The GOP cannot continue to attract urban and suburban voters if, in the name of ideology, its program is irrelevant to their problems.

V. A NOTE ON THE FUTURE

The South is in flux, with cross-currents and cross-winds. Moreover, there are, as Ralph McGill loves to say, many Souths with many political faces. There is not and is not likely to be any single and uniform pattern and rate of political movements and organizations. The diversity and complexity of the region prevent such a development.

In broad strokes, however, it is safe to say that, in certain sections of the Deep South, the Dixiecratic legacy will continue in the form of independent electors and splinter parties. In all probability, Wallace of Alabama will lead a splinter party in 1964. If Goldwater receives the GOP presidential nomination, most of the Dixiecratic elements will be unified behind him. If, however, Goldwater fails in his quest for the nomination, there is a possibility of an "independent electors" movement. The Negro voter registration movement will continue with steady but not dramatic increases. Political movements and organizations motivated and guided by resistance to desegregation will be perpetuated in certain areas of the region. But except for states like Mississippi and Alabama, support of them by state political leadership will continue to decline.

What is likely to be the ideological consequence of GOP advances in Dixie? Is there likely to be a realignment along conservative and liberal lines? Considerable speculation exists to the effect that, because of GOP competition, the Democratic party will be liberalized. In fact, pundits are insisting that GOP threats are already forcing Southern Democrats in Congress to abandon their historic coalition with conservative Republicans and to act more like national Democrats. The situation, however, is too fluid to justify the assumption that the GOP will liberalize the Democratic party. The opposite may well be true: perhaps in order to continue to win in the urban areas, the GOP will be forced to a more liberal position. At any rate, there is no likelihood that, in the foreseeable future, Southerners will have a choice between liberal and conservative parties.

The chances are that there will be no uniformity of strategy and policy on the part of either Democrats or Republicans. Playing the matter "by ear," the odds are that the parties and candidates will tailor their strategy, program, and appeal to fit the state and local situations. Hence the GOP in one state or local community may well be liberal, in another conservative, in still another "moderate" on certain issues. The same possibility exists for the Democrats. Both parties will carry their ideological water on both shoulders.

The problem of calculating the prospects is made impossible of solution by the great changes under way in the South. No one can anticipate the impact of legislative (and possibly congressional) re-apportionment, the nullification of Georgia's iniquitous county unit system, greater industrialization and urbanization, the slow growth of organized labor, the migration of Negroes, increasing education, the expanding Negro electorate, the imminent abolition of the poll tax, and a host of other evolving conditions. These developments will have a cumulative effect, but no one is wise enough to identify the precise political, organizational, and ideological consequences.

THE FEDERAL JUDICIARY AND POLITICAL CHANGE IN THE SOUTH

GEORGE W. SPICER

University of Virginia

INTRODUCTION

OVER THE PAST QUARTER century the federal judiciary, especially the Supreme Court, has assumed an increasingly important place in the American system of government. This development has been especially noteworthy since about 1950. Rarely, if ever, has the Supreme Court of the United States played a more extensive and significant role in the alteration of public policy, that is, in political change, than during the 1950's and the early 1960's. The impact of these changes although nationwide, has been, and will continue to be, most significant in the South.

Patterns of segregation in public education, in public transportation, in privately owned public accommodations, and discrimination in voting rights and legislative representation, that were thought by most Southerners to be permanently fixed, have been broken and may even be largely eliminated before the end of the decade of the seventies. Now the courts have not done, and cannot do, this alone. But until July, 1963, they have played the role of innovator, in so far as the government was concerned, in all of these movements. Only after much brave and agonizing work on the part of the courts, have the executive and legislative branches of the federal government begun to move with decisiveness and vigor.

It is the principal purpose of this essay to analyze in broad strokes the role of the federal courts, and especially of the Supreme Court, in effecting change in the public policy of the Southern states since 1950, in the above mentioned areas; and to set forth some of the probable long-range results of these judicial beginnings. Until now, as suggested, the legislative and executive branches of the national government and the state governments have left largely to the Supreme Court the task of finding new solutions to the long festering sores of racial discrimination and of deprivation and debasement of voting rights.

The suggestion that courts participate in the making of public policy is still shocking to many Americans, and perhaps even to a small number of judges and lawyers. But such a role for courts, in particular for the Supreme Court, is not new; it has grown with and out of the history of the American constitutional system. It is the responsibility of the courts, though not of the courts alone, to safeguard the constitutional rights of Americans against both national and state governments. In meeting this responsibility the federal courts, especially the Supreme Court, exercise the power of "judicial review," that is the power to pass on the validity of the acts of government—national and state.

In the exercise of this power the Supreme Court becomes the final arbiter of the federal system in the settlement of conflicts between the states and the national government; it fixes the boundaries between the different branches of the national government in proper cases; and most importantly it is the guardian of individual liberty against both national and state governments. Since 1937 judicial review has been largely confined to the field of civil liberties,[1] and here primarily to state action. In the judicial settlement of controversies here as elsewhere, the Court inevitably formulates policy. This is so because the specific language of the Constitution offers little guidance. Indeed it has often been said that one of the great virtues of the American Constitution is the generality of so many of its important provisions. If the meaning of all constitutional provisions was self-evident or unmistakably clear, there would be no constitutional cases. But the meaning of such phrases as "due process of law" and "equal protection of the laws" is not clear; and in interpretating them in constitutional cases the Court must pour meaning into them. In deciding cases in such a constitutional context, judges have a wide range of discretion. It is this discretion which has given the federal courts such an important role in changing the public policy of the South since 1950.

THE FEDERAL COURTS AND DESEGREGATION OF PUBLIC EDUCATION

The "equal but separate" doctrine which has been at the heart of the discussion of the problem of the desegregation of public schools since *Brown v. Board of Education* was first employed by the Supreme Court in the transportation case of *Plessy v. Ferguson*[2] in 1896, and, through that case, came to serve as the legal basis for the practice of segregation in education. Space does not permit

[1]Geo. W. Spicer, *The Supreme Court and Fundamental Freedoms* (New York: Appleton-Century-Crofts 1959), p. 4.
[2]163 U. S. 537 (1896).

an analysis of the Plessy Case here. Suffice it to say, that it would be difficult to gainsay the conclusion of Robert J. Harris that "The opinion of the Court in *Plessy v. Ferguson* is a compound of bad logic, bad history, bad sociology, and bad constitutional law."[3]

But the Plessy doctrine was destined to stand as the rationale of compulsory racial segregation for six decades. Still until 1954, the fact of segregation was never squarely challenged before the Supreme Court as a denial of equal protection of the laws. Instead, the complaint had generally been against inequality of the separate facilties.[4]

With the Gaines Case[4a] in 1938, the Court began to take seriously the "equal" part of the formula. It accepted the "equal but separate" formula, but for the first time held racial discrimination in education unconstitutional. It held that Missouri had denied equal protection of the laws to Gaines, a Negro, by refusing his admission to the University of Missouri Law School, and offering instead to pay his tuition fees in a law school of a non-segregated state. Equal protection can be afforded only within the jurisdiction of the state.

Although this case apparently recognized the legal validity of the "equal but separate" doctrine, its significance lies in the fact that its strict interpretation of the formula marks the beginning of the end of legally enforced segregation. From now on the Court consistently enforced a much more rigid test of equality. It insisted on reviewing more critically the facts of the cases brought before it to ascertain whether equality was in truth afforded.

The big surge towards repudiation of the "equal but separate" formula came in 1950, when the Court in two vitally significant cases unanimously condemned racial segregation in the professional and graduate schools of two state universities. In the first of these cases, *Sweatt v. Painter*,[5] the Court held that the barring of a Negro applicant from the University of Texas Law School had deprived him of the equal protection of the laws, even though Texas had provided a separate law school for Negroes within the state. In effect, the Court found that a segregated law school for Negroes could not pro-

[3]For support of conclusion see his *The Quest for Equality* (Louisiana State University Press, 1960), Chap. 4.

[4]See *Cumming v. County Board*, 175 U. S. 528 (1899); *Berea College v. Kentucky*, 211 U. S. 45 (1908); *Gong Lum v. Rice*, 275 U. S. 98 (1927).

[4a]*Missouri ex rel Gaines v. Canada*, 305 U. S. 337 (1938).

[5]339 U. S. 629 (1950).

vide them equal educational opportunities. In reaching such a conclusion the Court relied heavily on "those qualities which are incapable of objective measurement but which make for greatness in a law school." Chief Justice Vinson contrasted the two law schools with respect to such matters as the reputation of the faculties, the size of the student body and libraries, the influence and prestige of the large body of alumni of the University Law School as against the single alumnus of the Negro law school, the experience of the administration, and the traditions and prestige of the University Law School in general. The Court also pointed to the practical disadvantages incident to the state's exclusion from the Negro law school of 85 per cent of the population of the state—: a group which includes most of the lawyers, judges, jurors, witnesses and other officials with whom Negro lawyers would necessarily have to deal in the practice of their profession.

The Sweatt ruling was reinforced in the case of *McLaurin v. Oklahoma State Regents*,[6] where the Court held that enforced segregation of the activities of a Negro graduate student who had been admitted to the state university under court order was a denial of equal protection in that it handicapped him in the effective pursuit of his graduate studies.

Here the Court leaned even more heavily than in Sweatt upon psychological and other intangible factors; but in both cases the Court explicitly refused either to affirm or to reexamine the doctrine of *Plessy v. Ferguson.* In effect it rejected segregation in graduate and professional institutions without repudiating or overruling the "equal but separate" doctrine. But it raised the standard of equality to such a level as to make it extremely difficult for any scheme of racial segregation in education to meet the test of constitutionality. Thus the way was paved for the historic school segregation decision of May, 1954.

THE SCHOOL SEGREGATION CASES

When the Supreme Court convened in the fall of 1952, five cases in which racial segregation of children in public schools was squarely challenged as unconstitutional awaited its consideration. These cases were twice argued with elaborate briefs and the decision of the Court was not reached until May 17, 1954. Four cases arising from

[6]339 U. S. 637 (1950).

the states of South Carolina, Virginia, Delaware and Kansas were considered in a consolidated opinion under the style of *Brown v. Board of Education of Topeka.*[7]

Chief Justice Warren, again emphasizing the intangible factors of Sweatt and McLaurin, declared for the unanimous Court that such considerations apply with added force to children in grade and high schools. To separate children of the minority group from others of similar age and qualifications solely because of their race creates a feeling of inferiority as to their status in the community, and this sense of inferiority affects the motivation of the child to learn. The Court, therefore, concluded that the doctrine of "separate but equal" has no place in the field of public education, that "separate educational facilities are inherently unequal," and that the plaintiffs here involved "have been deprived of the equal protection of the laws guaranteed by the Fourteenth Amendment."[8]

In reaching this conclusion the Court considered "public education in the light of its full development and its present place in American life throughout the Nation." It was not possible to turn the clock back to the time of the adoption of the Fourteenth Amendment or even to *Plessy v. Ferguson* in 1896.

IMPLEMENTATION OF COURT'S DECISION: CRITERIA OF IMPLEMENTATION

The Supreme Court in its implementing decision a year later declared that "Full implementation of these constitutional principles may require the solution of varied local school problems."[9] It placed "primary responsibility for elucidating, assessing and solving these problems" on local school boards and assigned to the federal district courts the task of deciding "whether the action of the school authorities constitutes good faith implementation of the governing constitutional principles." The lower courts were directed to require that the school authorities "make a prompt and reasonable start towards full compliance" with the Court's ruling, and to use such procedures as will accomplish the objective of desegregated schools "with all deliberate speed."

[7]347 U. S. 483 (1954). The fifth case (*Bolling v. Sharpe,* 347 U. S. 497), relating to the District of Columbia, was decided under the *due process* clause of the Fifth Amendment.

[8]*Ibid.,* 495.

[9]*Brown v. Board of Education,* 349 U. S. 294, 298 (1955).

In effecting a gradual transition from segregated to non-segre-gated schools the courts "may consider problems related to the physical condition of the school plant, the school transportation system, personnel, revision of school districts and attendance areas into compact units to achieve a system of determining admission to the public schools on a nonracial basis, and revision of local laws and regulations which may be necessary in solving the foregoing problems." The burden of proof that any delay is necessary rests with the school board.

Although there is every indication in these prescriptions that reasonable time should be afforded for adjustment of difficult local situations, it is clear from the language of the Court that all of these procedures must look towards full compliance with its ruling at the earliest practical date. The opinion of the Court recognizes diversity of local conditions, and does not contemplate uniform compliance as of a given date. But it demands a prompt and reasonable start towards good faith compliance, and it clearly does not sanction indefinite delay in full compliance.

METHODS OF RESISTANCE TO THE COURT'S RULING

Although the foregoing standards seemed reasonable and suited to the conditions of the day in the South, their very reasonableness in affording time to assess problems and to plan methods of adjustment to the Court's far-reaching decision seemed to inspire the political leadership of some of the affected states to launch the most callous and unconscionable campaign of frustration, evasion, circumvention, defiance and distortion of the law that twentieth century America has known. Ironically all this was accompanied by loud protestations of "reliance on the Constitution as the fundamental law of the land." Space will not permit consideration here of all the complex developments of the past eight years in connection with the slow progress of, and resistance to, the desegregation movement. The most that we can do is to mention the principal devices of resistance employed and to comment briefly on one or two that continue to pose problems.

The difficulties of the district courts in deciding the validity of school board plans with all of the normal delays in legal procedure such as dilatory pleas, motions and objections, would have been enough to cause years of delay in the implementation of the Court's mandate. But in addition the courts were faced with an ever mounting volume of state legislative obstructions intended to prevent, if possible and if not, to delay, desegregation of the public schools. These legislative roadblocks included: resolutions concerning the long-discredited doctrine of interposition, statues relating to pupil placement and transfer, school closing laws, cutoff of appropriations to segregated schools, repeal of compulsory school attendance laws, tuition grants to "private" schools, and laws providing for segregation by choice.[10] In addition there have been laws and other legislative action designed to harass those who promote or advocate desegregation. These include compulsory production of NAACP membership lists before legislative investigating committees, and its punishment for the crime of barratry (i.e. the soliciting, inciting or fomenting of litigation), and statutes providing for the removal of teachers who belong to organizations which, or who personally, advocate the desegregation of the races.[11] Although most of these devices have been invalidated by the Court, some have continued to block the progress of desegregation and some have posed a real threat to public education.

Perhaps the school closing laws and the tuition grants to so-called private schools posed the most serious threat to public education. Virginia's school closing laws[12] were held unconstitutional by a three-judge federal district court in January 1959. The court declared that "no one public school or grade in Virginia may be closed to avoid the effect of the law of the land as interpreted by the Supreme Court, while the state permits other public schools or grades to remain open at the expense of the taxpayers."[13]

Likewise tuition grants to private schools in Prince Edward County, Virginia, where public schools had been abandoned, were held unconstitutional. The federal district court held that it was a denial of equal protection for the county to provide tuition grants to students in private schools as long as its public schools are closed.[14]

Even where public schools have been reopened on a non-segregated basis—as in Charlottesville, Norfolk and Front Royal, Virginia

[10]See 2 *Race Rel. L. Rep.* 889-891.
[11]*Ibid.,* 892-894.
[12]*Va. Acts of Assembly,* Ex. Sess., Ch. 68, p. 69.
[13]*James v. Almond,* 170 F. Supp. 331, appeal dismissed 359 U. S. 1006 (1959).
[14]See Book 2, U. S. Comm. on Civil Rights (1961), p. 215; *Allen v. Prince Edward School Board,* Civ. No. 1333, E. D. Va., 1960.

—the operation of segregated private schools with substantial support from state or local tuition grants would seem to rest on extremely shaky constitutional ground.

In the Little Rock Case, of 1958, the Supreme Court said that its Brown decision "forbids states to use their governmental powers to bar children on racial grounds from attending schools where there is state participation through any arrangement, management, funds, or property."[15]

State participation through "management" rendered segregation unconstitutional in the Girard College Case.[16] Here a college established and financed by a private trust was subject to the equal protection clause of the Fourteenth Amendment because of its administration by an agency of the City of Philadelphia. Surely state participation through substantial financial support renders segregation equally vulnerable.

Extension of the Brown Doctrine to Other Matters: It is well known that since 1954, the federal courts have been largely preoccupied with public school desegregation. But the Supreme Court did not confine this epochal change in judicial policy to racial discrimination in public education. It has moved steadily, if slowly, against other forms of racial discrimination. The implications of the Brown doctrine were later applied in a series of *per curiam* opinions, in which the Court held segregation on intrastate buses, on public golf courses, public beaches, parks and playgrounds to be a denial of equal protection. In all of these cases the Court simply cited *Brown v. Board.*[17] Without hearing argument the Court, in October 1962, affirmed a lower court decision invalidating discrimination in the terminal facilities of intra-state commerce. Louisiana's requirement that common carriers maintain and mark separate passenger-terminal facilities for whites and Negroes was held enjoinable by the United States.[18]

Segregation in interstate commerce had been largely eliminated before *Brown v. Board,* but this occurred under the Commerce Clause of the Constitution and the Interstate Commerce Act.[19] In

[15]*Cooper v. Aaron,* 358 U. S. 1, 4 (1958).

[16]*Pennsylvania v. Board of Directors of City Trust,* 353 U. S. 230 (1957).

[17]*Owen et al. v. Browder et al.,* 352 U. S. 903 (1956) ; *Baltimore v. Dawson,* 350 U. S. 877 (1955) ; *Holmes v. City of Atlanta,* 350 U. S. 879 (1955).

[18]*U. S. Law Week.* 1049, Oct. 9, 1962.

[19]See *Morgan v. Virginia,* 328 U. S. 373 (1946) ; *Henderson v. United States,* 339 U. S. 816 (1950).

this connection it is interesting to note that the "separate but equal" formula first applied by the Supreme Court in a transportation case, was never again applied in a transportation case. Equally interesting, if odd, is the fact that for a decade following the Morgan Case in 1946, the Commerce Clause served as a more effective weapon against racial segregation than the equal protection clause which was especially designed for that purpose.

Slow Progress of Desegregation: Although the basic law of desegregation as worked out by the federal courts in a long series of cases now seems clearly and firmly established, the actual effectuation of desegregation, thanks to the foregoing devices of evasion and delay, has proceeded slowly, spottily and painfully throughout most of the South.[19a] Only in the border states was there prompt and general desegregation following 1954. At the end of the 1962-63 session no more than 8% of the Negro school population was attending desegregated schools in the seventeen states which had segregation in 1954. In the eleven states of the former Confederacy the figure was no more than one half of 1%.

The success of the resistance tactics can be attributed in part to the nature of the implementation procedures laid down by the Supreme Court for the guidance of the lower courts in effecting, where local conditions warranted, a gradual transition from segregated to non-segregated schools. The use of equity principles in the application of the administrative factors prescribed by the Supreme Court enabled some district courts, under severe pressure from the forces of resistance, to apply these factors in such manner as to conform to the mores and prejudices of the community. Thus, instead of uniformity eight years of litigation has produced much diversity among lower court decisions as to what does, and what does not, satisfy constitutional requirements. These conflicting and confused decisions and the uncertainty which they create invite further litigation.

This situation has been abetted by the almost complete withdrawal of the Supreme Court from the battle of implementation until the 1960's. True the Court in the Little Rock Case,[20] of 1958, sought to clarify and amplify both the constitutional principle of state action announced in the school segregation cases and its instructions concerning implementation. But neither the sharper articulation of the principle of state action nor the clarification of the obli-

---

[19a]See 1961 *Report of U. S. Commission on Civil Rights,* Book 2, Ch. 4.
[20]*Cooper v. Aaron,* 358 U. S. 1, 7 (1958).

gations of implementation by the Court was sufficient greatly to reduce conflict and delay in the march towards the goal of eliminating racial segregation. The words of the Court were still not precise enough to shackle the "ingenious" and "ingenuous" forces of resistance. However, the Supreme Court, in the early 1960's made further advances in both of these areas which may have important consequences. In this development the chief tool of the Court has been an expanding interpretation and application of the concept of state action under the equal-protection clause. To these developments we now turn.

RACIAL DISCRIMINATION AND PRIVATELY OWNED PUBLIC FACILITIES: STATE ACTION

In the Civil Rights Cases[21] of 1883, the Supreme Court ruled that racial discrimination by theatres, inns, and private common carriers was not covered by the equal protection clause of the Fourteenth Amendment. It applied only to discrimination by the state, not to private invasion of individual rights. This sharp distinction between public and private action is by no means so clear in the complexities of the 1960's.

Since 1961, the Supreme Court has been exploring a new area of segregation involving a new application of the concept of state action. The central problem of the Court in these state action cases has been the determination of the nature and degree of governmental involvement necessary to justify the attribution of discriminatory action of private parties to the state.

In 1961, the Supreme Court held that a privately operated restaurant leased from a city could not constitutionally refuse service to Negroes. The Court concluded that the reciprocal advantages of the leasing agreement were sufficient to achieve "that degree of state participation and involvement in discriminatory action which it was the design of the Fourteenth Amendment to condemn."[22]

On May 20, 1963, the Court advanced much farther along the line of an expanding concept of state action. This step was taken in five cases arising from the states of North and South Carolina, Alabama and Louisiana, which involved "sit-in" demonstrations against segregation at lunch counters in privately owned stores in

[21]109 U. S. 3 (1883).
[22]*Burton v. Wilmington Parking Authority,* 365 U. S. 715, 724 (1961).

five cities. It was held in all five cases[23] that since the cities concerned had made *racial* segregation a public policy either by ordinance or by official declaration of their agents, they had become parties to such segregation in violation of the equal protection clause of the Fourteenth Amendment.

The essence of the Court's reasoning is set forth in the Peterson (Greenville, S. C.) and Lombard (New Orleans) Cases. In the former case ten Negro boys and girls were convicted under South Carolina's trespass law for refusing to leave a Kress store lunch counter in Greenville after the manager had announced that the counter was closed. It is important to note that the Negro "sit-ins" were not prosecuted under Greenville's segregation ordinance. It was the use of the trespass law to enforce the policy of segregation as declared by the ordinance that involved the state in racial discrimination in violation of equal protection. The convictions under the trespass law "had the effect . . . of enforcing the ordinance passed by the City of Gainesville, the agency of the state."

The most difficult of the cases was that of *Lombard v. Louisiana,*[24] for New Orleans had no segregation ordinance. When the sit-in demonstrations began, however, the Superintendent of Police and the Mayor severely criticized them and the Mayor issued a statement that the demonstrations would not be permitted.

Those official statements, said Chief Justice Warren, were equivalent to a declaration that the city as such "would not permit Negroes to seek desegregated service in restaurants. Consequently, the city must be treated exactly as if it had an ordinance prohibiting such conduct." So here, as in *Peterson,* the Chief Justice concluded, the convictions are linked to the command of the state for segregated service at the restaurant and cannot stand.

The Chief Justice freely conceded that under the Court's prior decisions "private conduct abridging individual rights does no violence to the Equal Protection Clause unless to some significant extent the state in any of its manifestations has been found to have become involved in it."[25] Does this mean that a restaurant owner in a city without a segregation ordinance or other official declaration

---

[23]*Peterson v. City of Greenville,* 83 S. Ct. 1119 (1963); *Lombard v. State of Louisiana,* Id. 1122; *Shuttlesworth v. City of Birmingham,* Id. 1130; *Gober v. City of Birmingham,* Id. 1130; *Avent v. North Carolina,* Id. 1137.

[24]*Lombard v. Louisiana,* 83 S. Ct. 1122 (1963).

[25]*Peterson v. City of Greenville, op. cit.,* 1134 quoting J. Clark in *Burton v. Wilmington,* 365 U. S. 715, 722.

of such a policy is free to refuse service to Negroes? If so, the Court's decision leads to anomalous results.

This difficult question the Court postponed until its 1963-64 Term. The cases scheduled for this term of the Court are more difficult in that they involve situations where there are no segregation laws and where the state and local officials are presumably neutral. So that here refusal of a restaurant or a store manager to serve Negroes results from the free expression of his own will. Would it be unconstitutional, as the demonstrators argue, for a government to use its power of arrest to enforce a policy of private discrimination by a restaurant or a store that solicits public patronage? How *public* does a privately operated commercial enterprise have to be before its discriminatory action becomes state action?

Besides upholding segregation in this situation, two conceivable courses seem open to the Court: one, it could apply the doctrine of the restrictive covenant cases[26] in which state enforcement of private agreements not to sell or lease property to members of the Negro race was held to be state action in violation of the Fourteenth Amendment. This reasoning of the Court, however, has not generally been followed, as it was not in the cases of May 20, 1963. The question in the application of this doctrine to the cases now pending would be whether police enforcement of a person's undirected private choice is sufficient to make his action state action. To hold that it is would seem to be a logical extension of the doctrine of the restrictive covenant cases, but such a holding might involve serious hazards to other rights as, for example, the right of private persons to police protection from trespass and other intrusions.

A second possible course open to the Court would be to follow the dissenting opinion of Justice Harlan in the Civil Rights Cases of 1883, in which he took the position that discrimination by railroads, inns and theatres is state action. Certainly it may be argued now that a store owner who solicits the patronage of the public generally has a much smaller claim to privacy than the private home or club.

The great significance of the reasoning of the Court in the sit-in cases is that the ban on racial discrimination which in the past has generally been held to cover only governmental action has now been extended to privately owned facilities in the circumstances indicated.

[26]*Shelley v. Kraemer,* 334 U. S. 1 (1948); *Barrows v. Jackson,* 346 U. S. 249 (1953).

It may not be assumed that the big stride in this direction will be followed by retreat in the cases still pending before the Court.

JUDICIAL SHARPENING OF PRINCIPLES OF IMPLEMENTATION

Judicial advancement in the implementation of the constitutional principles of racial desegregation enunciated in the second Brown decision is perhaps as significant as the previously considered extension of the doctrine of state action. On May 27, 1963, the Court, with Justice Goldberg as spokesman, unanimously refused to countenance further delay in the desegregation of the public parks and other recreational facilities of the City of Memphis—a delay which the lower court had sanctioned on the basis of the second Brown decision. This in itself was no occasion for surprise. The significance of the case lies in the Court's illumination of the precepts of the second Brown decision and its insistence on prompt compliance with the constitutional principles enunciated in the first Brown Case. The Court has shown a new sense of urgency in the vindication of the constitutional right against racial segregation by the State. After pointing out that the desegregation of parks and other recreation facilities does not present the same kinds of difficulties inherent in the elimination of racial segregation in schools, the Court declared that even the delay permitted by the second Brown decision was an exceptional "adaptation of the usual principle that any deprivation of constitutional rights calls for prompt rectification." The Court went on to emphasize that "The basic guarantees of our constitution are warrants for the here and now, unless there is an overwhelmingly compelling reason, they are to be promptly fulfilled."[27] Thus the "narrowly drawn" Brown decision "is not to be unnecessarily expanded in application."

Moreover, the Court in what may turn out to be a highly significant dictum said: "Given the extended time which has elapsed, it is far from clear that the mandate of the second Brown decision requiring that desegregation proceed with all deliberate speed would today be fully satisfied by types of plans or programs for desegregation of public school facilities which eight years ago might have been deemed sufficient." If, then, in 1955, the public interest in certain areas and in certain circumstances justified an exception to the traditional principle of prompt and complete vindication of personal con-

[27]*Watson v. City of Memphis*, 373 U. S. (1963).

stitutional rights, the time for such exception is now past. At least delay in the future will require the demonstration of "overwhelmingly compelling" reasons.

The Court's determination to speed up the pace of desegregation found further expression just one week after the Memphis Case in connection with its rejection of two public school transfer plans in Knoxville and Davidson County, Tennessee. The Court thought they had the effect of perpetuating segregation. Justice Clark for the unanimous Court, pointed out that the time formulas of "good faith compliance at the earliest practicable date" and "all deliberate speed" were designed to meet the local difficulties of the period of transition. Now, after eight years, said the Justice, "the context in which we must interpret and apply this language to plans for desegregation has been significantly altered."[28]

THE FEDERAL COURTS AND POLITICAL FREEDOM IN THE SOUTH

A. VOTING RIGHTS

For some two decades after the Fifteenth Amendment declared that "The right of citizens of the United States to vote shall not be denied or abridged by the United States or by any state on account of race, color or previous condition of servitude," the members of the Negro race were effectively disfranchised by violence, threats of violence, intimidation and the like. Later resort was had to more formal methods which, it was thought, could be brought technically within the limitations of the Constitution. Among these devices were so-called literacy tests, grandfather clauses, poll taxes and the "white primary." The principal purpose of all these measures was, of course, the elimination of Negro suffrage as a factor in elections.[29]

By all odds the most effective device for the elimination of Negro suffrage has been the white primary. But once the Supreme Court in the Classic Case[30] held that it was the right of a qualified citizen of the United States to vote in a congressional primary and to have his vote counted as cast, the white primary was doomed in states as well as in congressional contests. *Grovey v. Townsend*[31]

[28]*Goss v. Board of Education,* 83 S. Ct. 1405 (1963).

[29]For a discussion of these issues, see Geo. W. Spicer, "The Supreme Court and Racial Discrimination," *Vanderbilt Law Rev.* (June 1958).

[30]*United States v. Classic,* 313 U. S. 299 (1941).

[31]295 U. S. 45 (1935).

had in 1935, upheld the exclusion of a Negro voter from the Democratic primary in Texas under a resolution of the state Democratic Convention on the ground that the exclusionary action was not state action, but that of a private organization.

Then, in 1944, a significant landmark in the political history of the South was established by the decision of the Court in *Smith v. Allwright*.[32] By this decision the white primary was outlawed in state as well as national electoral contests and *Grovey v. Townsend* was overruled. This case, along with those which followed it for a decade wrought a mild revolution in the electoral freedom of the South.[33] Bold and ingenious devices of circumvention contrived by South Carolina and Alabama were struck down by the federal courts.[34]

The controlling issue in all of those cases was whether the action taken against the Negro was state action under the Fourteenth or Fifteenth Amendment. In the Allwright Case the Supreme Court declared that the constitutional right to be free from racial discrimination in voting cannot be nullified indirectly by a state through casting its electoral process in a form permitting a private organization to practice racial discrimination in an election. In later cases the principle was established that no election machinery can be sustained if its purpose or effect is to deny to the Negro, because of his race, an effective voice in the selection of his public officials or in the governmental affairs of his community.[35] A state, then, cannot escape the responsibility for unconstitutional discrimination by taking any action which permits a private organization to accomplish the same purpose. The state may not become actively identified with nor materially aid a private scheme of racial discrimination.

Debasement of the Vote: An effective variant on the more widespread methods of destroying equality of suffrage in the South has been the county unit system of Georgia, Maryland and Mississippi. This device does not deprive certain classes of citizens of the suffrage outright, but it has the effect of so diluting their votes as to render them relatively ineffective. Litigation on this scheme has been con-

[32] 321 U. S. 649 (1944).

[33] See O. D. Weeks, "The White Primary: 1944-1948," *The Amer. Polit. Sci. Rev.*, Vol. 42, No. 3, pp. 500-511; also Donald A. Strong, "The Rise of Negro Voting in Texas," *ibid.*, pp. 510-512.

[34] *Rice v. Elmore*, 165 F. 2d. 387 (1947); *Davis v. Schnell*, 81 F. Supp. 872 (1949).

[35] *Ibid.*, also *Terry v. Adams*, 345 U. S. 461 (1953).

fined largely to the Georgia system. In that state nomination of candidates for statewide offices and of candidates for the Congress was effected by a county unit vote rather than by popular vote until 1962.

Under this scheme each county was assigned twice as many unit votes as it had representatives in the lower house of the state legislature. The total unit vote of a county went to the candidate receiving a plurality of the popular vote of that county; and to win in the primary a candidate must have had a majority of the unit votes of the state. Under this device a resident of the least populous county had an influence in the nomination of candidates equivalent to 99 residents of the most populous county.

The victims of this system of electoral debasement met only defeat in the federal courts[86] until the spring of 1962 when they gained a partial victory in the federal district court,[37] which was made complete by the Supreme Court on March 18, 1963, in *Gray v. Sanders*.[38] Here the Court struck down a revised form of the Georgia County unit system. The revision involved the bracketing of counties into population groups and reduced substantially the disparities of the earlier system.

The district court had held that the amended act had some of the vices of the prior act and therefore denied equal protection to the plaintiffs. It did not, however, hold invalid the unit system as such. It still allowed a unit system to be used in weighting the votes if the system showed no greater disparity against a county than exists against any state in the most recent electoral college allocation, or if the disparity is not in excess of that which exists under the equal proportions formula for representation of the several states in the Congress.[39] Significantly the Supreme Court flatly rejected these analogies. "We think," said the Court, "the analogies to the electoral college, to districting and redistricting, . . . are inapposite." The Court insisted that this was only a voting case. Although Georgia gives every qualified voter one vote in a statewide election, she employs in counting those votes a unit system, which weights the rural vote more heavily than the urban vote.[40] The only weighting of votes permitted by the Constitution, the Court pointed out, is that

[86]See, for example, *South v. Peters,* 339 U. S. 276 (1950).
[37]*Sanders v. Gray,* 203 F. Supp. 158 (1962).
[38]372 Ct. S. 368 (1963).
[39]203 F. Supp. 170.
[40]*Gray v. Sanders, op. cit.,* 378.

involved in the allocation of two senators to each state and the use of the electoral college in the choice of the president. In sum, the Court concludes that "once the geographical unit for which a representative is to be chosen is designated, all who participate in the election are to have an equal vote—whatever their race . . . , and wherever their home may be in that geographical unit."[41] Nothing less is required by the equal protection clause of the Fourteenth Amendment.

The Court is careful not to tip its hand on the unsettled issues growing out of *Baker v. Carr* and now pending before the Court. This case, the Court emphasized, does not involve those issues, nor does it involve the related problem of *Gomillion v. Lightfoot*, where gerrymandering was employed to exclude a minority group from voting in municipal elections. Despite the Court's narrow confinement of its holding, it is difficult to see why the reasoning of the Gray Case would not apply to the debasement of urban votes in legislative mal-apportionment. The next term may reveal the Court's answer to this question.

Undoubtedly the boldest use of the gerrymander to debase the votes of the Negroes in the South was involved in an act of the Alabama legislature passed in 1957, altering the shape of the town of Tuskegee from a square to a twenty-eight-sided figure, thereby excluding from the city all but four or five Negro voters but leaving all white residents undisturbed. The result of the act, of course, was to prevent the excluded Negroes from voting in municipal elections.

The Supreme Court in *Gomillion v. Lightfoot*[42] held this act to be a violation of the Fifteenth Amendment, in that the excluded Negroes would be deprived of their right to vote. The opinion by Mr. Justice Frankfurter was neatly contrived to avoid opening up the broad problem of apportionment then pending before the Court in *Baker v. Carr*,[43] which rested upon the equal protection clause of the Fourteenth Amendment.

He avoided the broader language of this clause which, of course, has not been limited, in its application, to racial discrimination. This coupled with Justice Frankfurter's attempt to distinguish Gomillion from *Colegrove v. Green*[44] (where the Court refused to take jurisdic-

[41]*Ibid.*, 379.
[42]364 U. S. 339 (1960).
[43]369 U. S. 186.
[44]328 U. S. 549 (1946).

tion in an apportionment case because it involved a "political question") seems to give greater constitutional protection against debasement of the value of a vote because of race than because of urban residence.

The crucial point in the distinction of Gomillion and Colegrove was the argument that in no case involving the dilution of the value of the vote had the Court sanctioned unequivocal withdrawal of the vote solely from colored citizens. Of course, there was no unequivocal withdrawal of the vote from colored citizens in Gomillion. There was a clear racial discrimination against plaintiffs' right to cast an effective ballot, but they were free to vote in the political unit to which they were assigned. If then the debasement of the value of the electoral franchise can be challenged on the ground of racial discrimination, can it also be challenged on the ground of residential discrimination?

This question was dealt with by the Supreme Court in a case which is of nation-wide scope and influence but which could have an extraordinary impact on the South. Hence it is appropriate to consider here the case of *Baker v. Carr*.[45] Not since the segregation cases of 1954, has a case created so great legal and political maneuvering. But unlike the segregation cases the response here has in general been toward compliance rather than toward defiance.

The plaintiffs in this case claimed that the failure of the Tennessee legislature to reapportion its members in accordance with changes in population over the past sixty years as required by the state constitution had debased the value of their votes in violation of the equal protection clause of the Fourteenth Amendment. A three-judge district court dismissed this claim on the grounds that the court lacked jurisdiction in such a "political question," and that the complaint failed to state a claim upon which relief could be granted. The Supreme Court held that the dismissal was error.

Although the six opinions in the case cover a total of 165 pages, what the Court actually decided can be stated very briefly, as indeed it was by Justice Stewart in a concurring opinion. The Court simply held: (1) that the federal courts do have jurisdiction in malapportionment cases, (2) that the complaint presented a justiciable controversy, that is, it was capable of adjudication; and (3) that the appellants had standing to bring the suit. It also apparently

[45]369 U. S. 186 (1962).

decided that if the allegations of the appellants were sustained, they had been denied equal protection of the laws.

But the Supreme Court did not reach the merits of the case and the district court to which the case was remanded for trial on the merits of the allegations made was given no guide lines for the disposition of the case. It is not surprising then that much conflict and confusion characterize the torrent of decisions that have gushed from state and lower federal courts since March, 1962.

On June 10, 1963, the Court agreed to hear, on appeal, eight apportionment cases—six involving state legislative apportionment and two involving congressional apportionment. It is greatly to be hoped that the Court will make the consideration of these cases the occasion for the statement of a clearly reasoned doctrine that can serve as a dependable guide to lower courts.

In considering the possible impact of *Baker v. Carr* on the South, one can at this stage only speculate. Everything depends on what sort of standard the Supreme Court adopts to determine what sort of apportionment is, and is not a denial of equal protection of the laws to adversely affected voters. If the Court should approve the federal analogy argument which some state and federal district courts have, or if it should adopt—which seems unlikely—Justice Harlan's standard of rationality which justified even the Tennessee mal-apportionment, present inequities might even increase.

If, on the other hand, the Court should approve the standard applied by the federal district court in the Virginia Case of *Mann v. Davis*,[46] there could be a beginning of far-reaching progressive changes in the government and party politics of the Southern states.

In this case the district court laid down the rule that if inequality of representation on the basis of population is proved by plaintiffs, then the burden of proof shifts to defendants to show a rational basis for deviation from the primary standard of equality. In the language of the court, "Exactitude in population is not demanded by the Equal Protection clause. But there must be a fair approach to equality unless it be shown that other acceptable factors may make up for the differences in the numbers of people."

If the Supreme Court should require this standard, one result might well be, as Paul David has cogently suggested,[47] the develop-

[46]Civil Action No. 2604, Nov. 28, 1962.
[47]"One Man, One Vote?" Typescript copy of paper presented at a Seminar-Conf. of the Public Affairs Program, Univ. of Detroit (March 12, 1963), pp. 12-15.

ment of an effective two-party system in the South. The new Republicans in this region are concentrated in the cities and suburban area, whose voting power would be greatly increased by equitable apportionment on a population basis.

Virginius Dabney, in a recent Harper's article has suggested that such an increase in urban voting power might even "jeopardize the future of the Byrd machine" in Virginia.[48]

CONCLUSION

EFFECTIVENESS AND APPROPRIATENESS OF THE JUDICIARY AS AN INSTRUMENT OF POLITICAL CHANGE

How effective has the federal judiciary been as an instrument of change in the public policy of the South since 1950? Certainly it cannot be said that the millennium has arrived for Negro rights. The events of the summer of 1963, when mounting racial tension exploded into violence, bloodshed and murder, forcefully demonstrate the contrary. School segregation on a racial basis has not been eliminated. In the Deep South there is still little more than token desegregation nearly nine years after the Second Brown Case. But it was not expected, nor even desired, by most responsible leaders that widespread desegregation in such a sensitive and explosive area of human relations would come about overnight. True, the time allowed for adjustment has been misinterpreted and extended beyond all reason in many areas by white leaders determined to do the least possible rather than the most possible in the circumstances.

But progress has been made. The pattern of racial segregation in education has been broken in every state and desegregation is proceeding at a considerably accelerated pace in 1964. Less than a decade ago school segregation was complete in seventeen states and the District of Columbia. In some other fields the degree of desegregation ranges from substantial to complete elimination. Segregation in public transportation is virtually non-existent; in public recreational facilities it is rapidly vanishing under court orders or "voluntarily"; and even in privately owned public facilities it is crumbling under recent court decisions or "voluntarily" under economic pressure.

[48]"What the GOP Is Doing in the South," *Harper's Magazine*, May 1963, p. 91.

Although the right of the Negro to be free from racial discrimination in voting has been firmly established for more than a decade, few are permitted to vote in some states of the Deep South. But here, too, much progress has been made in the South as a whole. A generation ago few Negroes were able to vote in any of these states.[49] There is little reason to believe that much of this would have happened without the patient intervention of the federal judiciary.

There are sincere and responsible people who feel that regardless of the authority and effectiveness of the courts in bringing about social and political change, it is not appropriate that courts should enter these realms. These are matters "not meet for judicial determination." Certainly few will deny that it would have been more appropriate as well as more effective if the Southern states had taken the initiative and had exerted vigorous leadership in behalf of the constitutional rights of their citizens to be free from racial discrimination in public education, in transportation and in the exercise of the voting franchise. But they did not; instead they invoked the dogma of states' rights against the efforts of the national government to protect the civil and political rights of their citizens. Too often they have made a fetish of "states' rights" to deny rights to people.

Even in the face of this prostitution of constitutional theory, the federal courts have been slow to act. Take the two most important cases of the 20th century, *Brown v. Board of Education and Baker v. Carr.* In each of these cases the Court acted only as a last resort after repeated failure of other branches of the national government, as well as of the states, to act. In neither case was there a practical remedy. True, Congress has authority to enforce the equal protection guarantee of the Fourteenth Amendment, but Southern Congressmen, especially Southern Senators, have until recently been able to block such action.

If in 1946, when the Supreme Court refused to take jurisdiction in the Colegrove Apportionment Case, there was hope that rurally dominated state legislatures could be persuaded to respond to reason and justice with respect to legislative apportionment, that hope had vanished by 1962.

Thus in default of responsibility on the part of the states and the political branches of the national government, the federal judici-

[49]See generally, Voting: United States Commission on Civil Rights, Book I, 1961.

ary has intervened in proper cases to bring about potentially far-reaching social and political changes in the South. In this the Supreme Court was doubtless responding, as Anthony Lewis of the New York Times has pointed out, to a great moral imperative—"a demand of the national conscience" which "had found no way to express itself except through the Supreme Court."[50]

A LOOK AT THE FUTURE

The preceding pages have shown how federal judicial intervention launched two related "revolutions" in the South in mid-twentieth century. The first was the establishment of the constitutional right of the Negro to be free from discrimination because of race in public education, in transportation, in public recreational facilities; and from publicly influenced racial discrimination in privately owned public facilities. The second was the establishment of the right to be free from discrimination in the effective exercise of the right to vote either because of race or because of urban residence.

The ultimate destination of these "revolutions" will, of course, be determined by future events. The latter revolution, it will be recalled, was wrought by the white primary cases of the forties and early fifties, the 1963 county-unit case of *Gray* v. *Sanders,* and the historic apportionment case of *Baker* v. *Carr.* Although the full impact of the Baker case is still to be determined, it seems justifiable to speculate on the results if the Court follows through in the apportionment cases now pending. If Baker was more than an "exercise in futility," it seems reasonable to expect not only a "revolution" in the government and politics of southern states, but from this in turn a strong impact on national politics. The collapse of racial barriers in education and in the exercise of the franchise will greatly strengthen the position and influence of the Negro in the public life of the southern states.

Moreover, the achievement of approximate equality of voting power by the residents of urban areas will, as previously indicated, tend to strengthen the already growing Republican party in the South. This in turn will increase the strength and importance of the Negro vote, for the two parties would find themselves in the position of having to compete for the Negro vote and perhaps for the labor

[50]"Historic Change in the Supreme Court," *New York Times Magazine,* June 17, 1962, p. 38.

vote which tends to be concentrated in the cities. With two well-balanced and genuinely competitive parties operating in the South, the extremely conservative committee chairmen from the safe states and congressional districts of the area could be dislodged from their hitherto impregnable positions of disproportionate strength in both houses of Congress.

It would seem clear that competition between the two parties for the moderate or liberal vote would tend to have a liberalizing influence in Congress as well as in the Southern states. At any rate, if present trends continue, the South is not far from the day when discrimination, either because of race or because of urban residence, shall find no place in the public policy of any state. For these far-reaching and dramatic changes the federal judiciary has blazed the trail.[51]

[51]See 21 *Congressional Quarterly Weekly Report* (C Q W R) 997-999, 1030-1034 (June 21, 1963).

STATE LEGISLATURES IN SOUTHERN POLITICS

MALCOLM E. JEWELL
University of Kentucky

I N A SYMPOSIUM on southern politics of the last decade appearing
in the *Journal of Politics* in 1948, H. C. Nixon described the
typical southern legislature as "chiefly a body of Democratic, small-
town or rural white men, a majority of whom represent a minority of
the white population of the state, not to mention the restricted suffrage by which the members were chosen in a party primary."[1] More
than fifteen years later his description is still accurate: the legislature represents primarily rural, white Democrats. Despite variations
from state to state, the legislative pattern has been one of strong
conservative control, minimizing conflict within the legislature or
between the legislature and governor. Below the surface the forces
of change are already apparent, however. The Supreme Court decision in *Baker* v. *Carr* and the organizational effort of both Republicans and Negroes suggest that by 1970 there will be major changes
in the power structure of most southern legislatures, changes that
will make them more representative and that will increase the degree
of competition in legislative elections and the degree of conflict in
legislative sessions. In some legislatures the beginnings of change
are already apparent.

REAPPORTIONMENT AND URBAN REPRESENTATION

In March of 1962, when the *Baker* v. *Carr* decision was announced, not a single southern state had reapportioned both houses
fully on the basis of the 1960 census, but there was wide variation
among the states in the degree of malapportionment. In Arkansas,
Kentucky, and Virginia there were no major constitutional obstacles
to apportionment by population, the apportionments were no more
than ten or twenty years out of date, the smallest percentage of the
population that could elect a legislative majority averaged almost 40
percent, and the vote in rural counties (under 25,000 population)
was worth only about twice as much as the vote in the largest coun-

[1]H. C. Nixon, "The Southern Legislature and Legislation," *Journal of Politics*, X (1948), 412.

ties. In five other states the problem was somewhat more serious: Louisiana, Mississippi, North Carolina, South Carolina, and Texas had substantial constitutional obstacles to apportionment by population in one or both houses. The Mississippi apportionment was largely determined by the specific allotment of seats in the 1890 constitution. Each South Carolina county had a single state senator. Constitutional provisions discriminated against the larger counties in both houses in Texas and the lower houses in North Carolina and Louisiana. The smallest proportion of the population that could elect a legislative majority averaged about one-third, and the vote in rural counties was worth from two to five times as much as in the largest counties. (In South Carolina the apportionment was much better than this in the House and much worse in the Senate.)

In five states there were vast distortions in apportionment. These were caused by constitutional provisions in Florida and Georgia and in the Oklahoma House and by the failure to reapportion for half a century in Alabama, Tennessee, and in the Oklahoma Senate. A majority in the legislatures could be elected by about one-fourth the population, and in Florida by one-eighth. The value of the vote in rural counties ranged from three to fifteen times as much as in the largest counties in four states, while in Florida the ratio was thirty-to-one. In several of these states the apportionment also disadvantaged one region of the state; in Tennessee it discriminated against Republican areas. In Florida, where the apportionment was most distorted, it virtually guaranteed conflict between the legislature and a governor elected by urban as well as rural votes. In Georgia, on the other hand, the county unit system guaranteed that the governor, as well as the legislature, would be responsive primarily to rural voters.

The trend of population to metropolitan areas in the fifties and the pattern of inadequate or nonexistent reapportionment following the 1960 census meant that in the decade prior to *Baker* v. *Carr* the degree of malapportionment increased throughout the South. A comparison between 1955 figures (compiled by Dauer and Kelsay) and 1961 figures shows that the minimum percentage of the population needed to elect a majority dropped in every southern legislative body except two (the Louisiana House and Mississippi Senate). The median drop was 3 percent. The sharpest drops were in some of the most urban states: Virginia, Texas, Florida, and Tennessee.[2]

[2]Manning J. Dauer and Robert G. Kelsay, "Unrepresentative States," *National Municipal Review*, XLIV (1955), pp. 571-575. National Municipal

In the first sixteen months after the *Baker* v. *Carr* decision eight southern legislatures enacted new apportionment laws covering one or both houses. In most cases they acted after prodding by state or federal courts. In Florida and Mississippi the voters (primarily urban voters) rejected the first apportionment plans enacted as constitutional amendments, and the legislators were forced to try again. The apportionment laws passed in Tennessee, Virginia, Alabama, and Oklahoma were rejected by the courts. The Tennessee legislature made a second effort to meet the judicial requirements; the Virginia case was appealed to the Supreme Court; the court in Alabama imposed an apportionment plan based on some parts of the legislative plan; and the court in Oklahoma rejected a legislative compromise and imposed its own plan based strictly on population standards. The Georgia legislature reapportioned only one house, meeting the requirements of the federal court. The Kentucky legislature reapportioned both houses effectively enough to meet any likely judicial tests. Legislative and judicial action was prompt enough so that new apportionments formed the basis for the 1962 elections in Tennessee, Alabama, and Georgia, special elections in Florida early in 1963, and regular elections in Kentucky in 1963.

In five states the *Baker* v. *Carr* decision had no direct impact during the first sixteen months. In Texas, North Carolina, South Carolina, Louisiana, and Arkansas one or both houses had been reapportioned by the legislature (or in Arkansas by a state court prior to *Baker* v. *Carr*) following the 1960 census, although in all of these states constitutional provisions prevented the apportionments from being based fully on population. In most of these states the issue of reapportionment was attracting increased attention and was the subject of legislative debate if not action, in the months following *Baker* v. *Carr*.[2a]

It is too early to judge how full the tides of reapportionment will be in southern states. It is already evident that southern legislatures will go no further than is required by the courts. The Supreme Court will have to settle the contradictions which have already begun

League, *Compendium on Legislative Apportionment* (New York, 2nd ed., 1962), pp. iii, iv. The figures on the value of the vote are from: Paul T. David and Ralph Eisenberg, *Devaluation of the Urban and Suburban Vote* (Charlottesville: Bureau of Public Administration, University of Virginia, 1961).

[2a] A limited reapportionment of the Louisiana House withstood judicial challenge and took effect in the December primary. The North Carolina Senate was reapportioned in October.

to emerge from lower federal and state court decisions. Judicial standards of population equality have varied considerably in cases arising in southern states. A federal court required that the two largest counties in Oklahoma, with one-third of the population, have 34 percent of the Senate seats and 31 percent of the House seats. The federal court in Virginia invalidated an apportionment in which the maximum disparity was 2½ to 1 in the Senate and 4 to 1 in the House. Similarly, the federal court in Tennessee said that the reapportionment there fell short of constitutional standards when it gave the four metropolitan counties, with 43 percent of the adult population, just under one-third of the seats in each house. On the other hand, a federal court unanimously approved an apportionment in Florida (later rejected by the voters) as "rational" and "free from invidious discrimination" even though eleven urban counties with 72 percent of the population would have had 49 percent of the House seats and only 24 percent of the Senate seats.

The pattern of reapportionment in the South will also be clearer when the courts decide whether or not substantial equality is necessary in *both* houses. The federal court in Virginia asserted strongly that this was necessary, and this was the principle followed by the court in Oklahoma. In the Alabama case the federal court said that population must be used to some extent as the standard for both houses. In Tennessee the federal court said that population must be the only standard in at least one house. In Georgia the federal court stated that one house must be apportioned according to population and deliberately avoided a decision concerning what standard should apply to the other house. The efforts by legislators in Alabama, Mississippi, and other states to abandon the population standard entirely for one house indicates the importance of this question. It will also affect the chances for reapportionment in North Carolina, South Carolina, and Texas, where constitutional provisions have undermined or eliminated the population principle in one house.

The gradual growth of urban representation in southern legislatures resulting from legislative and judicial action will have a number of consequences, some more clearly discernible than others. It should increase competition in the legislative primaries. A study of recent legislative primaries in five southern states showed that, with few exceptions, metropolitan districts had a larger proportion of contested primaries and a larger proportion won by narrow margins than rural districts had. In Alabama and Louisiana there was a distinctly lower level of competition in black belt counties than in other rural counties.[3]   Reapportionment may affect the types of districts used in some states.   In those southern states which use multi-member districts for metropolitan counties, reapportionment is creating some unusually large districts. In Alabama, the number of representatives in the single legislative district of Jefferson county rose from 7 to 17, and those in Davidson county, Tennessee, increased from 6 to 9 under the new apportionment. Jefferson county has had from 23 to 36 candidates for 7 House seats in recent years, and Davidson county has had from 17 to 39 candidates running for 6 seats. The presence of so many candidates on the ballot is confusing to the voters and places a premium on well-known names.

Reapportionment may force changes in the rotation system common in some states.   Rotation agreements occur in a state Senate or the House when there are several counties in a district. Party committees in each county formally agree to rotate the legislative seat every two or four years from county to county.   Rotation agreements have been used by each party in some one-party House districts in Kentucky, and have been used in nearly all multi-county Senate districts in Alabama. In Tennessee and North Carolina, where there has been some use of rotation agreements, state law provides for primary voting only in the county from which the candidate is to be chosen if a rotation agreement is in effect. Until invalidated by a federal court following *Baker* v. *Carr,* Georgia law *required* rotation agreements in multi-county senatorial districts and permitted voting only in the county from which the candidate would come. The result was to discriminate against large counties joined in senatorial districts with small counties.

Unless a state increases the size of its legislature, a growth in urban seats is sure to increase the number of multi-county districts suitable for rotation agreements, although some districts may become so large as to make rotation impractical. If reapportionment is carried out regularly after each decennial census, it will become increasingly difficult to implement rotation agreements. (It may be no coincidence that two of the states with extensive and long-established rotation patterns, Alabama and Tennessee, had not reapportioned for half a century prior to *Baker* v. *Carr.*)   With the numeri-

[3]Malcolm E. Jewell, "Competition and Factionalism in Southern Legislative Primaries and Elections" (Paper presented at the 1962 meeting of the American Political Science Association, Washington, D. C., September, 1962), pp. 13-16.

cal growth of urban representatives, rural interests may decide that the principle of self-protection requires that legislative experience be given priority over rotation.

Perhaps the most important aspect of reapportionment, and certainly the most difficult to predict, concerns the effect of greater urban representation on voting patterns in the legislature. Are there significant differences between urban and rural representatives, and if so on which issues do these differences become sharpest? A study of past roll calls may be deceptive because a change in representation would affect the balance of power on committees and consequently the bills emerging from committee for a vote on the floor. Nevertheless, previous roll calls provide the most tangible alternative to sheer speculation about the effects of reapportionment on legislative voting.

The most detailed southern study of this question has been made in Alabama by Murray C. Havens. In a study of the 1955-1956 session of the Alabama House, he found statistically significant differences (at a level of significance of .05) in voting among urban, rural, and mixed representatives on only about one-fourth of the contested roll calls. The sharpest urban-rural differences were on the issue of reapportionment and racial questions. Urban-rural differences were sharply defined on only a few labor, health, education, and welfare issues. Nor were there many roll calls with significant urban-rural differences on other issues where they might be anticipated: taxation, municipal affairs, appropriations, and highways. Havens found, in a small sample of these roll calls, that factional differences (for and against the Folsom administration) were sometimes, but not consistently, more significant than urban-rural differences.[4]

One obvious shortcoming of roll call analyses is that they usually do not discriminate between major bills and trivial bills. Evidence from both North and South suggests that there are probably relatively few roll calls in most legislative sessions in which there are sharply defined urban-rural voting alignments. Yet these are likely to include some of the most important issues faced by the legislature. In addition to the Alabama study, evidence from Florida suggests that metropolitan or urban legislators are likely to have a more liberal attitude toward racial issues. Studies of both Florida and Alabama have cited "right to work" issues as another category on

[4]Murray C. Havens, *City Versus Farm?* (University, Ala.: Bureau of Public Administration, University of Alabama, 1957.)

which urban-rural alignments appear, and this might be expected on other labor issues as well. Evidence from states throughout the country suggests that malapportionment leads to a distribution of tax revenue, for such purposes as highways and education in particular, that is heavily weighted in favor of rural counties. In Florida, for example, revenue from race tracks is distributed evenly among counties—even though the largest county has more than three hundred times as many people as the smallest.[5]

There is no certainty that greater urban representation will produce a more liberal attitude toward social and economic issues in general. On some issues there may be a conservative coalition between suburban and rural legislators. The nature of urban representatives depends to a considerable extent on the districting practices followed in the cities. Where a metropolitan county is divided into single-member districts, there are likely to be differences in the voting behavior of legislators from low-income and high-income districts. Where, as in many southern states, legislators from the metropolitan districts are elected at large, greater uniformity in legislative voting during a session may be anticipated from those legislators.

In the North reapportionment is likely to have the greatest effect in those states where it leads to a change in the partisan balance of power and particularly where it reduces the incidence of divided government. Similarly, in the South reapportionment is likely to have the greatest effect in states where a small clique of rural legislators has been able to maintain tight control over one or both houses sometimes in conflict with the governor. Examples of this are found in the Georgia and Florida legislatures and in the South Carolina Senate. The implications of reapportionment for such state legislatures should be obvious from the description of their power structure in subsequent pages. Because the Negro vote and the Republican vote have been drawn primarily from metropolitan areas, reapportionment should also contribute to the growing importance of Negro and Republican representation in southern legislatures.

THE PROSPECTS FOR NEGRO REPRESENTATION

Negro registration increased rapidly in the late 1940's, following the demise of the white primary; during the 1950's the growth was

[5]William C. Havard and Loren P. Beth, *The Politics of Mis-Representation* (Baton Rouge: Louisiana State University Press, 1962), pp. 16-19, 79-82. Hugh Douglas Price, "Florida Politics and the Pork Choppers," in Malcolm E. Jewell, ed., *The Politics of Reapportionment* (New York: Atherton Press, 1962), p. 89.

slower. In the eleven states of the confederate South, estimated Negro registration rose from 600,000 in 1947 to 1,300,000 in 1960. How
rapidly Negro registration and voting will grow in the 1960's depends
of course on the vigor of Negro organizations, the effectiveness of
federal safeguards, and the strength of governmental resistance in
some southern states. The obstacles to Negro voting have been greatest in the deep South and particularly in those counties, primarily
rural, with a large proportion of Negro population. As a consequence, despite the existence of many rural legislative districts with
a population of from 40 to 70 percent Negro, there are few in which
the voting population is more than one-third Negro and almost none
in which it is over half Negro. Moreover, population trends in most
southern states are causing a decline in the number of southern
districts that are over 40 percent Negro. Progress toward more
equitable apportionment in southern states is being made more rapidly than progress in removing the obstacles to Negro voting, obstacles which tend to be least in metropolitan counties. All of these
factors support the prediction that Negro influence in the legislature
will grow more rapidly in metropolitan than in rural constituencies.
In several southern metropolitan counties the Negro registration is
close to 20 percent of the total registered voters.[6]

The extent of Negro influence in legislative elections depends
partly on the types of districts used in the metropolitan counties.
Although Negro political organizations may influence the choice of
white legislators through endorsements carrying great weight with
Negro voters, the acid test of Negro representation is the election of
Negro legislators. Since Negro population is usually concentrated in
certain sections of southern cities, the single-member district system provides Negroes with the best chance of concentrating their
vote and maximizing its effectiveness. The only metropolitan county
in the deep South having single-member districts is that containing
New Orleans, which assigns one, or occasionally two, members to
each of 17 wards and has single-member Senate districts. All other
counties in Louisiana having more than one House member elect
them at large. Negro registration has been as high as one-third in
two New Orleans House districts, but Negro influence on the Democratic primary has been reduced by the substantial proportion of
Negroes registered as Republicans. Two other states that might be

[6]Margaret Price, *The Negro and the Ballot* (Atlanta: Southern Regional
Council, 1959). U. S. Commission on Civil Rights, *Voting* (1961), p. 22.

more accurately classified as border states use single-member districts: Kentucky, which uses them exclusively, and Oklahoma, which uses them for some of the larger counties but has at-large elections in some two and three member House districts. Louisville has frequently had a Negro in the Kentucky legislature.

When the Georgia legislature reapportioned the Senate in October, 1962, the question of districting arose with regard to urban counties which, for the first time, were getting more than a single senator. Proponents of the at-large system warned that Negro legislators would probably be chosen from one or more districts if a district system were used, and this was one of the arguments that led the legislature to adopt an at-large system. (Districts were used as a basis of residence for candidates, and not for voting.) A constitutional amendment was also adopted to perpetuate the at-large system. After a hectic legal battle involving one federal court and two state courts, a state judge ruled that voting must be by districts in the 1962 election (and this permitted nomination of a Negro legislator without a runoff), but the constitutional amendment requiring at-large elections was approved. A brief filed in federal court charged that the at-large election "results in invidious dilution of a voter's vote due solely to his race." Although the federal court agreed that the at-large system "presents serious questions as to whether it is violative of the Fourteenth and Fifteenth Amendments," the court declined to rule on the point, leaving unanswered a constitutional question which could have far-reaching implications for Negro representation in state legislatures.

In all other southern states metropolitan counties electing more than one member to either house use at-large elections. In Arkansas, Georgia (in the House), North Carolina, South Carolina, Virginia, and (with one exception) Tennessee the metropolitan counties use a pure at-large system in which all candidates run against other. In Alabama, Florida, Mississippi, and Texas the metropolitan counties use an at-large system with places, in which candidates run for a specific place or position but are voted on by all voters in the county. The pure at-large system gives Negro voters, or any other group, a better chance to elect one or two legislators by voting only for these. Fear of such "one-shot" voting by Negroes led Shelby County, Tennessee, where Negroes constitute nearly one-third of the registered voters, to shift to the place system in 1960.[7]

[7]For a study of the consequences of a similar change in voting mechanics for city offices in Memphis, see William E. Wright, *Memphis Politics: A Study*

THE GROWTH OF REPUBLICAN REPRESENTATION

During the 1950's the southern legislatures could be divided into two categories: those that consistently had a small bloc of Republican members and those in which Republicans were rare or nonexistent. In the first category were only five of the thirteen states: Virginia, North Carolina, Kentucky, Tennessee, and Oklahoma. Most of the Republican legislators in these states were elected from traditional Republican counties, most of which were concentrated in the mountain areas of southwestern Virginia, western North Carolina, southeastern Kentucky and eastern Tennessee. In Oklahoma the traditional Republican counties are in the north-central part of the state. In almost one-fifth of the Kentucky House districts, for example, the Republicans won every election during this period, often without any Democratic opponent. In Tennessee there were ten House districts (out of one hundred) in which the Republicans won every election during the 1950-1960 period and in none of which the Democrats consistently ran candidates. In both states most of these districts incorporate counties traditionally Republican in presidential races, and most of the Tennessee districts had been electing Republican legislators consistently as far back as 1920. During the 1950's there were no Republicans in the legislatures of Louisiana, Mississippi, and South Carolina, and an insignificant number in the legislatures of Alabama, Arkansas, Georgia, Texas, and Florida.

The opportunities for *increased* Republican representation lie not in the traditional Republican counties, primarily rural, but in the metropolitan centers, usually those gaining seats in the new apportionments. It is in the metropolitan counties of the South that the Republican party had its largest percentage of the presidential vote in 1952, 1956, and 1960 (outside of traditionally Republican counties), and it is here that the largest number of Republican candidates for Congress have been found. It is also in the metropolitan South that the Republicans have made the greatest progress recently in running legislative candidates and, in a few states, winning additional legislative seats. Since 1950 the Republicans have run legislative candidates consistently in Louisville and frequently in other Kentucky metropolitan counties. In Alabama and Louisiana Republican candidates have been found almost entirely in metropolitan counties

in Racial Bloc Voting (Eagleton Cases in Practical Politics) (New York: McGraw-Hill Co., 1962).

(except for a handful of traditionally Republican Alabama counties).

The most significant Republican advances at the start of the 1960's, came in the two most urbanized southern states: Texas and Florida. The Republican party in Texas ran only 5 legislative candidates in 1956, 33 in 1958, 22 in 1960, and 101 candidates in 1962 out of a possible 181. Two-thirds of the candidates have been in the ten largest metropolitan counties, and in 1962 nearly complete Republican slates were run in several of the largest counties. The party won seven House seats in 1962, including six in Dallas, and a number of its candidates in metropolitan counties ran strong races.

The Republican party began to gain legislative seats in Florida during the 1950's, increasing from three in 1951 to seven in 1955 and 1957. The next advance came in the special 1963 election following reapportionment when the Republicans elected a second senator and increased House membership from 5 to 16. In the four elections from 1955 through 1962, the Republicans ran candidates, on the average, for one-fifth of the House seats; about 60 per cent of these candidates were in the seven largest metropolitan counties. The only county where the party consistently won was Pinellas (St. Petersburg). The potential impact of reapportionment on Republican legislative strength is more dramatically illustrated in Florida than anywhere else. Those seven counties, where Republican legislative strength is concentrated, increased their House representation from 18 to 46 seats in the 1963 apportionment. The Republicans ran candidates for 27 of those 28 new seats in the special 1963 election, and they won 11 of them.

THE TYPICAL LEGISLATIVE PATTERN: A LOW LEVEL OF CONFLICT

The underrepresentation of urban, Negro, and Republican voters has led to the minimizing of conflict in southern legislatures. It has meant that conflicts of interest are not usually structured with any continuity along partisan, factional, or urban-rural lines. The rural, conservative groups that have dominated southern legislatures have been able to maintain sufficient identity of interest and harmony within their ranks to prevent the development of clearly defined blocs in the legislature. In recent years this pattern, with some variations, has been the predominant one in most southern legislatures. In a few southern states, however, legislative conflicts have become sharply defined and legislative factionalism has become institutional-

ized. Analysis of the contrasts between these two legislative systems may suggest some of the probable consequences of changing
bases of representation in the 1960's.

In the typical southern legislature there is no evidence of factions in the organization of the legislature and in voting during the
sessions. Legislators representing urban areas, a particular section
of the state, or some other interest may band together in voting on
a single issue or group of issues, but this coalition falls apart when
other issues come to a vote. There is no continuity from session
to session and usually no continuity throughout a session for those
legislative blocs which do occasionally arise. Even in those states
where the Republicans constitute more than a trivial bloc, they
usually do not vote together with any consistency, unless it is in
support of the Democratic governor. Urban legislators find that
they must cooperate with the leadership to obtain legislation meeting urban needs, and consequently the likelihood of organizing an
urban bloc is reduced.

Samuel C. Patterson, in a study of the 1959 Oklahoma House
based on scaling techniques, found that in the absence of party organization or stable factional alignments "the patterns of voting in
the legislature are likely to be compartmentalized." Although legislative voting behavior was consistent enough to permit scaling with
regard to several major categories of issues, such as taxation, appropriations, schools, and labor and welfare, the voting of members
varied greatly from one category to the other. Patterson concluded
that, "in the absence of party as a reference group, the legislator is
likely, consciously or unconsciously, to respond to different pressures
in different voting areas."[8]

Any legislative body requires leadership, and in most southern
states—perhaps more than in most other states—that leadership
comes primarily from the governor. Most governors draw their power from a variety of sources: their constitutional authority to recom-
mend and veto legislation, their influence over public opinion, their
budgetary control, and their ability to control patronage—not only
jobs, but contracts, road projects, and other favors that can be made
available to a legislator, his political friends, or his district. All
southern governors, except those in Texas and Arkansas, are limited
to one four-year term. The North Carolina governor lacks the veto;
firm budgetary control; and patronage in some states is either limit-

[8]Samuel C. Patterson, "Dimensions of Voting Behavior in a One-Party
State Legislature," *Public Opinion Quarterly*, XXVI (1962), 185-200.

ed by civil service or diffused among a large number of elected officials free to dispense it as they wish. Nevertheless, most southern governors have a powerful variety of tools that they can use in exercising legislative leadership.

Southern governors lack one asset common in many other states: a disciplined legislative party through which to work. Legislative candidates usually run independently of the governor. They recognize that nothing the governor does will help them or hurt them at the polls, and consequently they have no political stake in the success of the governor's program. On the other hand, they have no stake in his failure, no reason to develop a legislative record of opposition. Most southern governors, even in states with some Republican legislators, do not have to deal with any group having the organizational structure or the motivation to constitute an "opposition party." This is of fundamental importance in explaining the strength of the southern governor.

In most southern states the governor exercises his leadership in part through having a dominant voice in the choice of legislative leaders: the president pro tem of the Senate, speaker of the House, his own floor leaders, and perhaps major committee chairmen. These leaders, like those in most legislative bodies, have powerful influence over the assigning of bills to committee, the reporting of bills from committee, and the conduct of legislative business on the floor. The committees seldom act independently on major bills, but respond to gubernatorial and legislative leadership. Alabama, Kentucky and Oklahoma are examples of states where the governor's influence over the choice of legislative leaders is particularly strong. This is generally true of Tennessee, but from 1953 through 1962 a strong and effective speaker held his post in the House under three governors.

South Carolina is typical of these other southern states in that it has been free of sharp conflict and institutionalized factions, but it is untypical in the weakness of its governor. V. O. Key's description still is accurate: "South Carolina's chief executive . . . can grant pardons, send messages to the legislature, and exercise the power of veto; yet he has the narrowest sort of power of direction of state administration. 'There's nothing to it except the honor,' is the common attitude. . . . It is the legislature, and primarily the senate, that gives direction, coherence, and continuity to the policy of the state."[9] The Senate continues to be dominated by a small

[9]V. O. Key, Jr., *Southern Politics* (New York: Alfred A. Knopf, 1950), pp. 150-152.

group of veteran leaders, who have served in the Senate from fifteen to thirty-five years. The president pro tem (described by Key as undoubtedly the most powerful man in the government) has served in that post and as chairman of the finance committee since 1942. Other major committees have been chaired by a group of four or five men, with some variation in specific responsibilities but no enlargement of the circle of power. The speaker of the House has served in that post (with the exception of two sessions) since 1937 and like the president pro tem comes from Barnwell county. There has been some greater variation in House chairmanships, but still more consistency of leadership than in most states. In Virginia, also the legislative leadership has remained concentrated in a few hands. The House speaker has held that position since 1950, and there have been few changes in the chairmanships of key committees since that date. A handful of senators have taken turns as president pro tem and have kept the important chairmanships. Most of these leaders in both houses started their legislative service in the 1930's or early 1940's. The governor has been effective only when he worked in harmony with the legislative leaders.

To say that the governor exercises strong legislative leadership in a state is not to say that he tries to influence legislative decisions on every bill; normally, he limits his efforts to a small proportion of legislative measures. The vast number of local bills (sometimes disguised to avoid constitutional prohibitions) are usually of no concern to the governor, but they are often of vital concern to individual legislators. The role of local bills in the legislative process differs from state to state. In Kentucky the governor and legislative leaders use their power to advance or delay the passage of local bills to win support of legislators for major bills. In Alabama and South Carolina, on the other hand, the legislature virtually always passes local bills without dissent once the members from the county involved have agreed on the text of a bill.[10] In Alabama the willingness of legislators to go along with the governor's program is sometimes attributed to their concentration on these local bills, and the frequency with which incumbents are defeated is sometimes blamed on voter resentment over handling these bills.

In states where the legislator bears such a heavy responsibility

[10]See Ralph Eisenberg, "The Logroll, South Carolina Style," in Richard T. Frost, ed., *Cases in State and Local Government* (Englewood Cliffs, New Jersey: Prentice-Hall, 1961), pp. 155-163.

for local legislation it is probably inevitable and logical that voters should give priority to local issues in legislative elections. Such localism is likely to doom alliances between gubernatorial and legislative candidates, campaigning on state issues.

Whether the governor is strong or weak, in most southern states there is an identity of interest between the governor and the dominant legislative forces. As a result there is seldom a deep gulf between the two or factional conflict within the legislature. Kentucky might appear to be an exception, because of the strength of factions within the Democratic party. But these factions are based more on personalities than they are on issues and clearly defined interests. The Kentucky governor is strong and can count on substantial legislative support from both factions in his first session. In the midterm primary elections the administration often seeks to re-elect or defeat legislators in some of the districts, though this intervention is not often well publicized in the district. In the governor's second session factional conflict is often sharper, but the governor usually prevails. In the 1958 session, Governor Chandler lost control over a majority of Democratic legislators but enacted most of his program because of his ability to attract the voting support of Republican legislators.

Governor Folsom's two administrations as Alabama's governor (1947-50) and (1955-58) were exceptions to the usual southern experience. Folsom represented the underrepresented northern and urban sections of the state. In the first administration he was unskilled and inexperienced and proved unable to enact much of his legislative program. In the second administration his leadership was more effective. During both periods pro-Folsom and anti-Folsom factions could be identified in the legislature and voted with varying degrees of cohesion on a limited number of issues. Alabama legislators seldom campaigned as pro-Folsom or anti-Folsom during gubernatorial elections (there are no midterm elections). Moreover, with the return of more conservative governors, these factions disappeared from view. Folsom left no heritage of factionalism.[11]

FACTIONS AND CONFLICTS IN THE SOUTHERN LEGISLATURE

For a preview of the conflict that may arise from changing representation we must look to three urban states with legislatures dif-

[11]Key, *op. cit.*, pp. 42-45. Coleman B. Ransone, Jr., *The Office of Governor in the South* (University, Alabama: Bureau of Public Administration, University of Alabama, 1951), pp. 96-98.

fering widely in every respect except in the existence of continuing factional patterns that structure the conflicts of interest. The states are Louisiana, Texas, and Florida.

Factional politics in Louisiana has a depth and continuity exceeding anything found in other southern states, not only because of the colorful personalities and controversial accomplishments of the Long dynasty but also because the factions are rooted in conflicting socioeconomic interests. Far more than in most states, these factions have extended into the legislature. Gubernatorial slates extending to all statewide offices have been a standard practice for three decades in Louisiana Democratic primaries, and this slating has often extended to legislative candidates. Legislative slating has been most common in New Orleans and in the southern part of the state, and it has varied in importance from election to election. It may have reached a height in the 1956 runoff when Earl Long, already victorious in the first primary, publicly endorsed about 40 candidates for the 70 legislative races with runoff contests, and about three-fourths of his candidates were nominated. In the 1959-60 primary, however, the Long forces were defeated and traditional factional alignments were weakened by the growth of the segregation issue.[12]

Factional blocs have also been evident during the many sessions of the Louisiana legislature. For example, from an analysis of roll calls in the 1958 Senate session it is possible to distinguish clearly between supporters and opponents of the Long administration. Thirty-one roll calls were selected as a measuring device; on each at least one-fifth of the legislators were in the minority and there was no dissension among six members of the Long leadership. There were 22 senators who usually supported leadership and six others who did so about two-thirds of the time. Six were about evenly divided and five others opposed the leadership at least two-thirds of the time. With two exceptions every committee chairman was a strong administration supporter. Every one of fourteen senators publicly endorsed by Long in the primary was a supporter; two of the three whose opponents he had endorsed voted against the leadership a majority of the time on these issues.

Political changes are occurring more rapidly in Texas than in most southern states. The strong, well financed Republican organi-

[12]Allan P. Sindler, *Huey Long's Louisiana* (Baltimore: Johns Hopkins Press, 1956), ch. 9. Jewell, "Competition and Factionalism in Southern Legislative Primaries and Elections," pp. 19-21.

zation has run impressive statewide campaigns; its extensive efforts to elect legislative candidates, already described, are almost certain to bear more fruit than in the past, with resulting changes in the legislative process in Texas. Texas Democrats are more sharply divided into ideological camps than is true in other southern states. This has been very evident in gubernatorial primaries, but in the past there have been no significant alliances between gubernatorial and legislative candidates. Recently in several of the metropolitan counties, notably those including Houston, Dallas, and San Antonio, there have been clearly identified legislative slates, usually with a liberal or conservative orientation. A separate, but related development has been the intensive campaigns waged by candidates for speaker of the House, who start campaigning in the preceding session and seek commitments of support from incumbent legislators and legislative candidates. While geographic considerations enter into these races, and chairmanships are offered as prizes for support, alignments in the speaker's race often have a liberal-conservative basis. Although the voters apparently seldom know or care about the commitments a legislative candidate has made in the speaker's race, this practice could be the forerunner of more clearly defined factions in the Texas primary. A further development is the endorsement of legislative candidates by various statewide labor and conservative groups. If legislative factionalism became more pronounced it would be logical to expect links between gubernatorial and legislative candidates, at least in some counties.

H. Dicken Cherry has pointed out that the blocs in the Texas House which are created by the contest for speaker maintain some voting cohesion in the legislative session. On a dozen major and closely contested roll calls in the 1961 session he found that the two blocs were opposed to each other and with few exceptions 70 to 90 percent of the members of each bloc were voting with it. These blocs proved to be more important than urban-rural differences. Moreover, the 1961 reapportionment bill was carefully designed to protect members of the majority bloc as much as was possible, particularly in districts losing seats. That bill was passed by a nearly straight-bloc vote, with some of the opponents being members of the minority bloc from metropolitan counties that stood to gain legislative seats.[13]

In 1950 V. O. Key described Florida's political structure as "an

[13]H. Dicken Cherry, "Texas: Factions in a One-Party Setting," in Jewell, *The Politics of Reapportionment*, pp. 123-126.

incredibly complex melange of amorphous factions. . . . In its politics it is almost literally every candidate for himself."[14] Since that time Florida politics has remained atomized, but a pattern has begun to emerge in gubernatorial primaries, particularly runoffs; according to Havard and Beth, it was evident in the 1948, 1954, 1956, and 1960 gubernatorial primaries. They describe the voting pattern as "a combination rural-urban and North-South political cleavage." Most, but not all, of the booming urban counties are in the South. The "urban" candidate for governor is likely to carry most or all of the urban counties in the South and to run a strong second in northern urban counties. The "rural" candidate is likely to carry northern rural counties easily and to carry most or all of the southern rural counties by smaller margins. The rapid growth of urban counties means that increasingly the governor of Florida represents urban interests, and even the governor elected by rural counties cannot ignore urban interests.[15]

The consequences are described by Havard and Beth: "Given the fact . . . that the legislature is stacked in favor of rural counties by the apportionment system, it is practically inevitable that there is going to be conflict between the governor and the legislature."[16] The apportionment existing in Florida prior to 1963 was probably the worst in the nation; it was the only state in which 15 percent of the voters could elect a majority to each house. Havard and Beth have shown how rural control over the legislature, based on malapportionment, has been solidified by the ability of rural legislators to elect one of their own as presiding officer and his determination to pack the key committees with legislators who represent rural constituencies or are willing to cooperate with the rural bloc. A small group of legislators in each house forms an interlocking directorate, serving in leadership posts and on the key committees. In the Senate this rural clique has been more cohesive and more secure than in the House; following the 1955 session in which an urban-oriented speaker served effectively as the governor's leader in the House, the rural bloc strengthened its organizational unity and re-established its control.[17]

Malcolm Parsons, in a study of the Florida Senate from 1947 through 1961, found strong evidence of bloc voting in the legisla-

[14]Key, *op cit.*, p. 82.
[15]Havard and Beth, *op cit.*, pp. 14-17.
[16]*Ibid.*, p. 21.
[17]*Ibid.*, pp. 131-149.

ture, beginning with the 1955 session. This was the beginning of Governor Collins' term, which marked the intensification of legislative factionalism. Parsons found that during the 1955-1961 period at least 60 percent of the northern senators opposed at least 60 percent of the southern senators on nearly half of the controversial roll calls, and that on almost as many roll calls the index of North-South likeness was less than 60. The North won on 84 percent of these latter roll calls. Both groups were highly cohesive on reapportionment, constitutional revision, and racial issues, and the southerners were highly cohesive on health and welfare issues. He concluded that, during the 1955-61 period "there has been a quite stable, cohesive bifactionalism in the one-party Florida Senate."[18]

The 1963 reapportionment has already changed the legislative process in Florida by significantly reducing rural control in the lower house. The seven largest counties, with 46 percent of the state's population, have 41 per cent of the House seats (compared to the previous 19 percent), but their representation in the Senate remains almost unchanged at 19 percent. Reapportionment, at least partial reapportionment, will not reduce conflict in Florida but shift its focus; the struggle between the governor and legislature will become a struggle within the legislature, in which the governor supports one side with the resources he can command (resources limited by constitutional obstacles and the lack of factional continuity in the gubernatorial primary).

Patterns of Change

The stable legislative patterns in the South are undergoing change, change induced by four interrelated factors: population trends to urban areas, judicially induced reapportionment, the growth of Republican strength in national and state elections, and the rising tide of Negro votes. In the three most urban states of the South, Louisiana, Texas, and Florida, we find examples of the varied patterns that this change may take. As out-groups begin to become more fully represented in the legislature, there will be a structuring of the increasing conflicts among these groups. This is likely to take the form of factions within the Democratic legislative party, fac-

[18]Malcolm B. Parsons, "Quasi-Partisan Conflict in a One-Party Legislative System: The Florida Senate, 1947-1961," *American Political Science Review,* LVI (1962), 605-614. The measurement of North-South likeness was based on the Rice Index of Likeness and the chi square test to assure that the probability of random distribution was not over .01.

tions that are evident in primary elections as well as in roll-call voting. The experience of Louisiana, where legislative factions have been more meaningful than in other states, suggests, however, that this trend toward factions is likely to be uneven, incomplete, and inconsistent over a period of years. The mechanical (i.e. districting) as well as political obstacles to the election of Negro legislators and the unity displayed by legislators in some states in opposition to school desegregation suggest that it will be a long time before Negro legislators are integrated into legislative factions.

The growth of legislative factions and the increase in Republican legislators in states like Florida and Texas result in part from the same causes. The trends are likely to develop along parallel lines and both will be intensified by reapportionment. But there is an inherent contradiction between the two trends. In a county, such as Dallas, the election of Republican legislators may put pressure on Democrats to abandon the divisive tactics of slating; in a state, such as Florida, Democrats might eventually have to unite to prevent the Republicans from holding the balance of power. Some southern legislatures may move from a one-party system to a "three-party" system, at least during a transitional period. Republicans, representing predominantly the more conservative, suburban interests in metropolitan counties, might vote with southern, urban Democrats in Florida on racial issues but would vote with the conservative wing of the Texas Democratic party on economic issues.

The trend of the 1960's in some southern states is toward increased legislative factionalism, but legislative factions seldom have the cohesion, organizational strength, or continuity that is characteristic of legislative parties. In most southern states the obstacles to a strong two-party system at the gubernatorial and particularly the legislative level remain formidable, despite reapportionment. In the 1970 legislature the various interests in southern states will be better—but not perfectly—represented. Conflicts among these groups will be structured more fully, but seldom neatly between two groups, whether called parties or factions. The legislative pattern will be more varied in the next decade than it has been in the past, and the writer describing southern legislatures in the 35th anniversary issue of the *Journal of Politics* will have even more difficulty making meaningful generalizations.

POLITICAL LEADERSHIP IN THE GOVERNOR'S OFFICE

COLEMAN B. RANSONE, JR.
University of Alabama

D URING THE TEN YEAR period from 1950 to 1960 the governors of the southern states gained considerably in stature as political leaders. This increase in prominence cannot be attributed to any substantial change in the legal position of the governor, although Tennessee increased the governor's term from two to four years during this decade. On the whole, the legal position of the governor in most southern states remained weak, although there is a wide variation in his legal position. The increasing role of the governor in providing the state with political leadership stems primarily from the fact that the unwieldy, poorly-organized, and non-representative legislatures of the southern states make leadership from these bodies virtually impossible. In the South, as in any other section of the country, the legislatures "make" the laws. However, their function is largely that of the ratification or rejection of the governor's proposals.[1] Furthermore it seems to be the nature of legislatures to cut down any aspiring single legislator who tries to assert leadership. When such a legislator occasionally does arise he is suspected, perhaps with good cause, to have designs on the governorship and hence is rejected as overly ambitious by his fellow legislators. He may be suspected also of the same ambitions by the incumbent governor who may assist in blocking the legislator's proposals.

One recent development which may be of great significance in executive-legislative relations is the current trend toward the reapportionment of state legislatures. The decision of the United States Supreme Court in *Baker* v. *Carr*[2] held that the citizens of a state had the right to challenge the apportionment of their state legislatures in the federal courts. The Court, however, left it up to the federal district courts to pass on reapportionment plans and even

[1]Note the discussion of the reasons for executive dominance of the legislative process by Robert B. Highsaw in "The Southern Governor—Challenge to the Strong Executive Theme" in the *Public Administration Review*, XIX (Winter, 1959), 8-10.
[2]369 U. S. 186, 1962.

(as it turned out in the Alabama situation) to order a reapportionment designed by the district court. This decision may have far-reaching consequences for the governor's political leadership. However, not all of the southern legislatures have yet been reapportioned and we are in the midst of only the first term of those governors in the states where reapportionment has occurred. Thus it is too early to judge the full impact of this change on executive-legislative relations.

As the situation now stands the lack of leadership by the legislature has created a vacuum in the legislative process. The southern governor has moved into this vacuum with a legislative program based, in part at least, on the program he used during the campaign in which he was elected. This process has become such standard operating procedure that when an occasional governor comes along who does not advocate a legislative program the process loses its real focus that must come from the governor's office. Hence when we speak of "political leadership" in the governor's office, we are dealing with no idle phrase but are discussing the very stuff of which state government can be made. With very few exceptions, the governor of a southern state is a program-oriented individual who sees the accomplishments of his administration in the light of program goals. One of those goals may be, as was the case with Governor John Patterson of Alabama, "no new taxes except for education," a pledge which incidentally the governor kept. But, on the whole, the governors of the South, with the possible exception of the Virginia variety, are not principally economy and efficiency minded. They are not afraid to spend money or even to propose new taxes to raise revenues for their favorite projects.

In addition to legislative ineptitude, we find that the governor alone has the advantage of a state-wide election and thus can advance a fairly valid claim to speak for the people of the state as a whole. His claim is particularly valid in regard to the city dwellers since they are under represented in the legislature and look to the governor to express their views on state policies. Thus the negative factor of the lack of legislative leadership coupled with the positive factor of the governor's role as the spokesman for the state as a whole has set the stage for increasing gubernatorial leadership. In addition, the governor has the best information via the executive departments on many of the complex matters of modern legislation. This balance of knowledge in favor of the executive is a matter of considerable importance in these days when the states are undertaking far-reaching programs in highly technical fields.

If we add to all this the tenor of the times, particularly the need for action called forth by the integration crisis, we had a situation favoring some sort of gubernatorial leadership in the 1950's. Hence the anomaly of political leadership from a group of governors who are traditionally weak legally is not as strange as it seems at first glance.

While any facet of the governor's office may affect his role as political leader, there are three primary areas which are most related to his success or failure in this field. The first of these is his legal position. Although the governor's legal powers are not the determining factor in his efforts to provide political leadership, some governors start from the advantage of a strong legal position; others must overcome the handicap of a weak position from which they begin their drive for the control of the state's administrative and legislative machinery. A second factor which seems to affect the governor's attempt at political leadership is the electoral base from which he drew his strength in his election. Although all the governors of this period were Democratic, there is some evidence that this Democratic dominance may be gradually changing in at least some of the southern states. A final factor influencing the governor's role in political leadership is really a combination of two closely related factors—the tenor of the times and the governor's own personality and political philosophy. This combination produces the governor's reaction to such recent challenges as the integration of the public schools. All southern governors in the last half of the period had to meet this challenge. How they met it varied considerably, according to both the climate of opinion in their state and their own political philosophy.

THE LEGAL POSITION OF THE GOVERNOR

In the South we have a wide variety of legal patterns most of which have not changed over the 10-year period under consideration. The legal position of the governors ranges from those with exceptional weak legal powers such as in Mississippi to those with a rather strong concentration of power in the governorship as in Virginia. For example, in Mississippi the "governor remains more of a 'chief observer' than a chief executive."[3] This assessment was based pri-

[3]Robert B. Highsaw and Charles N. Fortenberry, *The Government and Administration of Mississippi* (New York: Thomas Y. Crowell Company, 1954), p. 69.

marily on the governor's very limited appointing power, the absence of a real executive budget and the almost complete lack of those tools for the control over administration that tend to make for a strong executive position. In Virginia, on the other hand, the governor has a broad appointing and removal power, is responsible for the preparation of the executive budget, and has most of the recommended tools of management in his executive office. "The chief executive of the Old Dominion has emerged as the leader both of legislation and of administration."[4]

In spite of the wide range of gubernatorial powers in the South it is possible to rank the states' chief executives on the basis or their legal powers with some degree of success somewhere between the extreme of Mississippi, on one hand, and Virginia, on the other. In deciding on the strength of the governor's position vis-a-vis the executive branch, there are two factors which seem to be of the greatest significance for his control of that branch. One of these is the scope of his appointing power, and the other is his power to control the preparation and execution of the budget. A third factor, which is of lesser importance but still deserves mention, is the length of the governor's term and whether or not the governor immediately can succeed himself. If the governor has a broad appointing power, can control the preparation and execution of the budget, and has at least a four-year term he is in a relatively strong legal position and with some justification can be called the state's chief executive. If he lacks these powers he is likely to be only the first among many executives in the conduct of the state's administrative affairs.

In all of the southern states the governor's appointing power is limited by the presence of other elected officers most of whose offices are provided for by the constitution. This fact means that in all states the governor appoints only a part of his major department heads and that the remainder are elected by the people or appointed by the legislature. In some instances the loss of appointing power is more apparent than real since the office which he does not control has little policy significance. For example, this would be true in the case of the secretary of state. This office is usually elective but the department is not one which is generally concerned with substantive policy. Hence it is not a matter of real importance that the governor does not control this department. This is not true of other de-

[4]George W. Spicer, "Gubernatorial Leadership in Virginia," *Public Administration Review,* I (Autumn, 1941), 441.

partments which have real policy significance such as highways, welfare or education. If the governor lacks appointing power in such departments it is a matter for concern since it is in areas such as these that some of the governor's most important program proposals generally fall.

One or two examples will serve to illustrate this point. The superintendent of education is elected in seven states, the department operates under a board in one state, and the governor appoints the superintendent in only three states. Consequently, education is a function over which the governor has little direct control through appointments. In public welfare the governor fares little better since he appoints the department head in six states, while the department operates under a board in the remaining five states. In one of these the governor is a member of the board. Thus the governor controls through appointment the department of public welfare or its equivalent in slightly over one-half of the states. In highways the situation is much the same since the governor appoints the highway director in five states and in one other state the director is a division head in a department whose director is appointed by the governor. In the remaining states we find a board controlling in four states and in one the three highway commissioners are elected. Thus again the governor controls through appointment in slightly over one-half of the states.

These examples serve to illustrate that the governors in the southern states has a limited control of the executive establishment through appointment. Roughly speaking he now controls the major administrative offices in six or less of the eleven southern states. Furthermore, within a given state if the governor does not control one or more of the major offices, he is likely not to control the rest. For example, in Mississippi the governor appoints only the welfare director, and the remaining officers, including the heads of education and highways are elected. Much the same situation exists in South Carolina except that in that state the head of the department of education is elected and highways and welfare are under boards. Consequently, the governor appoints none of these officials in South Carolina.

In short the governors of the southern states lack substantial control over the executive branch through appointments except in a few states such as Virginia. Therefore, it follows that whatever control they exercise over the executive branch must be by other means, generally through their political leadership.

The question of whether or not the governor has budgetary control is one that cannot be answered with a flat positive or negative statement since the degree of control is more subtle than in the case of appointments. For example, the governor of Arkansas is clearly in the weakest legal position of any state in the group since in Arkansas the old legislative budget still persists.[5] However, there is not much grounds for a choice between such states as Florida and Mississippi. In the former state the governor is ex officio chairman of a budget commission which is composed of six elected department heads. In Mississippi, on the other hand, the governor is ex officio chairman of a commission made up of the chairmen of the house ways and means committee, the house appropriations committee, the senate finance committee, and the president pro-tem of the senate. Whether the governor of Florida is in a more advantageous position than the governor of Mississippi depends in large measure on a number of imponderables that vary from governor to governor, including his degree of influence in the legislature. If a Mississippi governor is in a strong position vis-a-vis a particular legislature, he may, in fact, be in a better position to have his political program reflected in appropriations, than the governor of Florida, who must deal with six independently elected department heads. On the other hand, if the governor of Mississippi is in a weak position vis-a-vis a particular legislature, he may be also in a weaker position on the budget than even his counterpart in Florida.

To take another example, what of the plight of the governor of Texas where he has the power to prepare an executive budget, but where a budget is prepared also by the Legislative Budget Board. Since the latter agency is the initial review agency for the legislature of both the budget of the governor and its own budget, it can, and generally does, throw out the governor's budget and submit its own for legislative consideration. In addition to these situations we have South Carolina where the budget is prepared by the State Budget and Control Board made up of the governor as chairman, the treasurer, the comptroller general, the chairman of the senate finance committee, and the chairman of the house ways and means committee. Under this arrangement the governor is also in a weak position to exercise budgetary control.

In the other states—Alabama, Georgia, Louisiana, North Caro-

[5]See *The Book of the States,* 1962-63, pp. 156-165, for a description of the various budget systems.

lina, Tennessee, and Virginia—some form of executive budget prevails, and the governor is in a stronger position. However, even here the situation varies. For example, in Alabama and Louisiana the budget director is under the civil service and cannot be removed by the governor for policy reasons. On the other hand, the budget director in Tennessee is not under the civil service and can be removed by the governor for policy reasons. However, in Tennessee the budget director is not automatically changed with a new administration unless there is a change in the faction controlling the governorship. Thus both law and custom provide for varying degrees of control even within the executive budget pattern, and it is not an easy matter to determine which governor has the greatest strength in terms of budgeting. Traditionally, in Tennessee and also to a considerable extent in Virginia, the governor has proven to be very powerful in the budget process, and consequently these two states probably rank at the top of the list whereas such states as Arkansas, Mississippi, and Florida would rank at the other end.

A review of the two foregoing criteria of gubernatorial strength vis-a-vis the executive branch shows that the same governors in the South are not always weak on both counts. There are some governors who are weak both in terms of budgeting and in terms of appointment. This situation prevails in both South Carolina and Mississippi, where the respective governors have very little appointing power and also a limited budget control. However, the other states do not fall into a neat pattern since Arkansas, which is the weakest state as far as the budget is concerned, is somewhat stronger in terms of appointing power, while Louisiana ranks fairly well in the budget but is rather weak in terms of appointments. However, for a given state a comparison of these two factors gives some idea of whether the governor is in a strong position or whether he must deal from one of weakness vis-a-vis the executive branch. This concept is tricky since the governor who is strong in the relationships with the legislature may be able to work through that body to achieve desired administrative ends. Much of the legislative policy, particularly that concerning appropriations, is really administrative politics, and we must be cautious about drawing too hasty conclusions as to the administrative position of the governor alone.

Another factor which affects the governor's legal position as well as his political position is his term of office. There has been one important change in his position in this regard in the period under consideration. In 1953 Tennessee adopted a constitutional amendment which lengthened the governor's term from two to four years effective with the 1954 term. However, the amendment also provided that the governor could not succeed himself in office. Hence the amendment gave with one hand and took away with the other. It added to the governor's power by eliminating the need for campaigning every two years and thus giving him a longer period in which to develop his programs. However, by preventing the governor from succeeding himself it also tended to weaken the governor's control over the legislature in the last two years of his office. Thus the Tennessee move was not an unmixed blessing, although on balance it appears to be a step in the direction of strengthening the office.

At the present time all the southern states have a four-year term except Arkansas and Texas, and all of the four-year states prohibit the governor's immediate re-election to office. Arkansas still has a two-year term and had, until recently, a very strong no-third-term tradition. However, this tradition was rudely shattered by Orval Faubus who has now been elected to five two-year terms. Several recent governors of Texas have served more than two terms. In fact, the entire period (1950-1960) was spanned by the terms of Allan Shivers and Price Daniel, who each served three two-year terms.[6]

Although the Tennessee move to a four-year term was a step in the direction of strengthening the governorship, it stopped short, as have its sister states, of making the four-year term a real instrument for democratic control. The accompanying provision in all the states with a four-year term that the governor may not be immediately re-elected tends to weaken the governor's position. This is particularly true of the last two years of his term when he is dealing with the legislature. Though the governor is not exactly a "lame duck," some of the same psychology is present and increases in intensity as the governor approaches the end of his term. Since we have no real two-party system in the South at the gubernatorial level and since the governor cannot succeed himself, he cannot perpetuate his policies in office unless he can throw his support to a new candidate with similar ideas. Such a transfer of support is generally hard to accomplish in the personal politics of the South. The result usually is that

[6]Allan Shivers first succeeded to the governorship in 1949, to fill the unexpired term of Beauford H. Jester. However, he was elected afterwards to three terms in his own right.

the governor has only four years to carry out any kind of a program. This relatively short tenure makes far-reaching change except on one or two key points extremely difficult. While the governor can run again after one term, not many are able to accomplish the feat of being re-elected after a four-year absence from the public eye. Consequently, it is noteworthy that four governors during this period were re-elected after an absence of four or more years from office. The first of these is James E. Folsom of Alabama, who was elected for a second term after four years out of office and who ran unsuccessfully for a third term after another four years. Louisiana produced two such governors. These were Earl K. Long, who was re-elected after a four-year layoff, and Jimmie H. Davis, who came back after being out of office in Louisiana for three terms. In addition, Frank G. Clement of Tennessee served one two-year term (1952-54), was elected to Tennessee's first four-year term in 1954 and returned for a second four-year term in 1962. These men seem to be exceptions to the general rule and what this self-denying ordinance probably does is to keep the people from passing on the worth of the governor's term at the time when it is fresh in their minds.

A four-year term with no bar to re-election would be a step in the direction of greater democratic control, but there seem to be no signs of a development in this direction. The discussion of this point in the Tennessee Constitutional Convention revealed general agreement among the delegates that four years were long enough. This particular legal provision, however, does have the effect of reducing the governor's influence with the legislature toward the end of his term and for this reason has important implications for his role in political leadership.

The Electoral Process

During the period under discussion, there was an upsurge of presidential Republicanism in the South with Eisenhower carrying four states in 1952 and five states in 1956. In 1960, the showing with Nixon was not quite as good but, even so, the Republicans carried three states—Florida, Tennessee, and Virginia. It is interesting to note that there was no comparable upsurge in gubernatorial Republicanism, although the Republicans did make a good showing in Texas in 1962 when they polled 45.6 per cent of the vote. Table 1 compares the percentage of the total vote received by the Republican candidates in the gubernatorial and presidential contests during the period 1952-1962.

There are certain conclusions which one can draw about the Republican gubernatorial vote on the basis of an examination of Table 1. The first of these is that the Republicans did not even bother to field a candidate in Georgia, Mississippi, or South Carolina during the period 1952-1962. Hence, these do not seem to be the states to which to look for an early Republican overthrow at the gubernatorial level. A second point is that in those states in which there were contests the gubernatorial candidate ran well behind the presidential candidate at the same election or in the gubernatorial election immediately following the presidential election. The comparison is not exact in this second case since two of the states elect their governors in even-numbered off years and Virginia elects in odd-numbered off years. However, in the presidential years the gubernatorial candidate ran substantially behind the presidential candidate except in North Carolina in 1960, where the gubernatorial candidate polled 45.5 per cent of the vote compared to 47.9 per cent for the Republican presidential candidate. In those states with off-year elections the Republican percentages for governor were consistently behind the Republican percentages for President in the preceding election. The lone exception is in Texas in 1962 when Jack Cox, the Republican candidate, polled 45.6 per cent of the vote which was very close to the 48.5 per cent of the vote polled by Nixon in 1960. The 1962 race by Cox is the best showing made by any Republican gubernatorial candidate during the period. Texas Republicans have steadily increased their percentage of the vote since 1952, when they did not field a candidate. On the basis of this steady growth it would appear that Texas is a likely state in which to look for a possible Republican governor in the next decade. Percentage-wise Virginia would appear to be the next best possibility but, except for the excellent race made by Ted Dalton in 1953, when he polled 44.3 per cent of the vote against Thomas B. Stanley, the Virginia percentage consistently hovers around 36 per cent in most elections. Unless this hard core can be considerably augmented, a Republican governor in Virginia does not appear to be as likely a development as one in Texas. Another possibility might be in Florida. Here the gubernatorial percentage has not risen above 40.2 per cent but the increasing urbanism of the state, very substantial in-

TABLE 1

PERCENTAGE OF TOTAL VOTE FOR PRESIDENT AND GOVERNOR RECEIVED BY REPUBLICAN CANDIDATES IN THE SOUTHERN STATES, 1952-1962[a]

STATE[b]	OFFICE	1952	1953	1954	1956	1957	1958	1960	1961	1962
Alabama	President	35.0			39.4			41.6		
	Governor									c
Arkansas	President	43.8	26.6		45.8		11.2	43.1		
	Governor	12.6		37.9	19.4		17.5	30.8		26.7
Florida	President	55.0			57.2			51.5		
	Governor	25.2		19.5d	26.3			40.2		
Louisiana	President	47.1			53.3			28.6		
	Governor	4.0			c			17.0		
North Carolina	President	46.1			49.3			47.9		
	Governor	32.5			33.0			45.5		
Tennessee	President	50.0			49.2			52.9		
	Governor	20.6		c e			8.3			16.0
Texas	President	53.1			55.3			48.5		
	Governor	c		10.4	14.8		11.9	27.2		45.6
Virginia	President	56.3			55.4			52.4		
	Governor		44.3			36.4			36.0	

a. This table is based in part on data taken from Bernard Cosman, "Republicanism in the Metropolitan South," unpublished Ph.D. dissertation, University of Alabama, 1960, p. 90. The figures on Louisiana for the entire period and the figures for the other states for the years 1960-62 have been added by the author.

b. There were no Republican candidates in Georgia, Mississippi, or South Carolina during this period.

c. No Republican candidate for governor.

d. Special election to fill two years of the unexpired term of Governor Dan McCarty.

e. The term of office for governor in Tennessee was increased from two to four years effective with the 1954 election.

migration and a very active Republican state organization make future increases seem likely.[7]

A point that does not appear in the statistics in Table 1 but which is apparent when similar figures are studied for the period 1920 to 1952 is that the Republicans, except in Texas, did not do appreciably better in the 1950's than they did earlier. For example, during the 1950's the Republican percentages were somewhat higher than during the 1930's. However, in comparison with the 1920's the Republican percentages in the 1950's actually show a decline.[8]

In spite of this negative finding as to Republican strength in the 1950's as compared to the 1920's, there is an interesting trend which developed in the 1950's which deserves further comment. This trend becomes apparent when we depart from a consideration of the total vote and concentrate on a breakdown of the Republican percentages themselves. Such a breakdown will enable us to develop an idea of who votes Republican for governor in the southern states and who is likely to do so in the future. There have been several studies of this nature on presidential Republicanism, one of the most recent being Donald Strong's *Urban Republicanism in the South*. This study concentrates primarily on the presidential races of 1952 and 1956. Strong makes a good case for presidential Republicanism and concludes that

> Eisenhower was strongest in 1956 in the larger cities. Within these cities his greatest strength was always in the upper-income neighborhood. . . . The question remains whether this support for Eisenhower is merely a flash in the pan or whether it is a harbinger of future developments. The author's guess is that it is an early step in the long-run trend toward an enduring presidential Republicanism accompanied by a lesser amount of the grassroots variety.[9]

Strong's forecast proved correct at least for the 1960 election. While the Republicans lost two states, their strength still lay in the larger cities in the upper-income neighborhoods with Nixon just as it had

[7]Another straw in the wind in Florida is the fact that the Republicans in 1963 captured 12 of the 40 newly created seats in Florida's reapportioned legislature. These victories gave the Republicans 2 of 45 senators and 16 of 125 house seats. These 18 members are the largest Republican representation in the Florida Legislature since Reconstruction days.

[8]This same conclusion was reached by Alexander Heard in *A Two-Party South?* (Chapel Hill: The University of North Carolina Press, 1952), p. 73.

[9]Donald S. Strong, *Urban Republicanism in the South* (University, Alabama: Bureau of Public Administration, 1960), p. 48.

with Eisenhower.[10]   The support for the Republicans did not drop to the pre-1952 level without the General.

From the point of view of this article the principal question is whether the same trend is evident in the voting for governor. One might also raise the question of whether the lesser amount of grass-roots variety of Republicanism of which Donald Strong speaks might be supposed to include an occasional gubernatorial breakthrough. There is some evidence to support the contention that a somewhat spotty development of grassroots gubernatorial Republicanism is taking place and that it follows much the same pattern, at a some-what lower level of intensity, as does presidential Republicanism. The first fact that might support such a conclusion is that the South is rapidly becoming more urban and that a larger and larger propor-tion of the population is now found in cities of fifty thousand or more. This urbanism is of particular significance for the guberna-torial races because they are statewide contests. In such a contest a candidate must pick up votes wherever he can find them. Hence, a city vote is just as important as a rural vote and there are now more and more votes to be had in the cities, which even in the South are rapidly developing into metropolitan areas containing the bulk of the state's population.[11]

Not only is the South becoming more urban but there is an in-creasing tendency of the voters in the cities in almost all the South-ern states to vote Republican for governor as well as for president. This tendency is clearly demonstrated when the Republican vote for governor is analyzed by looking at the behavior of the traditionally Republican counties, the urban counties, and the non-urban counties.

[10]See Bernard Cosman, "Presidential Republicanism in the South, 1960," *The Journal of Politics,* 24 (May, 1962), 303.

[11]Only Mississippi presents any real departure from a straight plurality deci-sion in the general election. Under an electoral system established in 1963 each county has as many electoral votes for governor as it has members in the state house of representatives. The candidate who has a plurality in a county is entitled to all of the electoral votes of that county In order to be elected gov-ernor a candidate must get both a majority of the popular vote and a majority of the electoral vote. If there is a tie or if no candidate wins both a popular and electoral majority, the house of representatives decides the election.

After an analysis of implications of the new system, Donald S. Vaughan concludes that ". . . the Mississippi electoral system is of no more consequence today than it has been in the past. Only the emergence within the state of a third factional alignment of substantial strength would threaten the automatic majority which the two-party system tends to produce." See "Mississippi's System For Electing A Governor," *Public Administration Survey* 10 (July, 1963), 5.

Most of the 142 traditionally Republican counties are found in a string of counties that generally follow the highlands in North Carolina, Tennessee and Virginia.[12] Included in this category are all those counties which gave at least 35 per cent of their vote to the Republican candidate in 75 per cent of the presidential elections between 1900 and 1948, excluding the election of 1912. The urban counties are those counties (some 43) which include a city of 50,000 or more in population according to the 1950 census. Added to this group are the five independent cities in Virginia with 50,000 or more population. This definition is roughly equivalent to the old census definition of a standard metropolitan area which was defined as a county, or group of counties, which contains a city of 50,000 inhabitants or more. The non-urban counties are those which remain after we have taken out the urban counties and the traditionally Republican counties. Consequently, when we speak of the non-urban vote in this section we mean the vote in a state outside the urban and traditionally Republican counties.[13] Table 2 gives a breakdown of the Republican vote on the basis of traditional, urban and non-urban counties for the period 1952-62. Figures on the urban and non-urban counties in Florida and Louisiana are included also even though there are no traditionally Republican counties in these states because of a Republican challenge in at least two elections during the period under consideration.

What this table shows is that the gubernatorial candidates, as one would expect, did best in the traditional Republican counties. It shows also that the Republican candidates ran stronger in the urban counties than in the non-urban counties.[14] This is the key finding from the point of view of our discussion. If the Republicans are running strong in the urban counties, and if the population of these counties vis-a-vis the rest of the state is growing, then if the projection continues to hold true in fact, we may expect a gradual increase in the percentage Republican of the urban counties. Of course, to win an election this percentage would have to be increased

[12]In addition there are five traditionally Republican counties in Texas, four in Arkansas, eight in Alabama, and six in Georgia.

[13]There are a few urban counties which are traditionally Republican such as Forsyth County (Winston-Salem), North Carolina; Guilford County (Greensboro), North Carolina; Hamilton County (Chattanooga), Tennessee; and Knox County (Knoxville), Tennessee. These counties are not included in the urban vote.

[14]The only exception to this pattern was in Tennessee in the 1952 election.

substantially, so that when it is added to the traditional Republican and non-urban counties it would give the gubernatorial candidate enough votes to carry the state. This increase did not occur during the period under consideration, since the closest vote was the 45.6 per cent polled by the Republican gubernatorial candidate in Texas in 1962. However, the increase in urban Republicanism is still of significance for the future.

One caveat may be injected at this point by noting that, while our evidence is not completely satisfactory, the evidence we do have indicates that the voters who support the Republican gubernatorial candidates are the same voters who vote for the GOP's presidential candidates. A disproportionate share of these Republican votes are drawn from the upper-income brackets. On the other hand, the blue collar segment of the white population and most of the Negro population are much less enthusiastic for the GOP standard bearers. Moreover, in the past these two groups have not been as politically active as the upper-income group.[15] If they do become politically active, then we have no reason to assume that they will necessarily vote Republican. In fact, if they follow the practice of the same type of voters in other parts of the country, they will probably vote Democratic both at the presidential and the gubernatorial level. Hence, what we may have in the growth of urban Republicanism may be a short term cyclical trend rather than a long term secular trend. Thus, when the lower income groups are heard from, the trend toward urban Republicanism may well be reversed. However, if we may assume that the trend toward urban Republicanism will grow at a faster rate than the contrary trend to political activism, we may find that some governors will be elected in the interim period from the upper-income urban vote. This is a good possibility in such outlying southern states as Texas and Florida before the reverse trend actually sets in. It is on this assumption that the author believes that we will have a spotty but steady increase in the urban Republican vote and that this vote will be enough to elect a governor in one of these states in the next decade.

It should be pointed out, however, that the reasons that cause many upper-income voters to become disenchanted with the national Democratic Party do not necessarily apply with equal force to the governor's race. At the state level we are not likely to get a contest

[15]See V. O. Key, Jr., *Public Opinion and American Democracy* (New York: Alfred A. Knopf, 1961), p. 105.

TABLE 2
Percentage of Total Vote for Governor Received By Republican Candidate in the Traditional, Urban, and Non-Urban Counties, 1952-1962[a]

State[b]		1952	1953	1954	1956	1957	1958	1960	1961	1962
Alabama	Traditional			35.0			25.1			c
	Urban			38.5			14.4			
	Non-Urban			18.5			5.6			
Arkansas	Traditional	40.4		37.6	32.6		33.7	44.9		34.1
	Urban	12.1		52.9	23.6		19.3	37.5		33.1
	Non-Urban	11.4		35.6	18.2		16.4	29.1		25.3
Florida	Traditional	30.0		23.0[d]	27.4			42.7		
	Urban	19.9		15.4	25.2			37.5		
	Non-Urban	e			c			22.6		
Louisiana	Traditional							14.4		
	Urban									
	Non-Urban									
North Carolina	Traditional	46.5			45.8			54.5		
	Urban	27.9			30.9			47.4		
	Non-Urban	20.0			20.9			35.7		
Tennessee	Traditional	33.8		c			11.0			24.7
	Urban	8.2					7.6			10.6
	Non-Urban	8.3					4.2			5.3
Texas	Traditional	c		16.6	30.3		23.0	38.3		54.1
	Urban			14.2	20.7		15.7	31.5		47.9
	Non-Urban			6.7	8.7		7.0	22.4		42.5
Virginia	Traditional		52.1			48.9			46.7	
	Urban		48.4			38.4			38.6	
	Non-Urban		38.6			30.7			31.0	

[a]This table is based in part on data taken from Bernard Cosman, "Republicanism in the Metropolitan South," unpublished Ph.D. dissertation, University of Alabama, 1960, p. 94.

[b]There were no Republican candidates in Georgia, Mississippi, and South Carolina during this period.

[c]No Republican candidate.

[d]Special election to fill two years of the unexpired term of Governor Dan McCarty.

[e]Republican candidate polled only 1.0 per cent of total vote in 1952.

between a liberal Democrat and a conservative Republican. Rather the race is more likely to be between a conservative Democrat and a conservative Republican. In this situation the old ties to the Democratic Party and the force of habit and tradition may prevent many life-long Democrats from voting Republican. Hence, we can expect a much slower rate of change at the gubernatorial level than at the presidential level. It may not be quite a glacial change, but we can expect it to be far from rapid particularly in the Deep South. On the other hand, conditions in Texas and Florida seem more favorable for such a shift. In Texas the Republican vote has been increasing steadily since 1952, and it appears that the urban vote added to the traditional Republican vote may push the total Republican vote into the winning column. In Florida the in-migration of Republican voters, particularly in the southern half of the state, coupled with the increasingly Republican urban vote and presence of an active party organization seems to indicate that in this state also the Republicans may push into the winning column in spite of the absence of a traditionally Republican vote on which to build a winning combination. Consequently, we may find ourselves with the first Republican governor in the South in one of these states since Alfred A. Taylor (1921-23) was elected in Tennessee.

The Tenor of the Times

Even if the southern governor were not basically a program oriented individual, the tenor of the times would force him to become program oriented on at least one issue—that of the desegregation of the public schools. *Brown* v. *Board of Education* forced all of the southern states to reassess the position which they had assumed on the basis of the separate but equal doctrine. This issue was one on which all the governors since 1954 had to take a stand. While the resulting stands varied, no governor could afford inaction in the face of this far-reaching decision. If he took no stand the courts might well decide his policy for him. Hence, he had to adopt some course such as proclaiming massive resistance, vowing to put himself in the school house door, or deciding to bow more gracefully to the Court's decision after going through the motions of combating the decision through "all legal means." In short, the governors of the southern states since 1954 had to do something about integration, and all of them did. The first example of gubernatorial leadership in this area came from Arkansas where Governor Orval Faubus was in his second term as the chief executive of that state. The evidence does not seem to suggest that Faubus was elected as an extreme segregationist candidate. He made no speeches about stationing himself in the school house door, and did not have in his original platform any program of massive resistance. Of course, he was publicly in favor of segregation as were all of the gubernatorial candidates of this era. However, in the primary in the Spring of 1956 Faubus, as a moderate, easily defeated State Senator James Johnson, Director of the Citizens Councils of Arkansas, who ran on a strong segregationist platform. Something of the original attitude of Governor Faubus may be seen from the fact that when Governor Marvin Griffin of Georgia was invited to Little Rock to address the Capital Citizens Council, Governor Faubus telephoned him for assurances that his talk would not be inflammatory. Upon such assurances, he then invited Governor Griffin to stay at the Governor's mansion for his appearance on August 22, 1957.[16]

In spite of what appeared to be a moderate beginning, the tangled chain of events in Little Rock led Governor Faubus to take a strong stand for what he called "law and order" by calling out the Arkansas National Guard to surround Central High School and prevent its integration. Thus he became the central figure in a struggle between federal and state power that ultimately resulted in the federalization of the Guard and the sending of federal troops to Little Rock to insure the integration of Central High School.

The fact that Central High eventually was integrated in spite of all that Governor Faubus could do seemed to be a lesson that was totally lost on Governor Ross Barnett of Mississippi. When his turn came some five years later with a court order for the integration of the University of Mississippi, he repeated the Faubus performance with some Mississippi variations. He defied the federal court order for integration at the University and actually stationed himself in the "school house door," or at least in the door of the Board of Trustees of State Institutions of Higher Learning, to prevent James Meredith from registering. The upshot of the whole affair was first the use of federal marshals and later federal troops to see that the court

---

[16]See Corinne Silverman, *The Little Rock Story* (Revised 1959), ICP Case No. 41, published for the ICP by the University of Alabama Press, University, Alabama, 1959, p. 5. This conclusion also seems to be supported by the comparatively moderate stand on segregation taken by Faubus in his campaign for a fifth term in 1962.

orders were enforced, although this was not accomplished without bloodshed. In July of 1963 the last of the federal troops were withdrawn and James Meredith was graduated in August, returning the University to its all-white status.

We may regard the actions of governors Faubus and Barnett as supplying leadership or merely as reflecting the opinion of their constituents. However, the fact remains that they took decisive action, sometimes with disastrous consequences, and that their actions apparently had a substantial degree of support within their respective states.

For a contrasting concept of leadership under the impact of the same crisis, we may turn to Georgia. Here we find a distinctly different attitude typified by the present Governor Carl E. Sanders. Commenting on the integration problem the governor said:

> I am a southerner by birth and at heart, and I believe sincerely in our traditional separation of the races. On the other hand, I am for progress. I am determined during my administration this state will move ahead—fast. And I know that we can't have real progress in the midst of social upheavals. Consequently, while I am governor we are going to obey the laws, we are not going to resist federal court orders with violence, and we are not going to close any schools. We have seen some pretty sorry examples of that kind of folly in the South, and I want none of it in Georgia.[17]

Of course, Governor Sanders, while he must be given credit for his reasonable attitude, did not arrive at his position unaided. Governor Sanders was preceeded by Governor Ernest S. Vandiver, who campaigned, in part, on a segregationist platform. However, during Governor Vandiver's administration Georgia repealed its massive resistance laws and integrated the University of Georgia. As of this writing not only has the University been integrated, but integration has also taken place at Georgia Tech, Emory University and Georgia State College. In addition, the public schools in Atlanta were integrated without incident in the fall of 1961. Both governors were materially assisted by the climate of opinion created by Ralph McGill of the *Atlanta Constitution,* who for several years prior to the attempt to integrate the University of Georgia had constantly hammered on a law and order and progress theme in his editorials. Then too, there had been a distinct change in the population pattern in Georgia for as cotton moved west thousands of farmers poured

---

[17]Quoted by Ben Hibbs in "Progress Goes Marching Through Georgia," *The Saturday Evening Post,* 236 (February 16, 1963) p. 70.

into the cities. This movement has been a fairly recent one since the rural population in 1940 was still 65.6 per cent of the total population. However, by 1950 it had fallen to 54.7 per cent and by 1960 to 44.7 per cent of the total population. Those farmers that remain diversified their farming and while cotton and tobacco are still being grown, other crops have become of great importance. What has happened to Georgia is that a mass movement to the cities has been coupled with diversified farming for those left on the farm. The farmers are in better financial shape than they have ever been before, as are the city folks who are working in industry, such as Lockheed which employs some 15,000 workers at its Marietta plant. This sense of general prosperity played a large part in backing the campaign for moderation by Ralph McGill and the business leaders in the state. All of this added together provided a favorable climate for the integration of the University of Georgia and later was influential in the governor's race which saw Sanders defeating the staunch segregationist Griffin in the primary.

The reapportioning of the Georgia legislature and the fact that the county unit system used in the Democratic primary was declared unconstitutional by the federal courts were steps in the direction of making the city vote more potent in the elections. Governor Sanders would have won the last election even if the county unit system rule had been in effect. However, its demise may be a key factor in future elections since the city folks will play a larger role in the gubernatorial races.

Not all of the recent southern governors have taken the Sanders' view. In Alabama George Wallace was elected on a strong segregationist platform and seemed determined to repeat the examples of Arkansas and Mississippi. Standing on the star on the capitol steps where Jefferson Davis had stood to take the oath of office of the Confederacy, Wallace at his inauguration declared "I draw the line in the dust and toss the gauntlet before the feet of tyranny. . . . I say segregation now, segregation tomorrow, segregation forever."

A test of the Wallace position came in June of 1963 after the Federal courts had ordered the admission of two Negro students to the summer session of the University of Alabama. On the day of their scheduled admission the governor took his stand in the doorway of Foster Auditorium and refused to stand aside when requested to do so by the Deputy Attorney General of the United States. While this confrontation was taking place the Negro students remained in the cars which had brought them to the auditorium. Consequently, technically they were not refused admission by the governor. After the governor's stand, the two students left the scene, but returned later in the day after the Alabama National Guard had been federalized. Faced with the Guard the governor stood aside and the students were registered. The registration took place without violence since the campus was completely surrounded with members of the state highway patrol and other law enforcement officers who maintained law and order under the direction of the governor. A few days later the state forces were withdrawn and the Alabama National Guard took over to maintain the peace. Later in the year the Guard was withdrawn, and the campus returned to normal. One of the students subsequently withdrew from the University; the other continued her studies. Negro students have also registered at two other state university centers without incident.[18]

At the same time that Wallace was inaugurated there was a change of administration in South Carolina. When Governor Ernest F. Hollings turned over the reins of government to his successor, Donald Russell, he made a strong statement to the incoming legislature in which he said that the General Assembly must make clear that South Carolina's choice would be a government of law rather than a government of men. Governor Russell apparently has approached his administration in the spirit suggested by Governor Hollings. The recent peaceful integration of Clemson College with the cooperation of the governor indicates that the new governor stands squarely for law and order in the enforcement of the mandates of the courts.

The general tenor of the statements of most recently elected governors, except Barnett and Wallace, seems to be of increasing moderation in segregation matters. For example, one of them has been quoted as defining a moderate in segregation by saying "In my case a moderate means that I am segregationist but not a damned fool." A few governors, including Governor Terry Sanford of North Carolina, have gone considerably beyond this point. Speaking to the North Carolina Press Association, he said, "The time has come to

---

[18]The situation in the public schools is more complex. The Federal courts have ordered integration in four cities. Integration has proceeded smoothly in Mobile and Huntsville. In Birmingham and Tuskegee (Macon County), there has been serious local resistance, but even here Negro students have entered the public schools.

quit unfair discrimination and to give the Negro a full chance to earn a decent living for his family and to contribute to high standards for himself and all men.. . ." Most of the southern states have not progressed to this point in their thinking, but the leadership from the governor's office seems to be headed in this direction.

The 1960's undoubtedly still hold seeds for further strife particularly in Mississippi and Alabama, but the tide seems to be flowing against the Barnetts and Wallaces and in the direction of the Sanders and Sanfords in the other southern states. We can look for the South's chief executives in the 60's to demonstrate continued gubernatorial leadership on segregation with the emphasis on moderation, continued steps toward integration and, above all, the maintenance of law and order. If the South is to progress, it must have a stable climate to attract industry. This is a point which the businessmen of Atlanta seem to have grasped but is one which is still eluding their counterparts in Alabama and Mississippi. Once this point has been established, the way may be paved for further progress in integration. However, we must remember that it is one thing to integrate a state university and quite another thing to integrate a primary school in a black belt county. The way to the latter will be long and hard, and the author does not foresee a complete integration of the secondary and primary system as a logical product of the next decade in spite of gubernatorial leadership in that direction.

THE NEXT DECADE

The most significant development in gubernatorial leadership in the 1950's seems to have been the leadership furnished by the governors in the integration crisis. In spite of the fact that many of the southern governors were not in a strong legal position in their respective states, all of them provided leadership either in compliance or defiance of the Supreme Court's decision in the realm of integration in education. The tide seems to be moving in the direction of compliance with the exception of Mississippi and Alabama. Even in the latter state it should be pointed out that the integration of the University of Alabama to date has been accomplished without violence and that law and order were maintained by the governor.

However, the way to further integration in education, to say nothing of the provision of equal opportunities in employment or the right to equal services in businesses serving the public, still would seem to be long and difficult. The possibilities of violence and the breakdown of law and order are ever present as the recent experiences in widely scattered cities throughout the South demonstrate. What we can expect in the 60's is a continuation of more enlightened gubernatorial leadership in the very difficult area of race relations, but we can also expect progress to be slow and setbacks to be frequent.

On another, if less spectacular front, we may expect what will be for the South a revolutionary change in voting behavior at the gubernatorial level. Republican opposition in gubernatorial races should grow and it is not unlikely that the next decade will see the election of a Republican governor in such rapidly industrializing and increasing urban states as Florida and Texas.

In legislative affairs we may look for continued gubernatorial leadership in spite of the governor's weak legal position in many southern states. It is not clear at this writing just what effect the reapportionment of state legislatures will have on the governor's role as a legislative leader. Such reapportionments should spread under the impetus of the decision in *Baker* v. *Carr* with a resulting increase in the urban representation in the legislature. Whether such an increase will give the governor a stronger basis for support remains to be seen.

The governor's legal position probably will not change substantially since there appears to be no widespread movement to strengthen his position by allowing him to succeed himself, by increasing his powers of appointment, or by providing him with a stronger voice in budgeting. However, isolated changes in any of these areas are possible as the 1954 shift from a two-year term to a four-year term in Tennessee illustrates.

The governor's role as spokesman for the state is likely to grow from the pressure of events, particularly in the race relations field.[19] It also seems likely that the Governor will speak with increasingly stronger urban overtones since continuing urbanization and realignment of population will give the urban voters a larger voice in the selection of the governor.

The 1960's will be a crucial time for state governments in the South. The problem of race relations has become in the last few

[19]One recent example of this role is the fact that both governors Barnett and Wallace testified in July of 1963 before the Commerce Committee of the United States Senate in opposition to the President's civil rights legislation.

months a nationwide rather than a regional problem. However, it will continue to be an extremely significant problem in the South because of the concentration of Negro citizens in most of our southern states. Hence, the question of the governor's political leadership will be of crucial importance in the 1960's. How well the governors fulfill their role may well be the difference between orderly progress and chaos.

THE SOUTH IN NATIONAL POLITICS

O. DOUGLAS WEEKS
The University of Texas

THE PRESENT MOMENT is a most difficult time to say anything definitive about the South in national politics—1950 to 1970. It is perhaps too soon to place any final interpretations on what the political events and changes of the 1950's and early 1960's have meant in the political life and institutions of the South and on its present place in national politics. It is hard to prophesy what confronts the Nation as a whole, as well as the South, for the next year, let alone the remainder of the decade. The present is no doubt a very critical time in the history of what has always been the controlling issue in the South and the chief shaper of her politics and political system. Are the organized Negroes and their friends about to force their way into full equality, or will their persistence produce a reaction in politics and otherwise which will set back their cause for years to come both in the North and South?

The race issue is always uppermost in Southern politics, but economic issues are never far behind. The South in general has in recent times undergone in effect an extensive economic revolution, which has not been completed by any means, but which has had and will have profound effects upon its political system and its place in national politics. To some extent the two revolutions are interrelated. What this will lead to by 1970 is difficult to foresee.

Much of the background for the concluding article of this symposium has been provided by the preceding articles, and yet the political customs, institutions, practices, and behavior patterns which have been subjected to the process of change must be understood before the changes are taken up in detail. In the present case the "Solid South" is what is undergoing change and possible dissolution.

THE SOLID SOUTH

From the end of Reconstruction and for nearly thirty years into the Twentieth Century, the eleven states of the South, except for a few areas and a few elective places, supported the Democratic ticket "from president to constable." Even though the Democratic party, because of its cleansing baths in Bryan populism in 1896 and Wilson progressivism in 1912, was considered the more liberal of the two major parties, the conservative South remained staunchly loyal to it and showed no signs of revolt until 1928, when its solidity or solidarity was cracked for the first time and the Republicans carried a majority of its vote for the presidency. The section had been two-party in the days before the Civil War, but for sixty years after Reconstruction and for the four times the Democrats attained the presidency in 1884, 1892, 1912, and 1916 and in many congressional elections the party was beholden to the support of the undivided South.

The Republican party, which had figured importantly during Reconstruction, continued on among the white voters in parts of Virginia, North Carolina, and Tennessee, and in certain smaller areas and counties of other Southern states where it still polls a considerable traditional vote and elects local officials, legislators, and members of Congress. The party was also generally supported by those Negroes who could vote until the period of Franklin D. Roosevelt and the New Deal. On the whole, the Republican party ceased to be important in most parts of the South after Reconstruction except as an occasional ally of the Greenback and Populist parties which gave the Democrats serious opposition throughout the South in the depression periods of the 1870's and 1890's.

After the elections of 1900 these third parties disappeared. At about the same time, many of the Southern states by a series of constitutional and legal devices largely eliminated the Negro from participation in politics. Thus, the Republican party was further reduced in importance. State-wide Republican organizations survived, but in all save the states with considerable Republican votes these organizations became machines for choosing and controlling delegations to Republican national conventions and for dispensing federal patronage when the party held the presidency. Thus, for the most part, these organizations became rotten or pocket borough affairs to be manipulated by Republican national leaders like Mark Hanna in 1896 in the nomination of McKinley and by Presidents Theodore Roosevelt and Taft in dictating the Republican nominations of 1908 and 1912. Republican nominating and campaigning functions were de-emphasized except where the party had local areas of strength. In most areas and for most election places the field of elections became frankly recognized as a Democratic monopoly.

While incomplete Republican tickets were nominated usually for some of the state-wide and district elective places, the party took little interest in campaigning for their election.

A factor which further solidified the Democratic South in the early Twentieth Century was the full emergence of the direct primary system of nomination which came to be invariably employed by the Democratic party, whether legally mandatory or not, to make state-wide and district nominations, and, therefore, applied to all congressional nominations, and might even apply to the choice of delegates to Democratic national conventions. For one reason or another the Republicans frequently did not hold primaries, and thus the voters tended to drift into the Democratic primaries and to regard them as the elections, which they came to be in effect, since the nominees of the Democratic primaries almost always won in the increasingly neglected general elections. Moreover, about half the Southern primary laws required parties to finance their own primaries, and this obviously proved to be a hardship on a minority party like the Republican. In approximately the same states the law required parties to administer their own primaries. These and other legal handicaps discouraged the growth of the Republican party and caused more and more voters to participate in the Democratic primaries. The run-off primary, which came to be required in many Southern states where a majority choice was not made in the first primary, was a perfect substitute for the general election. Also the white primary rules devised by party authorities to bar Negroes from participation in Democratic primaries proved more effective than the earlier registration and suffrage restrictions in keeping the Negro out of the political picture. In the black belt states, however, "custom" and "common knowledge" largely took care of the situation without need to invoke law or party rule.

This, then, was the shell or container for most of the politics of the Southern states built up by the Democratic party and within which most political decisions were in effect made. That is, United States senators, governors and other state-wide elective officers, and district and county elective officers were in effect chosen in the Democratic primaries except for the mountain areas of Virginia, North Carolina, and Tennessee and in a few areas in other states. Within the one-party system thus developed there evolved within each state a factional system which varied from state to state and served as a substitute for a party system.[1] In Virginia, for instance, conservative and liberal factions came to operate somewhat like opposing parties nominating complete slates all the way from governor to constable, united by common platforms and campaigning like parties. At the other extreme in states like Texas and Florida, no such permanent factionalism developed. The candidates for each office in the Democratic primary came to stand on their own legs, setting up their own campaign organizations, and adopting their own platforms. Most of the real interest in such systems has centered upon the principal state-wide races like those for United States Senate and governor. In most states the Democratic party as such did no campaigning and its primary was really nothing more than a mechanism for electing public officials and scarcely a partisan affair at all.

While Democratic primaries are concerned with congressional, state, district, and county politics, with what at the national level James MacGregor Burns[2] would call the Congressional Democratic party, the South was scarcely less solid at the presidential level for many years. Certainly, between the turn of the present century and 1928 the Republican presidential vote was at a low ebb. In that year, however, the Solid South experienced its first real split and at that level. The split was a real one, with Virginia, North Carolina, Tennessee, Florida, and Texas deserting the fold. Southern Democrats had never before divided in any very serious way over the Democratic nominees for the presidency, not to the extent at any rate of bolting the ticket. In this case the Catholicism of Al Smith, the Democratic candidate, his opposition to prohibition, and his ubanism, were too much for a staunchly protestant, dry, and still predominantly rural South. The states which bolted were all ones with relatively small Negro populations; Louisiana, Mississippi, and South Carolina with high Negro percentages produced very small Hoover votes. They were perhaps even more intensely prejudiced against what Smith stood for, but they could not go back on the chief reliance, the Democratic party. In the states that bolted it is also true that the largest traditional Republican areas were to be found, and the beginnings of the economic developments which were later to sweep the South were under way. This phenomenal first split

---

[1]These systems are fully described in V. O. Key, Jr., *Southern Politics in State and Nation* (New York: Alfred A. Knopf, 1949) Chs. 1-14. This work describes the Solid South in its prime.

[2]James MacGregor Burns, *The Deadlock of Democracy: Four-Party Politics in America* (Englewood Cliffs, N. J.: Prentice-Hall, Inc., 1963) pp. 271-279.

of 1928 was engineered by very little Republican effort and converted few voters permanently to Republicanism. Moreover, its underlying causes were quite remote, for the most part, from those that
were to produce the later splits. The conditions which in the thirty-
odd years since were to render insecure the superstructure and the
very foundations of the "Solid South" had not as yet developed.

STRAINS ON DEMOCRATIC SOLIDARITY

These conditions are familiar to everybody. They have revolu-
tionized the whole country as well as the South—economically, socially, constitutionally, and politically. We need only to mention
the Depression, the New Deal, World War II and its continuous
aftermath, the Fair Deal, New Republicanism, the New Frontier,
and the Nuclear Age to know what is meant. In the South, agricultural diversification, industrialization, population shifts, urbanization
and suburbanization have done their work. Wholesale political adjustments have been inevitable. The Negro and the Latin American
have made progress politically, labor has become a real power, a
great white-collar class has grown up, and many new immigrants
from beyond the South have come in with the developments. In
many respects these changes have made the South more like the rest
of the country.

With this came the general expansion of governmental power at
all levels, with phenomenal increases in the sphere of the national
government and a complex intermeshing of national and state government and politics. The fact that the Democratic party, the traditional friend and protector of the South and the historical defender
of states rights and rugged individualism, should have been the author of most of these political innovations did not ease the situation
in the South or conduce to harmony within the Democratic party in
the Southern states. While the "New Deal," the expansions and
restraints of wartime controls, the "Fair Deal" and the "New Frontier" have had their friends among Southern Democrats, the traditional loyalty to the party, so strong in the past, could not be expected to survive and flourish with the same vigor. The party shell,
certainly, could no longer serve as adequately as a commodious
container within which all political struggles could take place.

Obviously all this multiplied the special interests and created
many more powerful groups whose demands needed to be satisfied

or compromised politically.[3] In a growing community with many new interests and forms of wealth appearing, the predominant tone of politics tends to be conservative, although it is also true that liberal interests emerge to counteract and combat the more powerful conservative ones. This new emphasis on the extremes of right and left produced a more pronounced pattern of conservatism *versus* liberalism. The moderate center remained as the strongest element. In fact, it has even been greatly enhanced in importance, what with urbanization, suburbanization, and the growth of a white-collar class in general. Also, the many changes in agriculture toward diversification and mechanization and the progressive elimination of tenant farmers and unprofitable types of farming have made their contribution to the growth of the political center.

Political institutions and practices are more resistant to change, however, than those in other areas. In spite of all the stresses and strains, those of the South seem to hang on tenaciously and to retain much of their form and spirit. In short, the South still has substantially its one-party system in spite of many alterations and adjustments. Many are the signs that something different is on its way, but the South is adept at applying a delaying process in political matters which reduces greatly the rate of change. The system is by no means what it was in 1928 or even when V. O. Key, Jr. described it in 1949.[4] The changes, however, have been slow in coming and may well continue to be in the immediate future or at least for the remainder of the present decade.

The real beginning of the process of change in the political system of the South and its place in national politics did not fully get under way until the 1940's. In 1932 the South was engulfed in the depression along with the rest of the country, and reacted favorably to the first stages of Roosevelt's New Deal as the country in general did. It provided many outstanding leaders in Congress and elsewhere who were staunch supporters and lieutenants of the President. By 1936 considerable extreme right and left fringe group opposition had developed, some of which came from the South, but when the election of that year was over, Roosevelt was seen to have swept the whole country by an unprecedented landslide. In his second term, he shifted definitely to the left because the business interests had

[3]Marian D. Irish, "Political Thought and Political Behavior in the South," *Western Political Quarterly*, XIII, No. 2, June 1960, pp. 406-420.

[4]Key, *op. cit.*

deserted him and leftists had given considerable support to minority groups in 1936. This did not gain him support in the South.

In 1940 the sidetracking of Vice President Garner of Texas and the substitution of the leftist Henry Wallace as the President's choice for Garner's office, as well as his own candidacy for a third term, were not too popular in the South. Moreover, Senator Glass of Virginia had opposed Roosevelt's renomination and Senator Bankhead of Alabama had been Wallace's chief opponent for the vice presidential nomination. Wendell Willkie, the Republican candidate for president, attracted supporters in the South among economic conservatives and opponents of a third term for Roosevelt which resulted in a considerable increase in the Republican popular vote in the South. In 1940 it was almost equal to that of the later Republican vote of 1948.

The first real rift in the South which was to lead to more or less chronic cleavage came in 1944. In this year the Supreme Court of the United States invalidated the Texas white primary in *Smith v. Allwright*[5] which was met immediately in South Carolina by an elaborate attempt to circumvent the decision by repealing all references in the state constitution and statutes to political parties and primaries and thus taking them out from under any restraints of the Fourteenth and Fifteenth amendments. Real Democratic opposition to Roosevelt's nomination for a fourth term developed in some Southern states including Texas, Mississippi, and South Carolina. Here conventions withheld the pledging of party presidential electors pending the outcome of the Democratic National Convention. Conditions were laid down to be met by the the National Convention in return for electors being bound to vote for Roosevelt. These were: restoration of the old two-thirds rule for nominations; rejection of Henry Wallace as nominee for the vice presidency; and a "white supremacy" plank in the Democratic platform. Needless to say, except for the nomination of Harry S. Truman in the place of Henry Wallace for the vice presidency, the Convention did not meet these conditions. The rival delegations from Texas were both seated and the State's vote divided between them. The so-called Texas Regulars, who bolted after the Democratic National Convention, ran a separate electoral ticket in Texas pledged to Senator Byrd of Virginia which polled 135,439 votes as opposed to 821,605 cast for the Democratic electors. The South, however, again remained solid.

[5]321 U. S. 649 (1944).

While the racial issue made an entering wedge into the 1944 situation, the opposition within the Southern Democratic party came more from economic than racial issues. The racial issue had never really been forced by Roosevelt and the New Deal. That was to be the work of Truman and the Fair Deal, and it came in 1948. The Negro had been the real cause of the Solid South. The Democratic party had been the chief protector of the Solid South. When it ceased to be, the real split had come. How long would it remain one-party?

The presidential election of 1944 was the last one in which the South gave its entire electoral vote to the Democratic party. In the subsequent ones—1948, 1952, 1956, and 1960, the Solid South if not broken has at least been cracked. In fact after the death of President Roosevelt in 1945 the great coalition he had built up over the country in 1932 and had fairly well held together to 1944 seemed to be in the process of disintegration. Both houses of Congress went to the Republicans in the off-year election of 1946 for the first time in 18 years. If the usual signs held true, this would mean a Republican president in 1948.

Not until 1948 arrived, however, did the South show any serious indication of deserting the Democratic fold. In fact, late in 1947 it appeared as though President Truman might be in serious need of the old-time solid support of the Southern states if he were to remain in office. On December 29, 1947, former Vice President Henry A. Wallace, who had broken with Truman, announced he would seek the presidency on a third-party ticket which presumably would draw off the extreme left wing of the Democratic party. In spite of this defection, on February 2, 1948, the President sent a special message to Congress urging action upon a ten-point civil rights program not designed to hold the conservative Southern wing in line. It was based upon the proposals of his Committee on Civil Rights, submitted to him in October, 1947. The South was soon heard from. In March, 1948, seven of the fifteen members of the Conference of Southern Governors condemned the program and pledged themselves to oppose the nomination of any candidate who did not disavow it. They urged the selection of Convention delegates and presidential electors committed to this line of action. Southern state delegations to the Democratic National Convention were generally pledged not to support the Truman program. In the Convention, after much Southern maneuvering to sidetrack it, an amendment was adopted endorsing the civil rights program and demanding that Congress enact anti-poll tax, fair-employment practices, anti-lynching and anti-discrimination legislation. The Truman platform was thus victorious, and the Mississippi delegation and half the Alabama delegation walked out. Truman was nominated by 947½ votes. Senator Russell, the Southern choice, received a unanimous vote from each Southern state except North Carolina, which gave 13 of its 32 votes to Truman. Thus the Convention was split practically along the Mason-Dixon line, with the radical left of the Northern segment of the party organized into the so-called Progressive party. In the end, however, would the Southern Democrats split off in a solid block? There was not much chance of it.

As it turned out, the Southern revolt of 1948 was from the deep South and not from the rim as in 1928. It soon became organized and took the name of "States Rights Democrats," but was more familiarly known as the "Dixiecrats." In Alabama, Mississippi, Louisiana and South Carolina, it captured the machinery of the Democratic party; in the rest it was forced to assume the status of a third party. Most of the important Democratic leaders over the South refused to have anything to do with it. While the Dixiecrats ran tickets in all Southern states, their electors won only in Alabama (where the regular Democratic ticket was denied a place on the ballot), Mississippi, South Carolina, and Louisiana; in the first three by very large majorities; in the last by a smaller one. Only the states which had bolted in 1928 showed sizeable Republican votes, which was to have been expected, because they long had produced such votes. In this election the quarrel was within the Democratic party. The states which broke with the party were not yet ready to support the Republican candidates. The bolters tried to maintain the fiction that they were not bolting the Democratic party but that it was bolting them. The election of 1948 was a family quarrel among Democrats as was that of 1928. Shifting to the Republican party was still in the future, but its beginnings were soon to come. An amazing result of this election was that against all polls, prophecies, and expectations Mr. Truman was elected to a second term without the benefit of a left wing and a Solid South.

THE SOLID SOUTH CRACKS

Since 1948, the South had never settled back to its customary solidarity and political tranquility. The fifteen years since that date have witnessed more changes than even the previous fifteen and certainly more unsettling to the South's customary ways. Accelerated economic and social developments greatly altered the political outlook and disturbed political behavior patterns more than ever. The developments previously noted in the late thirties and early forties were multiplied: more new industries, more growth of cities, more population shifts, more immigrants from other parts of the country with ideas both liberal and conservative, more middle class, more effective labor and Negro political participation. This meant more complex and intense factionalism within the dominant Democratic party, much more activity on the part of powerful groups, and the emergence of the Republican party as a factor particularly in the part played by the South in national politics.

It might have been expected, perhaps, that under all the new conditions arising the peculiar race relationships long established in the South would not remain unquestioned and undisturbed. As a matter of fact, President Truman and his ten-point civil rights program really had set the ball rolling in 1948, followed by the United States Supreme Court putting the *coup de grace* on the white primary in *Rice v. Elmore*[6] and the Dixiecrat movement later in the year. From then on the civil rights question really never died down as a central issue in the politics of the South. The whole complex pattern of racial segregation and discrimination has been attacked and defended in every branch of the national government and of the governments of the Southern States.

The United States Supreme Court's decisions decreeing racial integration in the schools have led to the most continuous and widespread controversy and to varied and elaborate legislative subterfuges in some states designed to get around national policy. Executive action, both national and state, both civilian and military, have entered into the picture. Republican President Eisenhower had his Little Rock and Democratic President Kennedy his Oxford, Mississippi. Latterly, the whole controversy has gone beyond the South and has moved more or less out of the legal and governmental sphere into that of direct action. The practical results, one way or the other, had been so meager that the Negro grew restive and impatient and resorted to a variety of methods of mass demonstration, the most dramatic and latest being the "March on Washington," where in Congress a civil rights bill was and is pending at the time of writing.

[6]333 U. S. 875 (1948).

A most important result of all these economic and ethnic problems of the 1950's and 1960's has been the entry of the Republican party in a bigger and more permanent way not only into the rim but to some degree even into the black belt states of the South. National politics in the South between 1928 and 1948 was to a large extent still confined within the Democratic party and consisted of intra-party family quarrels. True, the Solid South was cracked in those two presidential election years. In 1928 five states—nearly half of the eleven—had voted Republican, and in 1948 four had deserted the national Democratic ticket but they had not gone Republican. The first five were rim states; the last four from the black belt. Only two states, Arkansas and Georgia, refused to bolt in both years, and have since refused in all subsequent elections. In the four presidential elections between 1928 and 1948 the provocations were great, but the old Confederacy stayed solid and the six states still held the record of never having gone Republican since Reconstruction.

Beginning with the presidential election of 1952, the Republican party seems to have moved in at the level of presidential politics on a rather permanent basis, because its presidential tickets have piled up immense popular votes in 1952, 1956 and 1960 and have carried some states each election. Four states (Florida, Tennessee, Texas, and Virginia) voted Republican the first year, five (Florida, Louisiana, Tennessee, Texas, and Virginia) the second year, and three (Florida, Tennessee, and Virginia) the last year. Also in 1960 Alabama had six independent electors and Mississippi eight, all of whom voted not for Republican candidate Nixon but for conservative Democratic Senator Byrd of Virginia. While Republican popular presidential votes in black belt states have tended to mount in these last three elections, Louisiana is the only state of this group that has so far gone over the line. The three consistent bolters to the Republican presidential ticket beginning in 1952 have been Florida, Tennessee, and Virginia. They also voted Republican in 1928. Texas went Republican in 1952 and 1956 and also in 1928. North Carolina has not voted Republican since 1928.

To a very large extent the activities in support of the Eisenhower ticket in 1952 were the work of dissident Democrats. "Democrats for Eisenhower" or temporary organizations with some such names came rapidly into existence and bore the brunt of the campaign. In most cases the Republican organization was inadequate to the task.

In Texas "Republicans for a day," who favored Eisenhower, in many cases swamped local Republican conventions and in the end took over the State party machinery.[7] Two years later Hodding Carter complained that even in the four states that went for Eisenhower in 1952 (Virginia, Florida, Tennessee, and Texas) very little effort had been made to build up a two-party system even down to the congressional level.[8] In other words, the sweeping victory in these states and big votes even in other states seemed to mean no more than the election of 1928. Would the South return to its normal Democratic loyalty as it had in 1932? Had it merely been swept off its feet by the personality and reputation of Eisenhower?

Analyses of the election of 1952[9] in the South seemed to indicate, however, that there were possibilities for building up something of a permanent Republican presidential opposition if people who professed to be Republicans or who said they wanted to see a two-party system would get to work. It was noted that a liberal versus conservative alignment was definitely discernible in most of the Southern urban areas. The facts showed that the Eisenhower strength was largely concentrated in these areas in Alabama, Arkansas, Florida, Georgia, Louisiana, Mississippi, North Carolina, Tennessee, and Texas. Only in South Carolina and Virginia was the city support of Eisenhower less pronounced. In some of the cities the pattern of voting was that of a strong Eisenhower vote in the upper income white precincts, a predominant Stevenson vote in the lower income white precincts, and a heavy Stevenson vote in the white laboring class and Negro precincts. The newer and more rapidly developing geographical areas added their strength to the cities in support of Eisenhower—the southern and newer half of Florida and the western, Gulf coast, and Rio Grande Valley areas of Texas as well as the newly industrialized areas in various other states. Also, the traditionally Republican areas of western Virginia, western North Carolina, eastern Tennessee, and the German counties of south central Texas added their weight. Joined with these elements were the

[7]O. Douglas Weeks, *Texas Presidential Politics in 1952* (Austin: Institute of Public Affairs, The University of Texas, 1953).

[8]Hodding Carter, "The Republicans Muffed the Ball in Dixie," *Saturday Evening Post,* August 21, 1954.

[9]See Donald S. Strong, *The 1952 Presidential Election in the South* (University of Alabama: Bureau of Public Administration, 1955); *The South,* Vol. 3 of *Presidential Nominating Politics in 1952.* Edited by Paul T. David, Malcolm Moos and Ralph M. Goldman (Baltimore: Johns Hopkins Press, 1954).

black belt whites in some counties of Alabama, Louisiana, Mississippi, and South Carolina, although similar areas in Georgia, North Carolina, Tennessee, Texas, and Virginia remained loyal to Stevenson.[10]

However, by 1954, it was felt by many that the Eisenhower coalition had disintegrated. Its constituent elements had by no means been converted to Republicanism or to Eisenhower. The vast majority dutifully returned to the Democratic primaries in 1954 and 1956. With the restoration of relative harmony in the national Democratic party in the latter year, many of the urban Eisenhowerites returned to the fold. Most of the Texas voters, for example, who were with the Shivers conservatives in 1952 shifted back to a shaky union with the liberal-loyalists in the 1956 conventions and primaries and shifted again to vote for Eisenhower in the general election. These people were not Republicans, nor were they about to become Republicans. As one writer put it:

> The Republicans did not convert the hosts of crusading amateurs who fought for Ike in '52 into a deep-going grass-roots organization, and The Republican "party" in Texas today could hold its caucus in a broom closet.[11]

In fact, the Democratic party in the South had remained as usual huge and all-embracing since 1952; nowhere had the Republican party become a party in any complete sense. It had made little progress in congressional, state, and local elections. Even in Florida, North Carolina, Tennessee, Texas, and Virginia, where respectable Republican organizations existed in certain areas, the one-party system still obtained. It was true that in 1956 more Republicans ran for Congress than in 1954 and 1952. They sought election to the House in 38 of the 94 congressional districts in nine Southern states as against 32 in 1954 of which they won seven and 30 in 1952 of which they won eight. In 1954 they gained only two seats and lost one they had won in 1952. In state and local politics, the monopolistic position of the Democratic party remained unassailed. Its primaries were still the determining elections.

Only the presidential break of 1956 was satisfactory to would-be Republican organizers, for it was even better than 1952 when Eisenhower had polled 48 per cent of the Southern popular vote. Now it was 49 per cent and was a plurality. These percentages stood out in

[10]Strong, *op. cit.*

[11]Harold H. Martin, "How Will the South Go"? *Colliers,* September 29 1956, p. 119.

strong contrast to Republican Dewey's 26 per cent in 1948 and his 25 per cent in 1944. The location of Eisenhower's support for 1956 followed that for 1952. In 1956 the Republican nominee did best in all states in the metropolitan counties and not quite as well in counties with smaller cities. Between 1952 and 1956 two shifts should be noted. Black-belt whites who were attracted to Eisenhower fell away in 1956, and Southern Negroes moved from a strong Democratic support in 1952 to about a 50-50 split in 1956. It has also been noted that Eisenhower did better in both elections in growing prosperous cities.[12]

Was the presidential election of 1956 another Republican victory to be explained largely on the popularity of Eisenhower? What would happen in 1960 when he could not be a candidate? This was the big question in the late fifties and as the election of 1960 approached. Both major parties put on the most steam ever in the history of national campaigns, and the efforts in the South were far more extensive and intensive than in 1952 or 1956. National Democratic and Republican headquarters looked upon much of the South as doubtful. Polls indicated several states safe for Nixon, only two or three leaning toward Kennedy and the rest uncertain. In previous campaigns the candidates for president and vice president did not make as many appearances. In 1960 Nixon appeared in every Southern State and Kennedy visited six. Senator Lyndon Johnson made a whistle-stop tour of eight Southern States covering 2,500 miles, a feat before unheard of in the South. This and the intensive efforts of Johnson and Speaker Rayburn in saving Texas by a hair's breadth, are as good an explanation for the election of Kennedy as anything else.[13] Moreover, the campaign of 1960 showed the Southern state and many of the local Republican party units as better organized and Democratic party organizations and Democrats for Nixon organizations as more effective than in the previous two elections.

Most noteworthy for 1960, however, were the facts that the voter increase was highest in the South and that the Nixon-Lodge ticket of the Republicans polled around a half-million more votes than the Eisenhower-Nixon ticket of 1956. Moreover, more votes

[12]See Donald S. Strong, *Urban Republicanism in the South* (University, Alabama: Bureau of Public Administration, 1960) for an analysis of the presidential election of 1956.
[13]O. Douglas Weeks, *Texas in the 1960 Presidential Election* (Austin: Institute of Public Affairs, The University of Texas, 1961).

were cast in 1960 for the former in nine of the eleven Southern states than before; only Arkansas and Louisiana fell behind. Like the rest of the nation, margins were close in most Southern states and very narrow in South Carolina and Texas. It is estimated that for the South as a whole there were 4.6 Republican votes for every five Democratic votes.[14]

In the nation at large it was estimated that Kennedy won 65 per cent of the vote of the large cities whereas Stevenson in 1956 won only 52 per cent. Even suburban areas, a source of Republican strength in recent elections, produced decreased Republican votes. The South followed this trend. The most important explanations for this were the strong Roman Catholic support of Kennedy, most notable in the cities, the solidification of the Negro vote for the Democrats, and the increased activity of organized labor in getting out the working-class vote and holding it for Kennedy. To a lesser extent did the religious issue unite the Protestants. Many Protestant ministers wore out the issue before the campaign was over. Also Kennedy's disarming statements about his faith overcame considerable Protestant opposition. Kennedy appealed strongly to the Negroes, while Nixon and the Republican campaigners neglected the Negro voters and muffled the civil rights issue in their eagerness to win conservative whites. The Eisenhower administration must have appeared in part responsible for the slow progress of integration. So far as white voters were concerned, the civil rights issue was somewhat neutralized. Both parties seemed to take about the same stand in their platforms and in the pronouncements of their candidates. Segregationists, having failed to get much consolation out of Eisenhower and eight years of Republicanism in the White House, settled down to contenting themselves with strong statements in state party platforms and returning to their traditional Democratic loyalty.

It should be noted that there was a greater degree of Democratic harmony among Southern party leaders in 1960 than there had been in 1952 or 1956. Arthur Krock attributes to Lyndon Johnson a great deal of the credit for creating this harmony:

> Johnson used his great influence to convince every important Southern party leader except Senator Byrd of Virginia that by party regularity they could restrain the "liberal" Democratic majority. Since they also depend on Democratic national victory and the seniority system for their powerful places in Congress and their states organizations, and

[14]*Austin American Statesman,* December 4, 1960.

on local party regularity for the offices they hold or seek, Johnson could use these arguments effectively. Also they "got the strong impression" (quoting one of them) and managed to persuade their resentful constituents, that Johnson would somehow see to it that the extreme proposals they bitterly resented in the Los Angeles platform would never become acts of Congress during a Kennedy-Johnson administration.[15]

Thus the hope of a continued Republican-Southern Democratic coalition in Congress emerged once again as the last ditch defense of the South together with the rule of seniority in a Congress with somewhat diminished Democratic majorities. Hunger for federal patronage after eight years of Republican control of the presidency was a further unifying factor.

There were signs of encouragement for the Republicans in the presidential politics of the South in 1960. The three old habitual bolters—Florida, Tennessee, and Virginia—were again in the Republican column. Texas was extremely close, and in all the other states except Alabama and Mississippi the Republican minority vote was quite large. Also, there were larger votes for Nixon in 1960 than for Eisenhower in 1956 in all eleven Southern States except Arkansas and Louisiana. This last fact definitely expelled the myth that Eisenhower's personality was the chief cause for breaking the Solid South in 1952 and 1956.

Not so encouraging was the Republican record in congressional, state-wide, and local elections in the eight years from 1952 to 1960. While the Republicans had gradually contested more elective places, their accomplishments had not been impressive. During the Eisenhower era, only five United States House seats had been gained. In 1960 none was added. Virginia in that year retained her two, and only Florida, North Carolina, and Texas had one each. There were no Republican United States Senators and the Republican gains in state and local elective places were negligible. It seemed, therefore, by the beginning of the 1960's that two-party rivalry had come to stay in presidential elections, but that in other elections the Solid South was still largely intact and the Democratic primaries were still in effect the elections for most congressional seats and state-wide and local elective offices.

[15]Arthur Krock, "In the Nation," *New York Times,* November 10, 1960. See also, "It Was a Johnson Victory Too," *U. S. News and World Report,* November 21, 1960, and *Dallas Morning News,* November 10, 1960.

A TWO-PARTY SYSTEM?

This situation, however, began to show some signs of change in 1961 and in the results of the congressional and state elections of 1962. The tremendous vote for Nixon in 1960 greatly encouraged Southern Republicans to think that they had a permanent chance thereafter to carry the South in presidential contests. A further boost came in the election of a Republican United States senator in Texas in a runoff of May 27, 1961, to fill the vacancy left by Lyndon Johnson's election to the vice presidency. In this election, John G. Tower won by a vote of 448,217 to 437,874 over interim Senator William A. Blakley. Tower had polled an unprecedentedly large vote against Johnson in the regular election of 1960 (926,653 votes as against 116,367 received by the Republican candidate for United States senator in 1958). Johnson, however, was candidate for Vice President as well as Senator in 1960 and many Texas Democrats resented this dual candidacy. In the special election run-off of 1961 both Tower and Blakley were ultra-conservative, and liberal Democrats were left with no choice except to refrain from voting or vote for Tower. Presumably many of them did the latter.[16] In any event the election of Tower seems to have been a shot in the arm to Republicans all over the South. Texas Republicans as a result ran candidates in 1962 for many more places than ever, but their victories were disappointingly few. Their candidate for governor, however, drew a very heavy vote, but he had only very recently been converted to the party, having run only in 1960 as a candidate for governor in the Democratic primary.

In November, 1961 a very significant conference of Republicans from 12 Southern States met in Atlanta. It consisted of 130 delegates. The Republican National Chairman, the Chairman of the Republican National Congressional Campaign Committee, and Senator Barry Goldwater of Arizona were present and addressed the meeting. Senator Goldwater was by then considered the South's favorite Republican presidential possibility for 1964. The conference talked much about building up a two-party system and concerned itself chiefly with the coming congressional election of 1962. Much evidence was also produced to indicate that healthy Republican organizations existed in most of the states, that many counties were in the process of being organized by businessmen and many

---

[16]Weeks, *Texas in the 1960 Presidential Election*, p. 74.

young persons. It was admitted that many of the local leaders were political amateurs. However, much growing enthusiasm and many permanent conversions were reported.[17]

Although the results in the election of 1962 in the South were quite meager so far as actual Republican gains were concerned, there were some reasons for advocates of a two-party system to feel some encouragement.[18] For one thing, the Republicans contested 62 U. S. House seats as against 42 in 1960 and 24 in 1958. Their candidates were, on the whole, abler and more influential people, in some cases converted Democrats of considerable prominence. Their party organization undoubtedly had been extended and improved and their leaders more competent. The Republicans also made a much more extensive effort to win state and local offices.

The results, however, were not impressive. In the congressional elections, the seven Republican U. S. House members held on and four new seats were gained (Florida, North Carolina, Tennessee and Texas). In a number of other districts Republicans lost by narrow margins. In all serious congressional contests, however, the races were between conservative Democrats and conservative Republicans as in the earlier Blakley-Tower case, and where liberal Democrats voted Republican because of hatred for conservative Democrats. One writer believes that this will work to the advantage of a Democratic national administration whose main troubles in the past have come usually from Southern Democrats in Congress. Defeating Southern Democrats with seniority in the end can only release committee chairmanships for Northern Democrats. He feels also that an ultra-conservative bloc of Southern Republican senators and representatives might come to be as embarrassing to Republican leaders as such a bloc often is to the Democrats.[19] It may be noted, however, that the congressional delegations of six states are still solidly Democratic and only Texas has a Republican U. S. Senator.

The efforts of Southern Republicans to pull conservative Democrats into the Republican party have made it too conservative and conservative Southern Democrats are wary of it. After all, even the national Republican party has not yet surrendered to Goldwater and there may yet be a chance for Rockefeller, Romney, or Scranton.

[17]*New York Times,* Nov. 19, 1961.

[18]See Virginius Dabney, "What the G. O. P. Is Doing in the South," *Harper's,* May, 1963, p. 86.

[19]Richard H. Rovere, "Letter from Washington," *New Yorker,* Nov. 17, 1962, pp. 205-206.

Most of the Republican inroads in the election of 1962 in the South were made by candidates who seemed to support segregation in various ways. This betrays the oldest Republican tradition and is bound to put Southern Republicans at odds with the national party.

In the election of 1962 Republican gains in statewide offices were nil even though Republican candidates for governor in Texas and South Carolina polled large votes. The meager legislative gains in a few states were negligible. Practically no dent was made in the Democratic monopoly in local offices. These places are held by people who are mostly moderate, conservative, and reactionary Democrats. They constitute after all the backbone of politics in all the Southern states and are sustained by a deep tradition still strong with many Southerners, and a well-established habit that makes Democratic primaries in effect the state and local elections.

All this would seem to indicate that the South is after all faced with a long slow process toward the realization of a two-party system. There is a great deal of disagreement as to what such a system is or ought to be. Many seem to have a rather idealistic picture of a two-party system as it is supposed to exist and operate outside the South. Some would insist that there can only be a genuine grass-roots two-party situation where both parties function effectively in congressional, state, district, county, and local elections, maintaining effective organizations, nominating candidates, staging opposing campaigns, and winning against each other at fairly frequent intervals. Such a system, however, exists in little more than one third of the fifty states. It exists nowhere in the South. The South seems to have attained the essence of this kind of rivalry so far only on the level of presidential politics. It may never come at lower levels except in some areas of some states. Certainly, no complete transformation will come anywhere by 1970, except perhaps in a few metropolitan counties. The matter that raises the most doubt is the impact of continuing Negro pressure through racial demonstrations and federal enforcement of strengthened civil rights legislation. The rising tide of presidential and urban Republicanism may well be contained within the sharp reefs of law-and-order symbolism successfully monopolized by the Democrats. It is by no means certain that moderate leadership of the state Democratic parties (outside Alabama and Mississippi) will be obliged to surrender to extreme segregationist elements, however much Freedom Marches may increase that possibility. If the disappearance of the one-party

South seems no longer in doubt, the development of two-party, competitive politics is still contingent upon the ability of the two rivals to take somewhat ambiguous, not-too-opposed positions on fundamental questions.

CONTRIBUTORS

ALFRED CLUBOK, JOHN DE GROVE, and CHARLES FARRIS, colleagues at the University of Florida, Gainesville, have collaborated on an interdisciplinary, comparative study of five Florida communities to observe the effects of rapid population increase and urbanization upon political structures and practices.

Professors ROBERT H. CONNERY and RICHARD H. LEACH, colleagues at Duke University, have collaborated on a major study, *The Federal Government and Metropolitan Areas* (1960).

SAMUEL DUBOIS COOK is Professor and Chairman of the Department of Political Science at Atlanta University, and is currently vice president of the Southern Political Science Association. He has contributed articles to several professional journals.

LESLIE W. DUNBAR took his Ph.D. degree at Cornell University and has taught political science at Emory University and Mt. Holyoke College. He is presently Executive Director of the Southern Regional Council, an association to attain the ideals and practices of equal opportunity for all peoples in the South, with headquarters in Atlanta, Georgia.

LAWRENCE L. DURISCH, Ph.D., Chicago, 1932, is head of the Government Relations and Economics Staff, Tennessee Valley Authority. He has taught for brief periods at several Southern colleges while on leave from TVA, and is currently professor at the University of Tennessee.

ALEXANDER HEARD, Chancellor of Vanderbilt University, is a former president of the Southern Political Science Association. He is the author of *A Two-Party South?* and *The Costs of Democracy.*

MALCOLM E. JEWELL, Ph.D., Pennsylvania State, 1958, Associate Professor at the University of Kentucky, is teaching during the current academic year at Duke University. He is the author of *The State Legislature* and *Senatorial Politics and Foreign Policy;* editor of *The Politics of Reapportionment;* and he has written several articles on legislative politics.

AVERY LEISERSON is Chairman of the Department of Political Science at Vanderbilt University and the Editor of *The Journal of Politics.* He is the author of *Administrative Regulation* and *Parties and Politics.*

Professors DONALD R. MATTHEWS and JAMES W. PROTHRO during the last three years have collaborated to make the University of North Carolina the center of sample survey work on Southern political attitudes. Matthews is author of *U. S. Senators and Their World;* Prothro is co-author of *The Politics of American Democracy.*

WILLIAM H. NICHOLLS is Kentucky-born, Professor of Economics at Vanderbilt University since 1948 and past president of the American Farm Economic Association and the Southern Economic Association. He is currently in Brazil conducting a study of causes of low productivity in Brazilian agriculture.

COLEMAN B. RANSONE, JR., Ph.D., is Professor of Political Science at the University of Alabama; author of *The Southern Governor* (1951) and *The Office of Governor in the U. S.* (1956); and co-author of *Constitutional Revision on Theory and Practice* (1962).

GEORGE W. SPICER is Professor of Political Science at the University of Virginia and past president of the Southern Political Science Association. He was consultant to the U. S. Commission on Civil Rights in 1959 and his most recent work is *The Supreme Court and Fundamental Freedoms* (1959).

O. DOUGLAS WEEKS, Ph.D., Wisconsin, 1924, is Professor of Government at the University of Texas. He has published many articles and short studies in the areas of American, Southern and Texas politics and the legislative process.